The big houses and landed estates of Ireland

Maynooth Research Guides for Irish Local History

GENERAL EDITOR Mary Ann Lyons

This book is one of the Maynooth Research Guides for Irish Local History series. Written by specialists in the relevant fields, these volumes are designed to provide historians, and specifically those interested in local history, with practical advice regarding the consultation of specific collections of historical material, thereby enabling them to conduct independent research in a competent and thorough manner. In each volume, a brief history of the relevant institutions is provided and the principal primary sources are identified and critically evaluated, with specific reference to their usefulness to the local historian. Readers receive step by step guidance as to how to conduct their research and are alerted to some of the problems which they might encounter in working with particular collections. Possible avenues for research are suggested and relevant secondary works are also recommended.

The General Editor acknowledges the assistance of both Professor Raymond Gillespie, NUI Maynooth and Dr James Kelly, St Patrick's College, Drumcondra, in the preparation of this book for publication.

IN THIS SERIES

Maynooth Research Guides for Irish Local History: Number 11

The big houses and landed estates of Ireland: a research guide

Terence Dooley

FOUR COURTS PRESS

Set in 10.5 pt on 12.5 pt Bembo by
Carrigboy Typesetting Services for
FOUR COURTS PRESS LTD
7 Malpas Street, Dublin 8
e-mail: info@four-courts-press.ie
www.four-courts-press.ie
and in North America by
FOUR COURTS PRESS
c/o ISBS, 920 N.E. 58th Avenue, Suite 300, Portland, OR 97213

A catalogue record for this title
is available from the British Library.

ISBN 978–1–84682–039–7 hbk
ISBN 978–1–85182–964–4 pbk

Printed in England
by MPG Books Ltd, Bodmin, Cornwall.

Contents

Illustrations

(appear between pages 96 and 97)

Acknowledgments

In writing this book I had reason to call upon the expertise and to tax the patience of a great many people. I am indebted to the following for their assistance, advice, guidance and forbearance: Dr Aoife Bhreatnach, Marie Boran, Donough Cahill, Mary Conefrey, John Joe Conwell, Patrick Cosgrove, Professor Vincent Comerford, Desmond FitzGerald Knight of Glin, Mary Fitzpatrick, Patricia Friel, Dr Irene Furlong, Professor Raymond Gillespie, Dr Brian Griffin, Hon. Desmond Guinness, Emmeline Henderson, Dick Hunter, Colette Jordan, Ciara Joyce, John Kearney, Dr Jennifer Kelly, Allen and Lorena Sanginés-Krause, Stephen Mallaghan, Conor Mallaghan, Catherine Mullan, Brian and Mary O'Carroll, Dr Finola O'Kane Crimmins, Dr Jacinta Prunty, Olwen Purdue, Terence Reeves-Smyth, Jake Reilly, Mattie Shinnors, Sara Smyth, Dr. Matthew Stout and Mick Wright.

I also wish to thank the staff of the following repositories: the Irish Architectural Archive, the Irish Georgian Society, the John Paul II Library NUI Maynooth, the National Archives of Ireland, the National Archives (London), the National Library of Ireland, the National Photographic Archive, the Public Record Office of Northern Ireland, and the Russell Library, Maynooth.

Since the establishment of the Centre for the Study of Historic Irish Houses and Estates at the National University of Ireland, Maynooth, in September 2004, I have benefited greatly from the expertise of those who have served on the CSHIHE's advisory committee: Sean Benton (Chairman of the Office of Public Works), Patrick Casement (Chairman of National Trust of Northern Ireland), Sir David Davies (Chairman of the Irish Heritage Trust), Desmond FitzGerald Knight of Glin (President of the Irish Georgian Society), Professor John Hughes (President of NUI Maynooth), Dermot McCarthy (Secretary General of the Department of An Taoiseach) and Klaus Unger (Assistant Principal Architect of the Office of Public Works). All have been extremely generous with their time and knowledge.

For the last number of years I have also learned a great deal about big houses, landed estates, landed families and sources from the undergraduate and postgraduate students I have had the privilege to teach at the Department of History, National University of Ireland, Maynooth. I am extremely grateful to them all. The continued fellowship of my colleagues in the Department of History at NUIM is greatly valued as is the intellectual stimulation that they provide.

I am particularly indebted to the series editor, Dr Mary Ann Lyons, who has been meticulous in her editorial efforts, generous with her time and patient in the extreme.

My greatest debt is, as ever, to my family whose unstinting support continues to be greatly appreciated.

Introduction

Throughout most of the period under consideration in this work, the vast majority of people living in Ireland belonged to landed estate communities whether they were landed magnates owning tens of thousands of acres; middlemen leasing large tracts of lands from head landlords and renting them in turn in smaller parcels of various sizes to tenant farmers (who more usually rented directly from landlords); cottiers who exchanged their labour for half an acre or so of potato ground; landless labourers who worked on estates or farms; or big house and demesne servants. Estates varied greatly in size from the smallest at around 500 acres to those of landed magnates such as the Marquis Conyngham who, by the nineteenth century, owned almost 160,000 acres. Smaller estates were typically concentrated in one county. There were, however, quite a few large estates of over 20,000 acres also concentrated in one county such as the Farnham estate in County Cavan and the Clonbrock estate in County Galway. More often large estates were distributed throughout two or more counties: by the nineteenth century Lord Ashtown's 37,300 acres were located in the eight counties (and three provinces) of Galway, Dublin, King's County, Limerick, Roscommon, Tipperary, Waterford and Westmeath. Not all estates were owned by individuals: Trinity College, Dublin, for example, was one of the largest landowners in Ireland[1], while twelve London companies had been granted lands in County Londonderry in the early seventeenth century in return for a financial contribution to the crown's scheme for the plantation of Ulster.[2]

At the heart of around 7,000 landed estates in nineteenth-century Ireland was the landlord's country residence, traditionally referred to in Ireland as the 'big house' by the wider community but now often referred to by a variety of other interchangeable terms: country house, mansion house, historic house and so on. The term 'big house' will be used in this work for a number of reasons: firstly, it captures the very essence of the *raison d'être* behind the building of these houses – to announce the economic and social strength of their owners in their localities and as a class as a whole, and to inspire awe in social equals and possibly encourage deference in the lower classes. Even the smallest landlord residence was big in comparison to any house inhabited by his tenant farmers, cottiers or labourers. Secondly, the term captures something of the historical resentment that was felt towards these houses by nationalist Ireland, particularly following the period of the

---

1 R.B. MacCarthy, *The Trinity College estates, 1800–1923: corporate management in an age of reform* (Dundalk, 1992); W.J. Lowe, 'Landlord and tenant on the estates of Trinity College, Dublin 1851–1903' in *Hermathena*, cxx (1976), pp 5–24. 2 Olive Robinson, 'The London companies as progressive landlords in nineteenth century Ireland' in *Economic History Review*, 2nd series, 15 (1) (Aug. 1962), pp 103–18; idem, 'The London companies and tenant right in nineteenth-century Ireland' in *Agricultural History Review*, 18 (1970), pp 54–63.

land war of the 1880s; Elizabeth Bowen (1899–1973), novelist and short story writer whose ancestral home was Bowen's Court in County Cork, once wrote that there was more than a slight inflection of hostility and irony in the wider popularity of the term 'big house'.[3] Whether intentional or not, the adjective 'big' declared the great social, economic, cultural (and even political and religious) divides that separated landed families from the majority of the surrounding community.

At the beginning of the nineteenth century, Ireland was a predominantly rural and un-industrialized economy where a rapidly expanding population was almost exclusively dependent upon land for a livelihood. In a society dominated to such an extent by agriculture, possession of land was venerated. Moreover, the nineteenth century witnessed the consolidation of the ideology that promoted land as the basis of the nation, where landownership became inextricably linked with the other great national issues of identity and independence so that by the post-famine period the development of nationality and nationalism was specifically bound up with the struggle for land. As a result it is probably fair to state that land and land-related issues dominate the historiography of nineteenth-century Ireland.[4]

Yet while 'land questions' dominate Irish historiography, relatively little has been published about either individual estates or individual big houses.[5] Sometimes the pretext is offered that an estate or house cannot be researched because family or estate records no longer survive. While it is true that this obviously causes great difficulty with regard to writing a total history of the house or estate, it should not be accepted as an excuse for avoiding an attempt; there are sufficient complementary sources to compensate for lacunae in the material which is available. One of the aims of this work is to highlight that very fact.

It is important from the outset to be clear as regards the aims and parameters of this work. This guide seeks to inform. Its methodology is devised according to the perceived needs of students over the last ten years or so who have taken this author's module on 'The decline of the big house in Ireland, 1860–1960' at the Department of History, NUI Maynooth. It is first and foremost a practical guide, the objectives of which are to identify, locate and describe the sources available for the study of Irish landed estates (chapter two) and Irish big houses (chapter four). Advice is offered on the strengths and limitations of these sources and suggestions are made as to how they might be used for further research into aspects of landed estate and big house life heretofore largely neglected by historians.

Before undertaking the study of a local estate or big house (or if one is very ambitious, both, which may be more challenging but ultimately more illuminating), the researcher should have a sufficient working knowledge of national history. He or she ought to be aware of what information is available regarding the history of the landed estate or big house. While each estate and each house was obviously unique, the researcher needs to appreciate that there were outside economic, social

---

3 Elizabeth Bowen, 'The big house' in Hermione Lee (ed.), *The mulberry tree: writings of Elizabeth Bowen* (London, 1986), p. 26.   **4** See chapter one.   **5** See chapters one and three for reference to what has been published.

and political forces at work which impinged upon them all and determined their management policy at various stages. Therefore, the first aim of chapter one is to provide a very broad outline of the history of landed estates in Ireland from their growth in the sixteenth century to their break up in the twentieth century, in particular investigating the outside influences which infringed upon estate life. In doing this, the researcher's attention is drawn to the most important secondary works published in this area. It is not proposed to offer a critique of the literature as such a task would be impracticable in the confines of a work such as this. The same applies to chapter three which, as well as offering an introduction to the historiography of the big house, is intended as a broad introduction to the growth, consolidation and decline of big houses in Ireland over a period of around four centuries. Of course, in sweeping surveys of this nature, one needs to remain constantly aware of the local anomalies not always identified in broad national generalizations.

Consulting secondary works prior to or simultaneously with the research of primary sources will provide the wider social, economic and political historical contexts to facilitate an investigation into whether what occurred on a particular estate was typical of what was happening elsewhere or peculiar to that estate. As a means of creating a comprehensive bibliography of relevant secondary works, the researcher should consider the benefits of consulting the many exhaustive bibliographies to be found in the works of some of the historians mentioned below.[6] Secondly, the researcher's attention is directed to www.irishhistoryonline.ie, a bibliography of Irish history created by Irish History Online in association with the Royal Historical Society Bibliography and London's Past Online. Funded under the Irish Research Council for the Humanities and Social Sciences Government of Ireland Projects Grants scheme, the IHO project is located in the Department of History at NUI Maynooth. This, as the website points out, is an authoritative guide (in progress) to what has been written about Irish history from earliest times to the present, which is free of charge to the user. Researchers may search via 'Simple search' or 'Full search'. If, for example, the researcher should enter the term 'land Ireland' under 'Simple search', he/she will find at least 500 works of relevance.

It should be noted that while this is a guide to sources relating to landed estates and big houses primarily, though not exclusively, for the period from the Act of

---

6 For the nineteenth and twentieth centuries, see for example (arranged in chronological order of publication), J.S. Donnelly jr., *The land and people of nineteenth-century Cork: the rural economy and the land question* (London, 1975); Paul Bew, *Land and the national question in Ireland, 1858–82* (Dublin, 1978); Samuel Clark, *Social origins of the Irish land war* (Princeton, 1979); T.W. Moody, *Davitt and Irish revolution, 1846–82* (Oxford, 1981); W.E. Vaughan, *Landlords and tenants in mid-Victorian Ireland* (Oxford, 1994); Samuel Clark & J.S. Donnelly jr. (eds), *Irish peasants: violence and political unrest, 1780–1914* (Manchester & Madison, W, 1983); David Seth Jones, *Graziers, land reform and political conflict in Ireland* (Washington, 1995); Terence Dooley, *The decline of the big house in Ireland: a study of Irish landed families, 1860–1960* (Dublin, 2001); idem, *'The land for the people': the land question in independent Ireland* (Dublin, 2004); Fergus Campbell, *Land and revolution: nationalist politics in the west of Ireland* (Oxford, 2005).

Union in 1800 to independence in 1922, neither chapter one nor chapter three actually begin or end at these dates. Chapter one begins in the seventeenth century and brings the history of estates in the twenty-six county area of the Irish Republic up to the 1980s when the Irish Land Commission was more or less dismantled, while chapter three begins with the Norman tower houses of the thirteenth century and brings the story of the big house in the same jurisdiction up to the present day. There is no discussion of the sources available for either landed estates or big houses in Northern Ireland after partition; because of the different social, political and cultural conditions which existed there, sources for the study of the big house in Northern Ireland post–1922 require and deserve a separate treatment.

The sources discussed in chapters two and four are not rigidly organized according to any hierarchy of importance, although the use of estate and family records is necessarily afforded detailed coverage. The conclusion briefly discusses some of the questions which can be asked of these sources. As Raymond Gillespie and Gerard Moran have stressed: 'Abundance of source material is of little value in increasing our understanding of the past unless we ask the right questions of these sources'.[7] The conclusion therefore briefly explores the areas of estate and big house life that require further examination by local historians.

---

7 Raymond Gillespie & Gerard Moran, 'Introduction: writing local history' in Raymond Gillespie & Gerard Moran (eds), '*A various country*': *essays in Mayo history, 1500–1900* (Westport, 1987), p. 22.

CHAPTER I

Irish landed estates

THE EVOLUTION OF IRISH LANDED ESTATES
PRE-NINETEENTH CENTURY

The history of the evolution of landed estates both at national and local level in early modern Ireland has been visited by a number of scholars.[1] What emerges from their studies is a rather complex picture of land transfer which began in the sixteenth century with Tudor ambitions to conquer Ireland. The Tudor government's simultaneous desire to impose Protestantism as the state religion on Ireland (and its other dominions) very quickly bound religion with the land question. At first the government (and private investors) flirted rather tenuously with the idea of colonization and plantation, that is encouraging the migration of Protestants to Ireland to settle in colonies on estates confiscated from the existing occupiers as one possible means of expediting conversion and beyond that asserting state control. The first counties to be settled were King's County and Queen's County (later Offaly and Laois). In the 1580s a much more ambitious, and arguably strategic, scheme to plant the southern province of Munster was undertaken, again with mixed degrees of success. The other major scheme was in Ulster where private entrepreneurs exploited both the vacuum created by the departure of the Gaelic earls from that province in 1607 and the subsequent confiscation of their lands, as well as the increasing indebtedness of those who remained and who were having difficulties adjusting to the new capitalist environment in order to purchase their estates at bargain prices.[2]

---

1 Excellent starting points include such works as T.C. Barnard, *A new anatomy of Ireland: the Irish Protestants, 1649–1770* (New Haven & London, 2003); S.J. Connolly, *Religion, law, and power: the making of Protestant Ireland, 1660–1760* (Oxford, 1992); L.M. Cullen, *The emergence of modern Ireland* (London, 1981); idem, 'Economic development, 1691–1750; 1750–1800' in T.W. Moody & W.E. Vaughan (eds), *A new history of Ireland, iv, eighteenth-century Ireland* (Oxford, 1986), pp 123–58, 159–95; David Dickson, *Old world colony: Cork and south Munster, 1630–1830* (Cork, 2005); see also David Dickson, *New foundations: Ireland, 1660–1800* (Dublin, 1987; 2nd ed., Dublin, 2000); for more local studies see W.H. Crawford, *The management of a major Ulster estate in the late eighteenth century: the eighth earl of Abercorn and his Irish agents* (Dublin, 2001); P.J. Duffy, 'The evolution of estate properties in south Ulster, 1600–1900' in W.J. Smyth & Kevin Whelan (eds), *Common ground: essays on the historical geography of Ireland* (Cork, 1988), pp 84–109; W.A. Maguire, *The Downshire estates in Ireland, 1801–1845* (Oxford, 1972); Peter Roebuck, 'The making of an Ulster great estate: the Chichesters, barons of Belfast and viscounts of Carrickfergus, 1599–1648' in *Proceedings of the Royal Irish Academy* (hereinafter *R.I.A. Proc.*), C, lxxix (1979), pp 1–25; William Roulston, 'The evolution of the Abercorn estate in north-west Ulster, 1610–1703' in *Familia*, xv (1999), pp 54–67.   2 Over

By the 1640s an estimated 15,000 English and Scotch Protestants had settled in Ulster and up to 22,000 English Protestants in Munster. But there was also immigration to many other parts of the country as the new landlords began to encourage settlement on their lands. For quite obvious reasons such settlement caused resentment, particularly amongst the dispossessed. During the late sixteenth and early seventeenth centuries, settlers (commonly referred to as planters) in Queen's County, King's County and the province of Munster found themselves frequently under attack, most notably in Munster in 1598 and Ulster in 1615. Traditionally it was believed that the most infamous of the revolts in Ulster in 1641 was an attack on the Ulster plantation. However, it has since been shown that the rebels were conspicuously debt-ridden scions of families who had benefited rather than suffered from the plantation.[3] When the rebellion moved out from Ulster, it laid the foundation for the Confederate War, which was to last down to 1653. While the motives behind rebellion and war were complex and varied, the outcome had major repercussions for the long-term future of the land question in Ireland.

The suppression of the 1641 rebellion gave rise to further social engineering. The Cromwellian plantation of the 1650s was ostensibly intended to meet the cost of large-scale military operations; almost 35,000 soldiers were to receive their arrears of pay in Irish land. Invariably, the soldiers sold off their smallholdings to the officer class so that probably around 7,500 Cromwellian soldiers eventually settled on larger estates than most of them might initially have hoped for.[4] Similarly around 1,000 so-called adventurers who had invested money in the campaign were also to be rewarded with lands and at least half of those took up the offer. The need to provide this land gave the pretext for the further confiscation of Catholic lands on a dramatic scale and their redistribution amongst new Protestant proprietors. While Catholics had owned around 60 per cent of the land in 1641, the success of the Cromwellian plantation meant that this proportion plummeted to around 20

---

the last thirty years or so, there has been an outpouring of extremely important works on sixteenth- and seventeenth-century Ireland. Rather than listing them all here, the reader might be advised, as a starting point, to take a look at Toby Barnard's chapter 'Further reading' in T.C. Barnard, *The kingdom of Ireland, 1641–1760* (Basingstoke, 2004), pp 181–93. **3** Plantation records fall outside the scope of the sources discussed in this work but for an introduction to the same, see Raymond Gillespie, 'Plantation records' in William Nolan & Anngret Simms (eds), *Irish towns: a guide to sources* (Dublin, 1998), pp 79–85; Professor Gillespie's many published works which offer an excellent insight to seventeenth-century developments at national and regional levels include *Colonial Ulster: the settlement of East Ulster, 1600–1641* (Cork, 1985); 'The end of an era: Ulster and the outbreak of the 1641 rising' in Ciaran Brady & Raymond Gillespie (eds), *Natives and newcomers: essays on the making of Irish colonial society, 1534–1641* (Dublin, 1986), pp 191–214; *The transformation of the Irish economy, 1550–1700* (Dundalk, 1991); 'Explorers, exploiters and entrepreneurs: early modern Ireland and its context, 1500–1700' in B.J. Graham & Lindsay Proudfoot (eds), *An historical geography of Ireland* (London, 1993), pp 123–57; 'Destabilizing Ulster, 1641–1642' in Brian MacCuarta (ed.), *Ulster 1641: aspects of the rising* (Belfast, 1993), pp 107–21; 'A manor court in seventeenth-century Ireland' in *Irish Economic & Social History*, xxv (1998), pp 81–7. **4** Connolly, *Religion, law and power*, pp 15–16.

per cent by 1688.[5] (David Dickson has shown that the proportions in southern counties such as Cork and Kerry were a little higher at around 25 per cent and 33 per cent respectively.)[6] However, the plans of 1653 to segregate the remaining Catholic landowners west of the Shannon did not come to fruition.[7]

When the Commonwealth fell in 1659 Catholics began to question the legal efficacy of the redistribution scheme which was under way. In late 1660 a royal declaration announced that Catholics who had not involved themselves in rebellion in 1641 or after or who had served the crown in exile were to have their lands restored. However, adventurers and soldiers already in possession were confirmed.[8] At the time James Butler (1610–88), first duke of Ormond and later lord lieutenant of Ireland, made the famous remark that if the declaration were to be implemented: 'there must be discoveries made of a new Ireland, for the old will not serve to satisfy these engagements'.[9] (In the 1920s, others were to make very similar remarks when the Irish Land Commission proposed the redistribution of compulsorily acquired lands to uneconomic holders, the landless and a variety of other interested groups.)[10]

In 1662 the Act of Settlement gave legal force to the declaration. In early 1663 a Court of Claims began to hear representations from those seeking the restoration of their lands. But before more than one-seventh of the claims had been heard the government suspended the court. There were possibly others like Ormond who quickly realized how much of a logistical nightmare it would be to progress any further. The Restoration land settlement was completed or more accurately abandoned in 1665 with Catholics marginally increasing their share of land. It was, as S.J. Connolly remarks, nothing more than a 'crude lottery' and those who had their claims heard in the Court of Claims were lucky to have recovered their estates through personal connections or the king's direct favour.[11]

Conflict regarding landownership continued. In 1685 the Catholic King James II succeeded his brother, Charles II. Two years later he began to devise a scheme which proposed that Cromwellian and post-Cromwellian grantees would be required to restore one-half of their estates to their former owners. By 1689 the Irish parliament had been packed with the Catholic majority that would be necessary to carry legislation to put James's plans into effect. Around the same time, Ireland had become a major theatre of war in what was essentially a European conflict. The Williamite victory in 1690–1 meant that the order established in the preceding decades was merely confirmed and King James' plan to undo the Restoration land settlement did not come to fruition. His defeat by William III, prince of Orange, opened the way for a further round of confiscation of his supporters' lands and prompted the introduction of a series of so-called penal laws.[12]

5 Ibid., p. 13; Toby Barnard puts this figure at 14 per cent in Barnard, *The kingdom of Ireland*, p. 4. **6** Dickson, *Old world colony*, p. 61. **7** Barnard, *The kingdom of Ireland*, p. 4. **8** Connolly, *Religion, law, and power*, p. 13. **9** Quoted in ibid., p. 14. **10** See below. **11** Connolly, *Religion, law, and power*, pp 14–15. **12** See, for example, S.J. Connolly, 'The penal laws' in W.A. Maguire (ed.), *Kings in conflict: the revolutionary war in Ireland and its*

Simply stated, these laws were a series of discriminatory measures which represented the culmination of previously ad hoc attempts to exclude Catholics from landownership and positions of political and administrative influence and to repress Catholic worship. An act of 1697, for example, provided that the lands of a Protestant heiress who married a Catholic should be forfeited to her Protestant next of kin. Over the next decade or so, there was to be a more direct assault on Catholic landed property. Under the Act to Prevent the Further Growth of Popery (1704), Catholics were prohibited from buying land, inheriting land from Protestants or holding leases for longer than thirty-one years. The concentration of lands in Catholic hands was further weakened by the stipulation that the lands of a deceased Catholic landowner had to be divided equally amongst all of his male heirs if they remained Catholics. In order to avoid the loss of estates, many Catholic owners simply converted to the Established Church.[13] In 1780, by which time the era of mass plantation had long come to an end, the Catholics' share of land had fallen to 5 per cent and Protestant landed ascendancy had become very much a reality.[14] Those few Catholics who managed to retain ownership of their estates – mainly in Connaught but to a lesser extent in counties such as Meath, Dublin, Louth and Kerry – did so for a variety of reasons ranging from luck to subterfuge (often with the connivance of a separate branch of the family who had converted to Protestantism in order to secure their own lands).

By the end of the seventeenth century, landownership in Ireland was therefore the preserve of a privileged minority of probably no more than 5,000 families, almost exclusively members of the Established Protestant Church (even if a landlord was Catholic, his lifestyle was invariably that of the Protestant ascendancy), while the majority of their tenants over most of the country tended to be Roman Catholics. The landed class in the seventeenth century or at any time afterwards was not a homogenous body. At the top were the landed magnates owning tens of thousands of acres and monopolising to a very large extent the political power of the country. Most were noblemen, some holding numerous titles. But there were large landowners who remained commoners such as the Conollys at Castletown in Kildare in the eighteenth century (Lord Midleton once argued that if William

aftermath, 1689–1750 (Belfast, 1990), pp 157–72; K.J. Harvey, *The Bellews of Mount Bellew: a Catholic gentry family in eighteenth-century Ireland* (Dublin, 1998); J.R. Hill, 'The meaning and significance of "Protestant Ascendancy", 1787–1840' in *Ireland after the Union: proceedings of the second joint meeting of the Royal Irish Academy and the British Academy, London 1986* (Oxford, 1989), pp 1–22; T.P. O'Neill, 'Religion, land and laws in eighteenth-century Thomond' in *North Munster Antiquarian Journal*, 33 (1991), pp 78–83; W.N. Osborough, 'Catholics, land and the popery acts of Anne' in T.P. Power & Kevin Whelan (eds), *Endurance and emergence: Catholics in Ireland in the eighteenth century* (Dublin, 1990), pp 21–56. **13** Connolly, *Religion, law, and power*, p. 310; Barnard, *The kingdom of Ireland*, p. 53. **14** Monica Brennan, *The making of the Protestant ascendancy in County Kilkenny landownership* (Michigan, 1987); W.A. Maguire, 'The land settlement' in Maguire (ed.), *Kings in conflict*, pp 139–56; on Protestant ascendancy see J.G. Simms, 'The establishment of Protestant ascendancy, 1691–1714' in Moody & Vaughan (eds), *A new history of Ireland, iv, eighteenth-century Ireland*, pp 1–30.

Conolly were to be given a peerage, it would have to be at a level equal to his 'birth and education', otherwise there would be those lords 'who may be piqued at seeing one of his birth and condition put over their heads')[15] and also the Shirleys at Lough Fea in Monaghan. Beneath them were the gentry, powerful in their localities and who along with the magnates largely controlled local offices. Below them again were the lesser gentry whose social status was largely confined to the parish.

EIGHTEENTH-CENTURY ESTATE MANAGEMENT

The land question in the eighteenth century has been more successful in attracting the attention of historians than the seventeenth century, but still falls some way behind the nineteenth century.[16] At local level, W.H. Crawford's work on agents and estate management structures and policies on the Abercorn estate in the eighteenth century points to the need for many more such studies in evaluating changing relationships between landlords and tenants, the latter and their sub-tenants, the rôle of landlord patronage in the economic and social development of an estate and the strategies devised (if any) by landlords and tenants to cope with periods of economic crises. Similarly, Joe Clarke's *Christopher Dillon Bellew and his Galway estates, 1763–1826* (Dublin, 2003) bears ample testimony to the fact that tenants were not always willing to participate in a landlord's grandiose plans to create a form of rural idyll. His work covers a period that was in many respects crucial in ending the old world of ascendancy Ireland. Land issues in some counties such as Tipperary have been particularly well served: T. P. Power's study of *Land, politics and society in eighteenth-century Tipperary* (Oxford, 1993) identifies many of the considerable changes which characterized rural society in that county and shows clearly that the presence of a strong Catholic farmer and middleman class curtailed the operation of the penal laws.[17]

The eighteenth century saw rural society undergo considerable change and become much more stratified.[18] The probability is that it witnessed a widening of

15 Connolly, *Religion, law, and power*, p. 65. **16** See note 1 above; also Mervyn Busteed, 'The practice of improvement in the Irish context – the Castle Caldwell estate in County Fermanagh in the second half of the eighteenth century' in *Irish Geography* (hereinafter *Ir. Geography*), 33 (1) (2000), pp 15–36; David Large, 'The wealth of the greater Irish landowners, 1750–1815' in *Irish Historical Studies* (hereinafter *I.H.S.*) xv, no. 57 (1966), pp 21–46; Power & Whelan (eds), *Endurance and emergence*; Peter Roebuck, 'The economic situation and the functions of substantial landowners, 1600–1815: Ulster and Lowland Scotland compared' in Rosalind Mitchison & Peter Roebuck (eds), *Economy and society in Scotland and Ireland, 1500–1939* (Edinburgh, 1988), pp 81–92; idem, 'Landlord indebtedness in Ulster in the seventeenth and eighteenth centuries' in J.M. Goldstrom & L.A. Clarkson (eds), *Irish population, economy and society* (Oxford, 1982), pp 135–54; idem, 'Rent movement, proprietorial incomes and agricultural developments 1730–1830' in Peter Roebuck (ed.), *Plantation to partition* (Belfast, 1981), pp 82–107. **17** See also Miriam Lambe, *A Tipperary estate: Castle Otway, 1750–1853* (Dublin, 1998); D.G. Marnane, *Land and violence: a history of west Tipperary from 1660* (Tipperary, 1985). **18** For an informative local analysis see W.H.

the social base of the landed class, particularly in the ranks of the lesser gentry. Economic necessity probably resulted in the fragmentation of many great estates which covered Ireland at the beginning of the century. This fragmentation may have been motivated by the need to sell in order to remain affluent, or even the desire to provide younger sons, denied access to the core estate through the rule of primogeniture, with a place in the landed class. Although the balance in landownership was altered, it was still very much the preserve of an élite corps of predominantly Protestant landlords.

By 1800 as many as one third of landlords owning Irish land were absentees.[19] But absenteeism did not necessarily go hand-in-hand with poor estate management; some of the best managed estates were run by efficient estate agents.[20] Olive Robinson has found that it was efficient resident agents who successfully managed the Londonderry estates of the London companies,[21] and W.H. Crawford has shown that even though a landlord such as the duke of Abercorn could be absent, this did not necessarily mean he was incapable of maintaining a hands-on approach to estate management:

> Abercorn visited his Irish estates and resided in the family seat at Baronscourt in west Tyrone on only a few occasions: in 1746, 1749, 1751, 1752, 1756, 1761, 1777 (April to December 'after an absence of fifteen years'), and 1782. He was an absentee landlord by all the definitions of that term and yet the scale, the range and the substance of the correspondence he maintained with his Irish agents, reveals the extent and depth of his knowledge of life on the estates.[22]

The employment of agents (except in the case of smaller estates managed by their owners) was the most common form of estate management by the late eighteenth century. Some of the greater estates employed a number of agents with the duties of sub-agents (with responsibility for outlying estates) supervised by the chief agent who, in turn, was accountable to the landlord himself. Agents were responsible for collecting rents (which were usually collected twice a year on appointed gale days in May and November and often in local hotels or estate offices in nearby towns), eliminating arrears, keeping accounts, drawing up leases and ensuring that their covenants were adhered to by tenants, choosing new tenants,

---

Crawford, 'Economy and society in south Ulster in the eighteenth century' in *Clogher Record* (hereinafter *Clogher Rec.*), viii, no. 3 (1975), pp 241–56.   **19** Melvyn Jones, 'The absentee landlord's landscape: the Watson-Wentworth estate in eighteenth-century Ireland' in *Landscapes*, 1 (2) (2000), pp 33–52; A.P.W. Malcomson, 'Absenteeism in eighteenth-century Ireland' in *Irish Economic & Social History*, i (1974), pp 15–35; for the early nineteenth-century management of an absentee estate see 'The journal of Sir John Benn-Walsh relating to the management of his Irish estate, 1823–64', ed. J.S. Donnelly jr. in *Journal of the Cork Historical & Archaeological Society* (hereinafter *Cork Hist. Soc. Jn.*), 79 (230) (1974), pp 86–123; 80 (231) (1975), pp 15–42.   **20** For information on the rôle of agents in the eighteenth century, see Barnard, *A new anatomy of Ireland*, pp 208–38.   **21** Robinson, 'The London companies as progressive landlords', pp 114–15.   **22** Crawford, *Ulster estate*, p. 4.

supervising estate expenditure, overseeing improvements, carrying out evictions, and valuing property. They often had to arrange borrowing on behalf of their employer and seek abatements of interest on existing loans. They had to liaise between landlords and tenants, receiving petitions from tenants particularly for reductions of rent.[23] At its most rudimentary level, land agents were responsible for all aspects of estate administration and for almost all the income and expenditure on estates. As J.S. Donnelly jr. points out: 'estate agents in nineteenth-century Ireland enjoyed a much greater measure of autonomy in the management of landed property than did their counterparts in England.'[24]

Besides his estate duties, an Irish agent often served as resident magistrate, represented his employer at poor law guardian meetings (after 1838) or on grand juries and organized voters at elections. The importance of these functions allied to the (moderate) financial rewards on offer the attracted younger sons of landlords to the profession throughout the eighteenth and nineteenth centuries. Agents were often local solicitors (a knowledge of the law was an obvious advantage) or retired army officers. Invariably, because social respectability was considered desirable, they were well-connected or wealthy gentlemen. J.S. Donnelly jr. quotes William R. Townsend, a noted writer on Irish agricultural matters, who in 1816 condemned the idea of 'keeping as an agent one of the lower orders one of the people's selves' because such a person was 'incapable of improving the farms or farmers' and was 'generally both corrupt and oppressive'.[25]

Other more routine administrative duties on an estate were carried out by bailiffs, stewards and agriculturalists. Larger estates sometimes employed surveyors and valuators although individual landlords and their agents often carried out these duties themselves.[26] In the early part of the nineteenth century Lord Downshire employed a permanent surveyor and valuator who was attached to his estate office at Hillsborough for routine survey work and the drawing of maps for inclusion in his leases. The obvious advantage of employing a professional valuator was to give new rents the authority of an independent and impartial observer. Some valuators were local men; others were members of valuation firms such as Brassington and Gale, based in Dublin, who in the nineteenth century had clients all over the country. The day-to-day running of an estate office, where established, was the duty of an accountant. Large estates also employed a number of clerks and often the agents paid for their own clerks. The likes of Lord Devonshire or Lord Ormonde employed an auditor to oversee accounts and a law agent to undertake all legal transactions such as the preparation of leases and notices to quit. While larger

23 For memoirs of nineteenth-century land agents see S.M. Hussey, *The reminiscences of an Irish land agent* (London, 1904); W.S. Trench, *Realities of Irish life* (London, 1868); for functions and social backgrounds of agents see Donnelly, *Land and people of Cork*, pp 173–87; Maguire, *The Downshire estates*, pp 155–205. **24** Donnelly, *Land and people of Cork*, p.173. **25** Ibid., p.178. **26** Maguire, *The Downshire estates*, p.157. A study of estate papers from the mid-1850s onwards show, however, that most landlords by then seem to have relied on the government valuation, better known as Griffith's valuation.

landowners obviously had the finances to employ professional administrators, there was also the need for them to do so in order to administer large properties. It is perhaps because of this more professional approach by larger landowners that surviving estate records belong predominantly to this class. Smaller estates had less finances and less need for such a high degree of administration.

On a more general level, landlords or their agents in the eighteenth century showed little enthusiasm for investing in permanent improvements on tenant holdings such as the construction of new dwelling houses, farm offices or drainage schemes and so throughout the century Irish agriculture remained backward compared to England. The founding of the Dublin Society in the 1730s marked an important attempt to circulate new farming ideas throughout the country, but the fact that it attracted only 300 members spoke volumes for the levels of interest amongst the gentry. In the main, they were not farmer-landlords; instead they remained content to draw income from rent-paying tenants.

The eighteenth century also witnessed a significant growth in the middleman class, who David Dickson points out were often referred to in contemporary terms as '*tiarnaí beaga*' (small landlords). Many were drawn from the old Catholic landowning families and usually held large tracts of land from 100 to 1,000 acres and upwards on leases for up to ninety-nine years (although in theory, after the passing of the 1704 penal law Catholics were prevented from receiving leases in excess of thirty-one years' duration.)[27] Initially landlords may have perceived the middleman system to be a convenient means of relieving them from the troublesome collection of rents from a mass of tenants; however, it was a system that was to fall out of favour with them before the century had drawn to a close.

Dickson's authoritative work on Munster points out that by the eighteenth century 'estate practice in south Munster was remarkably standardized: the lease was the near-universal form of legal contract governing relations between landowners and their direct tenants'.[28] From the landlord's point of view, leases simplified the running of the estate; there was no need to enter into annual negotiations with tenants. From the tenants' point of view an extended lease, for around twenty-one years or more, provided the security to begin long-term planning. This, in turn, could benefit the estate; an improving and solvent tenant who invested in farm improvement was an obvious asset. Having improved farmhouses, ditches,

---

27 Dickson, *Ireland 1660–1800*, p. 112; see also idem, 'Middlemen' in Thomas Bartlett & D.W. Hayton (eds), *Penal era and golden age: essays in Irish history* (Belfast, 1979), pp 162–85; G.E. Christianson, 'Landlords and land tenure in Ireland, 1790–1830' in *Éire-Ireland*, ix (1974), pp 25–58; see also D.G. Gahan, 'Religion and land tenure in eighteenth-century Ireland: tenancy in the south-east' in R.V. Comerford et al. (ed.), *Religion, conflict and coexistence in Ireland* (Dublin, 1990), pp 99–117; K.J. Harvey, 'Landords and land usage in eighteenth-century Galway' in Gerard Moran & Raymond Gillespie (eds), *Galway: history and society. Interdisciplinary essays on the history of an Irish county* (Dublin, 1996), pp 297–318; Kevin Whelan, 'An underground gentry? Catholic middlemen in eighteenth-century Ireland' in J.S. Donnelly jr. & K.A. Miller (eds), *Irish popular culture, 1650–1850* (Dublin & Portland, 1998), pp 118–72. 28 Dickson, *Old world colony*, p. 181.

agricultural production and so on during his tenure, an improving tenant was better placed to renegotiate with a landlord or his agent once the twenty-one year period had expired. Extended leases to middlemen allowed for the emergence of a Catholic squirearchy or 'semi-gentry', despite the existence of the penal laws, the characteristics of which Dickson very well defines:

> Close affinity to a landowning family; patrilinear descent from a forfeiting landowner; close affinity to high-status functionaries abroad (officers in French service, etc.); a lifestyle which was predominantly non-productive, and the resources and the facilities to provide extended hospitality. This social group transcended religious affiliation, and even within the region it was quite heterogeneous. But by definition it was comfortable in material terms, ambitious for its children and the family name, and increasingly conscious of upper-class fashions as mediated by urban display and the world of print culture.[29]

The middleman occupied something of an ambiguous position in Irish society. If some landlords considered them an easy method of collecting rents from the masses, others resented long leases granted to them in previous generations as obstacles to modernization and their own attempts to improve their financial position, particularly during periods of economic growth such as 1750 to 1815 when there was a steep rise in agricultural prices.[30] However, the big house-building boom that characterized this period brings into question the extent to which many were financially straitjacketed.[31]

While middlemen were often castigated by social commentators for their willingness to acquiesce in subdivision, a system that was undoubtedly contributory to poor agricultural practice and the creation of an underbelly of impoverishment, a continuously rising population meant access to land became a late eighteenth- and nineteenth-century imperative over which middlemen were possibly unwilling or unable to exert any control. Indeed, if the middlemen exploited this land hunger they were often less resented than the prosperous farmers – the large graziers and the strong mixed farmers – who were more determined to consolidate their holdings or who refused to sublet them (except to labourers and then usually at exorbitant rents).[32] This is probably evidenced in the fact that agrarian unrest was most pronounced during the late eighteenth and early nineteenth centuries in counties such as Tipperary and Limerick and belts of the Midlands, where large grazing farms predominated which failed to provide adequate employment or conacre. But one should not lose sight of the fact that the motives for agrarian unrest were often much more varied and complex and often regionally determined.[33] Middlemen were undoubtedly, as L.M. Cullen contends, 'important

---

29 Ibid., p. 188.   **30** For rent movements at this time see Large, 'The wealth of the greater Irish landowners', pp 21–47; also Roebuck, 'Rent movement and proprietorial incomes', pp 82–101.   **31** See chapter three.   **32** Cullen, *The emergence of modern Ireland*, p. 103. **33** Thomas Bartlett, *The fall and rise of the Irish nation: the Catholic question, 1690–1830* (Dublin,

social brokers in the countryside' and when they disappeared 'the conflicting social interests of rural Ireland confronted one another much more directly'.[34]

As in the eighteenth century, landlords in pre-famine Ireland do not seem to have done as much as their English counterparts to prohibit bad farming practices or to encourage better husbandry on their estates by including covenants to that effect in their leases. Edward Wakefield, a commentator on agricultural matters, claimed in 1812 that few leases contained 'clauses by which the tenant is bound to cultivate the ground in particular manner'.[36] Some agents were undoubtedly more concerned with the collection of rents on behalf of their absentee employers than the promotion of good farming practice. However, the estate management policy of even some of the more stringent agents needs more examination. For example, Patrick Duffy's reassessment of William Steuart Trench's early career as agent to the absentee Evelyn Shirley in County Monaghan in the early 1840s shows that Trench was not impressed by his predecessor's management policy 'of making a profit on every trifling transaction'. Instead Trench advocated the positive effects on the tenants if they perceived that the landlord was willing to 'bear and share' their burdens with them. This, he believed, would entice them to improve their situation and prevent them from joining the 'enemy's ranks'. Duffy concludes that the report from which these quotes are drawn, written by Trench for Lord Shirley in 1843, indicates that he was 'a champion of tenants' rights, a humane and enlightened advocate for the material and moral welfare of the tenantry'.[37] His management policy on the Lansdowne estate in Kerry in the post-famine period certainly fitted in with the more rigorous management practices that were put in place on many estates from the 1830s as landlords such as Lansdowne tried to correct the business errors of their predecessors who had allowed arrears to accumulate, their property to become hopelessly fragmented, their tenantry to slide into abject poverty, and their own indebtedness to grow.[38]

The pre-famine period also witnessed a trend towards the repossession of lands occupied by middlemen and tenants by landlords, both individuals and institutions;

1992); Kevin Whelan, *The tree of liberty: radicalism, Catholicism and the construction of Irish identity, 1760–1830* (Cork, 1996); Gearóid Ó Tuathaigh, 'Political history' in L.M. Geary & Margaret Kelleher (eds), *Nineteenth-century Ireland: a guide to recent research* (Dublin, 2005), pp 8–9.   **34** Cullen, *The emergence of modern Ireland*, p. 104.   **35** See for example: Peter Connell, *The land and people of County Meath, 1750–1850* (Dublin, 2004); Donnelly, *Land and people of Cork*; Lambe, *A Tipperary landed estate*; MacCarthy, *The Trinity College estates*; Kevin O'Neill, *Family and farm in pre-famine Ireland: the parish of Killeshandra* (Madison NJ, 1984). **36** Edward Wakefield, *An account of Ireland statistical and political* (2 vols, London, 1812), i, 245. **37** P.J. Duffy, 'Management problems on a large estate in mid-nineteenth century Ireland: William Steuart Trench's report on the Shirley estate in 1843' in *Clogher Rec.*, xvi, no. 1 (1997), pp 101–22.   **38** See Gerard Lyne, *The Lansdowne estate in Kerry under the agency of William Steuart Trench, 1849–72* (Dublin, 2001).

Olive Robinson points out that three of the London companies repossessed large tracts of lands in 1817, 1820 and 1821 on the expiry of leases in order to improve their estates, while the other London companies did so in the period from the early 1830s to the early 1870s. If the experience of the London companies is representative, then it seems that by the early nineteenth century the middleman system was perceived to be detrimental to estate improvement; both the Fishmonger's Company and the Grocers' Company found that lands leased to middlemen had fallen into a neglected state and were populated with far too many impoverished under-tenants holding minute farms and with no resources to improve them.[39]

The 1817–21 repossession of the London company lands also coincided with the economic downturn that resulted from the ending of the Napoleonic wars in 1815.[40] As in other phases of economic depression, the smallholders, cottiers and labourers who lived in more or less permanent impoverishment once again became sacrificial lambs to adverse weather conditions, poor harvests, diseased potato crops and another cyclical slump in the agricultural and linen markets. Meanwhile Ireland was experiencing a rapid demographic expansion which saw the population rise from 2.5 million in the early 1750s to 8.2 million by the time of the 1841 census. This population explosion was most heavily concentrated at the lower end of the rural class structure. Joseph Lee has calculated that cottiers (holders of less than five acres), small farmers (holders of between five and fifteen acres) and agricultural labourers were four times more numerous than large farmers (holders of more than fifteen acres) on the eve of the Great Famine.[41] The need for access to land in an unindustrialized society kept the level of rents higher than was warranted by agricultural prices. Force of competition between labourers meant farmers could easily exploit the price of conacre. If the labourer had to pay for his conacre in advance and then his crop failed, he had nothing to fall back on. Therefore, labourers became the most vulnerable class in Irish society. In many instances, they were also the most socially aggrieved – many were the sons of farmers who had become products of downward social mobility, losing their status in life with little prospects of regaining it.

Landlords of all grades who had broken up their grazing lands to gain from rents payable by small tillage farmers were not readily convinced when the war ended in 1815 that rent levels should fall.[42] Instead, they 'sought to tighten the management

39 Robinson, 'The London companies as progressive landlords', pp 103–4.   40 Cormac Ó Gráda, 'Poverty, population and agriculture, 1801–45' in W.E. Vaughan (ed.), *A new history of Ireland, v, Ireland under the union, I, 1801–70* (Oxford, 1989), p. 108.   41 J.J. Lee, *The modernisation of Irish society, 1848–1918* (Dublin, 1973), p. 2; see also W.E. Vaughan & E.J. Fitzpatrick (eds), *Irish historical statistics: population, 1821–1971* (Dublin, 1978); P.J. Duffy, 'Irish landholding structures and population in mid-nineteenth century Ireland' in *Maynooth Review*, iii (1977), pp 3–27; for an example of population study on a local level at this time see G. Alwill, 'The 1841 census of Killeshandra parish [Co. Cavan]' in *Breifne*, v (1976), pp 7–36.   42 George Sigerson, *History of the land tenures and land classes of Ireland with an account of the various secret agrarian confederacies* (London, 1871), p. 170; A. Atkinson, *Ireland exhibited to England* (London, 1823), p. 109; L.M. Cullen, *An economic history of Ireland since 1660* (London,

of their properties, with the result that they became more demanding and less tolerant of the loose practices permitted on estates in the eighteenth century and during the wartime prosperity'.[43] Rather ironically, one of the main reasons for the tightening of financial belts was the growth of indebtedness that had characterized the previous half-century or so. The big house building boom of the Georgian period was but one cause. Extravagant living, often well beyond the means of some families, was another. The rôle of spendthrift landlords has tended to be exaggerated in this growth, particularly in works of fiction such as Maria Edgeworth's *Castle Rackrent*, but spendthrifts did exist and some landlords spent lavishly on the building of palatial mansions at this time. The earl of Kingston, for example, spent £220,000 on the building of Mitchelstown castle during the 1820s. To facilitate the building or renovations of big houses or simply to maintain the lifestyle of their predecessors meant that the early part of the nineteenth century was characterized by a high degree of landlord borrowing. W.A. Maguire, who has scrutinized the vast collection of Downshire papers, found that Lord Downshire borrowed £185,500 between 1810 and 1840. His study enlightens on the constraints within which landlords (or their representatives) managed their estates in pre-famine Ireland and illuminates the financial restrictions under which landlords operated. Downshire was constrained by his indebtedness, which came in large part from his over exuberance for generous credit facilities.[44] Landlord indebtedness, therefore, was by no means a consequence of the Great Famine: even before its outbreak in 1845, almost 900 Irish estates with a combined annual rental of £750,000 were in the Court of Chancery.[45]

From 1815 to 1816 rural Ireland was effectively a time bomb awaiting to explode in which there were disgruntled landlords, discontented middlemen and large tenant farmers and aggrieved smallholders, cottiers and labourers. A dramatic increase in agrarian disorder became inevitable.

Agrarian unrest was not exclusively a pre-famine phenomenon but it was probably more widespread and at least as complex in its origins than at any stage in the eighteenth century.[46] The 1760s and 1770s had witnessed large-scale agrarian disorder in many parts of Ireland. The Munster (and Kilkenny) disturbances of the 1760s focused on enclosures, high conacre rents and tithes. The emergence of secret societies such as Whiteboys and Levellers who bound themselves together by oaths, raided farmhouses, leveled fences, intimidated those who transgressed their moral laws became a ubiquity of Irish rural society for generations to come. In the 1790s the Dublin Castle administration and local resident landlords had frequently perceived outbreaks in terms of an assault on propertied Protestants, essentially

1972), p. 120.   **43** 'General Introduction' in Clark & Donnelly (eds), *Irish peasants*, p. 9; see also Enright Flannan, 'Pre-famine reform and emigration on the Wyndham estate in Clare' in *The Other Clare*, 8 (1984), pp 33–9.   **44** Maguire, *The Downshire estates*.   **45** J.S. Donnelly jr., *The great Irish potato famine* (Stroud, 2001), p. 162.   **46** For a very good introduction to the literature on agrarian crime, see Brian Griffin, *Sources for the study of crime in Ireland, 1801–1921* (Dublin, 2005), pp 11–17.

tying land and religion together. The rise of Defenderism in Ulster in the 1780s had certainly given organizational strength to lower class Catholics who felt they had grievances which had to be addressed,[47] but the so-called Armagh troubles of the 1780s and 1790s offer a very good example of how difficult it is to separate religious, agrarian and political motives.[48] While this episode of agitation has traditionally been seen in terms of sectarian-based disputes over access to land, more recent studies argue that their real basis lay in the political developments of the last quarter of the nineteenth century when the arming of Catholics through the Volunteer movement was perceived to be a threat to Protestant ascendancy.[49] Protestant Peep O' Day Boys began a campaign of nocturnal raids on Catholic homes for arms; Catholic Defenders reacted assuming the rôle of self-protecting vigilantes. As tensions escalated thousands of Catholics were forced to leave their homes in 1795–6 and migrate, some to neighbouring counties, others further west to Mayo, which, in turn, probably facilitated the rise of secret agrarian societies there at a later stage.[50]

In 1973 Joseph Lee's pioneering article 'The Ribbonmen' made the case that agrarian crime was not just about disputes between landlords and tenants; it more often was the product of intense class conflict between cottiers, labourers and small farmers on the one hand and large farmers (who may very well have been the formers' landlords because of varying degrees of sub-letting) on the other.[51] Perceived inequalities in tenurial arrangements, the desire to control the local agrarian economy by stabilizing rent levels or curbing landlord powers of eviction undoubtedly gave rise to the ubiquitous collective activity of pre-famine Ireland.[52]

---

47 Marianne Elliott, 'The Defenders in Ulster' in David Dickson, Dáire Keogh & Kevin Whelan (eds), *The United Irishmen: republicanism, radicalism and rebellion* (Dublin, 1993), p. 223. **48** D.W. Miller, 'The Armagh troubles, 1784–95' in Clark & Donnelly (eds), *Irish peasants*, pp 176–7; Jim Smyth, *The men of no property: Irish radicals and popular politics in the late eighteenth century* (Dublin, 1992) p. 5. **49** Dáire Keogh (ed.), *A patriot priest: the life of Fr James Coigly, 1761–1798* (Cork, 1998), pp 6–7; Smyth, *Men of no property*, p. 48; see also Donal A. Kerr, 'Priests, pikes and patriots: the Irish Catholic church and political violence from the Whiteboys to the Fenians' in S.J. Brown & D.W. Miller (eds), *Piety and power in Ireland, 1760–1960* (Belfast & Notre Dame, 2000), pp 16–42. **50** Keogh (ed.), *A patriot priest*, p. 11. **51** J.J. Lee, 'The Ribbonmen' in T.D. Williams (ed.), *Secret societies in Ireland* (Dublin, 1973), pp 26–35. **52** The best contemporary analysis is G.C. Lewis, *On local disturbances in Ireland; and on the Irish church question* (London, 1836); for later national and local studies see M.R. Beames, 'Rural conflict in pre-famine Tipperary: peasant assassinations in Tipperary, 1837–1847' in *Past & Present*, no. 81 (1978), pp 75–91; idem, *Peasants and power: the Whiteboy movements and their control in pre-famine Ireland* (Brighton & New York, 1983); idem, 'The Ribbon societies: lower class nationalism in pre-famine Ireland' in Philpin (ed.), *Nationalism and popular protest*, pp 245–81; John Belchem, 'Freedom and friendship to Ireland: Ribbonism in early nineteenth-century Liverpool' in *International Journal of Social History*, no. 39 (1994), pp 33–56; Gaelen Broeker, *Rural disorder and police reform in Ireland, 1812–36* (London & Toronto, 1970); Clark & Donnelly (eds), *Irish peasants*; J.S. Donnelly jr., 'The Rightboy movement, 1785–8' in *Studia Hibernica* (hereinafter *Studia Hib.*), nos 17–18 (1977–78), pp 120–202; idem, 'The Whiteboy movement, 1761–5' in *I.H.S.*, xxi, no. 81 (1978), pp 20–54; idem, 'Hearts of Oak, Hearts of Steel' in *Studia Hib.*, no. 21 (1981), pp 7–73; idem, 'Irish

There are, however, difficulties associated with using the term 'Ribbonmen' in the generic sense to describe all agrarian agitators (as, indeed, contemporary authorities were inclined to do.) These difficulties have been most clearly described in Jennifer Kelly's fascinating study of Ribbonism and popular mobilization in pre-famine Leitrim in which she questions the validity of seeing Ribbonism in terms of either a political or agrarian combination but instead portrays it as: 'essentially a self-contained organization which gave young men in pre-famine Leitrim opportunities to exercise a *machismo* which may have been otherwise constricted by family and economic structures'.[53] Her study provides an excellent template for the many other regional studies which are required to complete the historical landscape of Ribbonism and the various other societies which were responsible for outbreaks of rural disorder in 1813–16, 1819–22 and the early 1830s.

It should be noted that in each of these pre-famine outbreaks, as well as the Whiteboy outbreak in the 1760s and the Rightboy outbreak of the 1780s, the issue of tithes – taxes imposed on landholders to support the Church of Ireland clergy – also figured prominently.[54] From 1735 to 1823, livestock and livestock products had been exempt from liability to tithes. When the shift from pasture to tillage occurred in the eighteenth century more farmers came into the tithe net. Catholic farmers, who were also liable for the payment of exacting dues to their own clergy, resented the extra financial burden of a compulsory contribution to the upkeep of a minority church. Under the Tithe Composition Act of 1823, pasture as well as tillage lands became liable for tithes, arousing the resentment of the large livestock farmers who up to now had largely remained aloof from any type of agrarian protest movements. By the early 1830s as many as twenty-two counties were involved in the so-called Tithe War, a campaign against tithe payment that at times and in different areas moved from passive resistance to violent affray.[55]

agrarian rebellion: the Whiteboys of 1769–76' in *P.R.I.A. Proc.*, dccciii, no. 12 (1983), pp 293–331; idem, 'The social composition of agrarian rebellions in early nineteenth-century Ireland: the case of the Carders and Caravats, 1813–1816' in P.J. Corish (ed.), *Radicals, rebels and establishments: historical studies xv* (Belfast, 1985), pp 151–69; idem, 'The Terry Alt movement, 1829–31' in *History Ireland*, 2 (4) (1994), pp 30–5; Elliott, 'The Defenders in Ulster'; Tom Garvin, 'Defenders, Ribbonmen and others: underground political networks in pre-famine Ireland' in C.H.E. Philpin (ed.), *Nationalism and popular protest in Ireland* (Cambridge, 1987), pp 219–43; D.G. Marnane, 'Land and violence in 19th century Tipperary' in *Tipperary Historical Journal* (1988), pp 53–89; Desmond Mooney, 'The origins of agrarian violence in Meath, 1790–1828' in *Ríocht na Midhe*, viii, no. 1 (1987), pp 49–67; A.C. Murray, 'Agrarian violence and nationalism in nineteenth-century Ireland: the myth of Ribbonism' in *Irish Economic & Social History*, xiii (1986), pp 56–73; Shunsuka Katsuta, 'The Rockite movement in County Cork in the early 1820s' in *I.H.S.*, xxxiii, no. 131 (2003), pp 278–96; David Ryan, 'Ribbonism and agrarian crime in County Galway, 1819–1820' in *Journal of the Galway Archaeological & Historical Society* (hereinafter *Galway Arch. Soc. Jn.*), 52 (2000), pp 120–34. **53** Jennifer Kelly, 'An outward looking community? Ribbonism & popular mobilization in pre-famine Leitrim, 1836–1846' (unpublished Ph.D. thesis, Mary Immaculate College, University of Limerick, 2005). **54** M.J. Bric, 'The tithe system in eighteenth-century Ireland' in *R.I.A. Proc.*, C, dcccvi (1987), pp 271–88. **55** Clark & Donnelly (eds), *Irish peasants*, pp 30–1; see also Niamh

The late eighteenth and early nineteenth centuries, therefore, represented a period of great change in Ireland. It was a time when a huge number of rural combinations, some oath-bound, others probably not, came into existence. Some of these were of impressive magnitude such as the Caravats and Shanavests operating in east Muster in the first decade of the nineteenth century, or the Rockites concentrated in an area south of and including Kilkenny.[56] Other combinations were probably little more than roaming bands of banditti who had self-aggrandisement more than the collective good of the lower classes in mind. The rise of all of these coincided with the development of more national movements that had associational features including the O'Connellite movements of the 1820s to the 1840s but also movements bound by more agrarian issues such as tithes. The Great Famine did much to diminish the activity of these regional movements, but it by no means eradicated them as there would be sporadic outbreaks of so-called Ribbonism in counties such as Monaghan, Armagh and Westmeath in the 1850s and continued unrest in counties such as Limerick and Wexford during the 1860s.[57] The post-famine period saw instead the rise of much larger, more national associational movements such as the Land League and the National League which were to become linked to the Home Rule movement, inextricably tying land and politics together and bringing the strong farmers to the forefront of Irish nationalist politics.[58]

THE GREAT FAMINE, 1845–51

The sesquicentenary of the Great Famine produced an outpouring of publi-cations,[59] of disparate standard, going some way towards making up for the rather

Brennan, 'The Ballagh barracks riot of 1815: an early tithe protest in Co. Tipperary' in Bob Reece (ed.), *Irish convicts: the origins of convicts transported to Australia* (Dublin, 1989), pp 49–80; M.J. Bric, 'Priests, parsons and politics: the Rightboy protest in County Cork, 1785–1788' in Philpin (ed.), *Nationalism and popular protest in Ireland*, pp 163–90; J.S. Donnelly jr., 'Irish agrarian rebellion: the Whiteboys of 1769–76' in *R.I.A. Proc.*, C, dccciii, 12 (1983), pp 293–331; P. O'Donoghue, 'Causes of the opposition to tithes, 1830–38' in *Studia Hib.*, no. 5 (1965), pp 7–28; idem, 'Opposition to tithe payments in 1830–31' in *Studia Hib.*, no. 6 (1966), pp 69–98; idem, 'Opposition to tithe payments in 1832–33' in *Studia Hib.*, no. 12 (1972), pp 77–108; Michael O'Hanrahan, 'The tithe war in County Kilkenny, 1830–1834' in William Nolan & Kevin Whelan (eds), *Kilkenny: history and society. Interdisciplinary essays on the history of an Irish county* (Dublin, 1990), pp 481–505. **56** Other more regional studies include: Maria Luddy, 'Whiteboy support in Co. Tipperary, 1761–1789' in *Tipperary Historical Journal* (1989), pp 66–79; Eoin Magennis, 'County Armagh Hearts of Oak' in *Seanchas Ardmhacha*, 17 (2) (1998), pp 19–31; W.A. Maguire, 'Lord Donegall and the Hearts of Steel' in *I.H.S*, xxi, no. 84 (1979), pp 351–76; Ryan, 'Ribbonism and agrarian violence in County Galway'. **57** Pat Feeley, 'Whiteboys and Ribbonmen: early agrarian secret societies' in *Old Limerick Journal*, 4 (1980), pp 23–7. **58** Alvin Jackson, *Ireland: 1798–1998* (Oxford, 1999), p. 87. **59** A search under 'Ireland famine' on the www.irishhistoryonline website reveals around 700 publications, the bulk of which are related to the Great Famine.

glaring lacuna in famine studies until then.[60] Given the centrality of the landed estate to Irish rural society and economy, it seems remarkable that in this outpouring of works, there remained a dearth of focus on the effects of the famine on individual Irish estates, big houses or landed families.[61] Instead as Gearóid Ó Tuathaigh has put it: 'ideology has loomed large in many of these publications, together with studies of the politics of poor relief, the politics of resistance and the politics of recrimination'.[62] Until the mid-1990s, only the relevant chapters in James S. Donnelly jr.'s *The land and the people of nineteenth-century Cork* (London, 1975) and his comprehensive chapters in W.E.Vaughan (ed.), *A new history of Ireland, v, Ireland under the Union, i: 1801–1870* (Oxford, 1989) shed much light on the effects of famine on landed estates and their associated communities. In 2001 he drew much of this work together in *The great Irish potato famine* (Stroud, 2001). Robert Scally's *The end of hidden Ireland: rebellion, famine and emigration* (New York, 1995) is a useful experiment in micro-history that helps unveil the world of the tenantry at local level – a County Roscommon townland – in the years before and after the Great Famine.

The death of one million people and the further depopulation of the country by the emigration of 1.5 million more in only ten years (1845–55) inevitably caused major dislocation in Irish rural society.[63] Those who suffered most were the cottiers

<hr />

60 See 'Introduction' in Donnelly, *The great Irish potato famine*, pp 1–40. **61** However, see P.J. Duffy, 'Aspects of famine and the Farney landscape' in *Journal of the County Louth Archaeological & Historical Society*, 23 (1996), pp 393–404; Patrick Feeny, 'Ballysaggart estate: eviction, famine and conspiracy' in *Decies: Journal of the Waterford Archaeological & Historical Society*, 26 (1984), pp 5–12; Dermot James, *John Hamilton of Donegal: this recklessly generous landlord* (Dublin, 1998); S.P. Mac Manamon, 'Landlords and evictions in County Mayo during the Great Famine' in *Cathair na Mart*, 18 (1998), pp 125–34; Desmond Norton, 'On Lord Palmerston's Irish estates in the 1840s' in *English Historical Review*, 119 (484) (2004), pp 154–74. **62** Ó Tuathaigh, 'Political history', p. 13; amongst the major works which appeared around this time were M.E. Daly, *The famine in Ireland* (Dundalk, 1986); R.D. Edwards & T.D. Williams, *The Great Famine: studies in Irish history, 1845–52* (Dublin, 1956); Peter Gray, *Famine, land and politics: British government and Irish society, 1843–50* (Dublin, 1999); Jacqueline Hill & Cormac Ó Gráda (eds), *'The visitation of God'? The potato and the great Irish Famine* (Dublin, 1993); Liam Kennedy et al., *Mapping the Great Irish Famine: a survey of the famine decades* (Dublin, 1999); Donal A. Kerr, *'A nation of beggars'? Priests, people and politics in Famine Ireland, 1846–52,* (Oxford, 1994); Christine Kinealy, *This great calamity: the Irish famine, 1845–52* (Dublin, 1994); Joel Mokyr, *Why Ireland starved: a quantitative and analytical history of the Irish economy, 1800–1850* (London, 1983); Cormac Ó Gráda, *Black '47 and beyond: the Great Irish Famine in history, economy and memory* (Princeton NJ, 1999); idem, *The great Irish famine* (London, 1989); Cathal Póirtéir (ed.), *The great Irish famine* (Cork, 1995); for a very useful discussion of recent Famine historiography, see S.J. Connolly, 'Revisions revised: new work on the Irish Famine' in *Victorian Studies*, xxxix (1996), pp 205–16; for a chronology of the famine, see T.W. Moody, F.X. Martin & F.J. Byrne (eds), *A new history of Ireland, viii: a chronology of Irish history to 1976. A companion to Irish history, part I* (Oxford, 1982), pp 320–9. **63** For a concise overview see Donnelly, *The great Irish potato famine*, pp 132–68; also W.E. Vaughan, 'Reflections on the Great Famine' in *Ulster Local Studies*, 17 (2) (1995), pp 7–18.

and landless labourers who died in their hundreds of thousands; those who were better off emigrated in equal numbers simply because they could more afford to do so.[64] Many of those who emigrated were assisted by their landlords, some out of benevolence, others anxious to clear their estates of impoverished tenants and to consolidate their small holdings into more viable farms. One of the largest such assisted emigration schemes was carried out on the Lansdowne estate in Kerry from where 4,600 people were emigrated in the early 1850s.[65] How many tenants in total were provided with passages to America and elsewhere is difficult to determine but Oliver MacDonagh has estimated the number at around 50,000.[66]

In 1847 an amendment to the Poor Law Act of that year, the so-called 'Gregory clause', named after its proposer, Sir William Gregory, barred from public relief anyone holding more than a quarter of an acre of land. It was, therefore, only by surrendering their smallholdings that the poorer classes could receive necessary public assistance. Once they had been surrendered, many landlords used the opportunity to demolish the vacated simple dwellings, and, thereby cleared their estates of impoverished tenants. For those in the more congested poorer regions of the west, clearances also relieved landlords of the burden for all the rates (property taxes) of holdings valued at £4 or more for which they had been liable since August 1843. Lord Clanricarde, who had extensive estates in Galway, thus declared in late 1848: 'The landlords are *prevented* from aiding or tolerating poor tenants. They are compelled to hunt out all such, to save their property from the £4 clause.'[67]

Estate clearances (which had begun in some areas in 1846 before the introduction of the Gregory clause) gathered momentum in the following years and by 1853 an estimated 70,000 families had been evicted. W.E. Vaughan has found that there were 141 clearances where more than forty families were removed simultaneously from the same estate between 1850 and 1853.[68] Amongst the most notorious of these were the mass evictions that took place in the Kilrush poor law union in County Clare in the late 1840s, where an estimated 1,000 people were evicted from the Vandeleur estate and 2,800 people had their houses leveled on the neighbouring estates managed by Marcus Keane.[69] Whether we will ever know the true extent of evictions or clearances during the Great Famine is debatable. Even from 1849, when the constabulary began to record statistics on the same, they were only recording those evictions which had come to their attention. Like agrarian crimes, many undoubtedly went unreported.

64 See Oliver MacDonagh, 'Irish emigration to the United States of America and the British colonies during the famine' in Edwards & Williams (ed.), *The Great Famine: studies in Irish history, 1845–52* (new edition with a new introduction by Cormac Ó Gráda (Dublin, 1994), pp 319–88). 65 Donnelly, *The great Irish potato famine*, p. 141. 66 MacDonagh, 'Irish overseas emigration', p. 335. 67 Quoted in Donnelly, *The great Irish potato famine*, p. 138. 68 Vaughan, *Landlords and tenants in mid-Victorian Ireland*, pp 24–6; see also J.S. Donnelly jr., 'Mass eviction and the Great Famine' in Póirtéir (ed.), *Great Famine*, pp 155–73; T.P. O'Neill, 'Famine evictions' in Carla King (ed.), *Famine, land and culture in Ireland* (Dublin, 2000), pp 29–70. 69 Donnelly, *The great Irish potato famine*, pp 144–52; Ignatius Murphy, *A people starved: life and death in west Clare* (Dublin & Portland, OR, 1996), pp 53–80; see also, Tom

Between 1845 and 1851 approximately 25 per cent of farm holdings became available as occupiers died, emigrated or vacated them in favour of the workhouse. Landlords and strong farmers benefited as a result: landlords were able to consolidate holdings on their estates on an extensive scale,[70] which meant that many post-famine farmers worked larger, more viable holdings. James S. Donnelly jr. has shown that farms above fifteen acres in size increased dramatically in proportional terms from less that a third of all holdings in 1845 to almost half by 1851 and concludes: 'There was never again so sudden and drastic a change in the structure of landholding in Ireland as that which occurred during and immediately after the famine.'[71] This in turn sped up the expansion of commercial livestock farming and signaled a move away from tillage. New expansive grass ranches began to form in the east, the Midlands and even in areas of Connaught such as Roscommon, east Galway and south Mayo. There was a new landlord determination to 'populate' their estates with improving farmers; an unapologetic Marcus Keane argued that after the clearances in Kilrush he took the land from the 'bad and enlarge[d] the holdings of the good'.[72] For new purchasers of estates, one of the incentives to buy, as sometimes indicated in the Encumbered Estates rentals, was that the estate had been cleared of 'superfluous', undoubtedly meaning impoverished tenants.[73]

The middlemen were the other class to suffer most from the Great Famine. Donnelly contends that: 'They were ground into dust between the upper and nether millstones.'[74] They hardly starved to death, but their way of life was radically changed as the Great Famine provided many landlords with the opportunity to eradicate them from their estates – for different reasons they were perceived as no less of a nuisance than impoverished tenants – and some did so calculatedly by refusing to grant abatements on their rents.[75]

Many landlords did not have the luxury of simply having to concern themselves with getting rid of middlemen; they had to worry about their own financial survival. There were a few who impoverished themselves by helping their destitute

Yager, 'Mass eviction in the Mullet Peninsula during and after the Great Famine' in *Irish Economic & Social History*, xxiii (1996), pp 24–44. **70** For local studies of estates during the famine see, James Dermot & Seamus Ó Maitiu, *The Wicklow world of Elizabeth Smith, 1840–1850* (Dublin, 1996); Patrick Feeney, 'Balysaggart estate: Eviction, famine and conspiracy' in *Decies*, no. 27 (autumn, 1984), pp 4–12; Eileen McCourt, 'The management of the Farnham estates during the nineteenth century' in *Breifne*, iv (1975), pp 531–60; *The Irish journals of Elizabeth Smith, 1840–50*, ed. David Thomson & Michael McGusty (Oxford, 1980); for more general studies of the effects of famine on estate management, see relevant chapters of Donnelly, *Land and people of Cork*; Cullen, *Econ. Hist. Ireland since 1660*; also of interest, J.M. Goldstrom, 'Irish agriculture and the great famine' in Goldstrom & Clarkson (eds), *Irish population, economy and society*, pp 155–71; Cormac Ó Gráda, *Ireland before and after the famine: explorations in economic history, 1800–1925* (Manchester, 1988); T.P. O'Neill, 'The Irish land question, 1830–50' in *Studies*, xliv (autumn, 1955), pp 325–36. **71** Donnelly, *The great Irish potato famine*, pp 161–2. **72** Quoted in ibid., p. 152. **73** Ibid., p. 159. **74** J.S. Donnelly jr., 'Landlords and tenants' in Vaughan (ed.), *A new history of Ireland, v, Ireland under the union, I*, p. 333. **75** Donnelly, *The great Irish potato famine*, p. 134.

tenants through famine relief schemes but the majority of those who fell foul of the crisis were probably more likely to have been victims of falling income levels and rising indebtedness. It remains to be seen to what extent rent levels fell on the majority of Irish estates, but a decline of more than 50 per cent on individual estates from 1846–7 to 1852 may not be improbable.[76] A great number of already heavily burdened landlords were, therefore, pushed to bankruptcy. By 1849 there was property with an estimated rental of £2 million (out of a total national rental of around £13 million) under the control of the Courts of Equity.

In the pre-famine period, legal complexities made it extremely difficult to prove title on heavily encumbranced estates and this, in turn, was a major obstacle to their sale. The Encumbered Estates Act of 1849, superseding a similar act of the year before, was designed to simplify the transfer of encumbered property by breaking entail and conferring on the purchaser a parliamentary or indefeasible title.[77] (Philip Bull makes the important point that the act also witnessed 'the beginning of active intervention by parliament in the problems of land tenure and management in Ireland'.[78]) Under the auspices of a newly established Encumbered Estates Court,[79] the three judges were given authority to order the sale of any estate upon the application of a single encumbrancer if the level of annual debts was greater than half of its net annual income.[80] The court could oversee the sale of estates held in fee, leaseholds in perpetuity, or viable leases which had up to sixty years to run. Within a year a total of 1,200 petitions for sale had been lodged with the court, many of which had been brought to insolvency by the effects of the Great Famine.[81] Over the next thirty years an estimated 25 per cent (or five million acres) changed hands, the biggest transfers taking place in the early 1850s.[82] Another point worth mentioning is that the judges were empowered to arrange exchanges between landlords (even if one was not the owner of an estate to be sold in the court.) The extent to which this facilitated major change in the Irish rural estate landscape remains to be seen, but there certainly were many examples of landlords consolidating their estates in more compact units by exchanging outlying areas with another neighbouring landlord.

Unfortunately for landowners who sold under the act in the early years, the market value of land was at rock bottom. While landed property had sold in Ireland for an average of 20 to 25 years' purchase of current rents in the 1830s, prices realized in the 1850s were as low as 10 to 15 years' purchase.[83] This undoubtedly

76 Ibid., p. 136.   **77** 12 & 13 Vict., c. lxxvii (28 July 1849).   **78** Philip Bull, *Land, politics and nationalism: a study of the Irish land question* (Dublin, 1996), p. 2.   **79** Later the Landed Estates Court and later still the Land Judges Court.   **80** For an introduction to sales under the courts, see M.C. Lyons, *Illustrated incumbered estates: Ireland, 1850–1905* (Clare, 1993).   **81** Donnelly, *The great Irish potato famine*, p. 162.   **82** See P.G. Lane, 'The Encumbered Estates Court, Ireland, 1848–49' in *Economic and Social Review*, 3 (1972), pp 413–53; idem, 'The general impact of the Encumbered Estates Act of 1849 on counties Galway and Mayo' in *Galway Arch. Soc. Jn.*, 33 (1972–3), pp 44–74; idem, 'The impact of the Encumbered Estates Court upon the landlords of Galway and Mayo' in *Galway Arch. Soc. Jn.*, 38 (1981–2), pp 45–58.   **83** J.S. Donnelly jr., *Landlord and tenant in nineteenth-century Ireland* (Dublin, 1973),

appealed to speculators; within a few years of the ending of the Great Famine when the economy recovered, some of the 'new' landlords were petitioning for the sale of their own estates, suggesting that there had been considerable purchasing simply to sell at generous profits when the time was right. In 1851 Vincent Scully, MP for Cork for most of the 1850s and early 1860s, bought the Castlehyde estate near Fermoy for just over £14,400 and resold it nine years later for £45,000.[84] However, the traditional view that new proprietors were mainly businessmen/speculators is now not as widely accepted, for it seems that in fact at least as much property was purchased by the wealthier landlords who had survived the Great Famine. Moreover, it would make for an interesting study to establish how many younger sons of landlords, grandsons and so on who had made careers for themselves outside land (in the business or professional worlds) availed of the opportunity to buy back into the social respectability of the landed class. It might be found that the extent to which the base of the original landowning class in Ireland was diluted by the influx of 'outsiders' was marginal.[85]

POST-FAMINE IRELAND

The dominant position of the land question(s) in the post-famine period and the fact that land and politics became inextricably entwined, if it was not already so, has provided one of the most fertile research areas for historians of the mid- to late Victorian period.[86] Until the 1970s, much of what was accepted about landlords and landlordism emanated from two works published at either end of the 1930s: J.E. Pomfret, *The struggle for land in Ireland, 1800–1923* (Princeton, 1930) and Elizabeth R. Hooker, *Readjustments of agricultural tenure in Ireland* (Chapel Hill, 1938). As W.E. Vaughan pointed out in his erudite assessment of landlord and tenant relations in Ireland in the period 1850–78, enshrined in these works was 'the picture of a peasantry oppressed by high rents, insecure in its holdings and goaded into violence by its grievances.'[87] From the 1970s a small group of historians and economists began to put forward an alternative interpretation.[88]

p.49; twenty-five years purchase of current rents means the yearly rental of the property sold multiplied by 25.   **84** Donnelly, *The great Irish potato famine*, p. 165; see also P.G. Lane, 'The Encumbered Estates Court and Galway landownership, 1849–58' in Moran & Gillespie (eds), *Galway: history and society*, pp 395–417; Lindsay Proudfoot, 'The estate system in mid-nineteenth-century County Waterford' in William Nolan, T.P. Power & Des Cowman (eds), *Waterford: history and society: Interdisciplinary essays on the history of an Irish county* (Dublin, 1992), pp 519–40.   **85** For Cork, see Donnelly, *Land and people of Cork*, p. 131.   **86** Paul Bew, *C.S. Parnell* (Dublin, 1980); Sally Warwick-Haller, *William O'Brien and the Irish land war* (Dublin, 1990); Donal McCartney (ed.), *Parnell: the politics of power* (Dublin, 1991); Bull, *Land, politics and nationalism*.   **87** W.E. Vaughan, 'Landlord and tenant relations in Ireland between the Famine and the land war, 1850–1878' in L.M. Cullen & T.C. Smout (eds), *Comparative aspects of Scottish and Irish economic and social history, 1600–1900* (Edinburgh, 1977), pp 216–26; see also idem, *Landlords and tenants in mid-Victorian Ireland*, p. vi.   **88** The most important of these works include: R.D. Crotty, *Irish agricultural production* (Cork, 1966); Donnelly, *Land and*

Barbara Solow's *The land question and the Irish economy, 1870–1903* (Cambridge, MA, 1971) threw existing orthodoxy on its head when she argued that tenant farmers had not been exploited in the aftermath of the Great Famine; if they were insecure it was not because they lived in dread of evictions but because their rents were (too) low and they wanted to keep them that way.[89] Four years later James S. Donnelly jr. brought the reappraisal of the land question a stage forward in his authoritative *The land and the people of nineteenth-century Cork* (London, 1975). Through a forensic examination of a much more formidable array of sources than that used by Solow (who largely depended upon parliamentary papers), including over thirty sets of estate records, he observed that rent movements were not exorbitant and that generalizations about a capricious and rackrenting class of landlords could not be sustained. Seven years later, W.E. Vaughan's *Landlords and tenants in mid-Victorian Ireland* (Oxford, 1994) dealt, in his own words, with 'certain aspects of relations between landlords and tenants in mid-nineteenth-century Ireland: evictions, rents, tenant rights, estate management, agrarian outrages, and conflicts between landlords and tenants' in an attempt to move further away from works which 'gave the predatory landlord a central place in nineteenth-century Irish history'.[90] Already in 1977, Vaughan's important paper on landlord and tenant relations in Ireland (1850–78), building on his own and others' recent research, had succinctly and convincingly debunked much of the Pomfret and Hooker orthodoxy. Since the publication of these studies by Donnelly, Solow and Vaughan, there has been an outpouring of books and articles which have reshaped thinking on a variety of land-related issues from 1853, some of the most important of which will be noted in the brief discussion which follows. One local study worth mentioning is Gerard Lyne's award-winning and meticulously researched *The Lansdowne estate in Kerry under the agency of William Steuart Trench, 1849–72* (Dublin, 2001). The most comprehensive local study of estate management in the post-famine to the early 1870s period published to date, this substantial work of eighteen chapters illustrates the potential of estate studies, particularly where the author has a comprehensive estate collection to work with that he or she can supplement with a vast array of other primary sources, in Lyne's case parliamentary papers, local newspapers, local government archives, the Kerry diocesan archives (the diary of Fr O'Sullivan) and folklore archives.

What is now clear is that by the early 1850s, the Irish economy was beginning to recover from the calamitous effects of the Great Famine and except for a

---

people of Cork; L.P. Curtis, 'Incumbered wealth: landlord indebtedness in post-famine Ireland' in *American Historical Review*, 85 (1980), pp 332–67; Terence Dooley, 'Landlords and the land question, 1879–1909' in King (ed.), *Famine, land and culture in Ireland*, pp 116–39; Cormac Ó Gráda, 'The investment behaviour of Irish landlords, 1850–75: some preliminary findings' in *Agricultural History Review*, xxxiii (1975), pp 139–55; Robinson, 'The London companies', pp 103–18; B.L. Solow, *The land question and the Irish economy, 1870–1903* (Cambridge, MA, 1971); Vaughan, *Landlords and tenants in mid-Victorian Ireland*.   **89** Solow, *The land question*, p. 51. **90** Vaughan, *Landlords and tenants in mid-Victorian Ireland*, p. iv.

temporary interruption in the early 1860s, this economic prosperity continued until
the late 1870s.[91] Irish agricultural output and prices rose steadily between then and
the mid-1870s (despite a temporary fallback in the early 1860s): output increased
by 47 per cent from the early 1850s to the mid-1870s; the price of cereals rose by
46 per cent; livestock products by 81 per cent; and butter by 86 per cent. Overall,
the annual average value of agricultural output rose by 40 per cent from 1851–5 to
1871–5; farmers' incomes increased by an estimated 77 per cent over the same
period, while bank deposits increased by 400 per cent from 1845 to 1876.[92] Rent
increases over the period were moderate, on average by around 20 per cent when
the market could have accommodated a rise of 40 per cent.[93] Rents were generally
being paid in full and on time and, indeed, arrears that had accumulated during the
Great Famine were being cleared.[94] Vaughan has estimated that rents collected
between 1851 and 1880 amounted to £354 million (but also notably that if they
had increased in line with agricultural output, step by step, the total would have
been £400 million, or 13 per cent more).[95]

Prosperity was arguably reflected in the peace of the countryside; agrarian
outrages exceeded 500 per annum in only seven years between 1850 and 1880,[96]

---

91 J.S. Donnelly jr., 'The Irish agricultural depression of 1859–64' in *Irish Economic & Social
History*, iii (1976), pp 33–54; Vaughan, 'Landlord and tenant relations between the famine and
the land war', pp 216–26; idem, 'Agricultural output, rents and wages in Ireland, 1850–80' in
L.M. Cullen & F. Furet (eds), *Ireland and France, 17th–20th centuries: towards a comparative study
of rural history* (Paris, 1990), pp 85–97; idem, 'An assessment of the economic performance of
Irish landlords, 1851–81' in F.S.L. Lyons & R.A.J. Hawkins (eds), *Ireland under the union:
varieties of tension. Essays in honour of T.W. Moody* (Oxford, 1980), pp 173–99; Liam Dolan,
Land war and eviction in Derryveagh, 1840–65 (Dundalk, 1980); P.G. Lane, 'The management of
estates by financial corporations in Ireland after the famine' in *Studia Hib.*, no. 14 (1974), pp
67–89; T.P. O'Neill, 'From famine to near famine, 1845–79' in *Studia Hib.*, no. 1 (1961), pp
161–71.   **92** M. Winstanley, *Ireland and the land question, 1800–1922* (London, 1984), p. 9.
93 In a study of rentals for fifty estates, W.E. Vaughan found that rents had increased by an
average of 20 per cent over this period. J.S. Donnelly jr., while finding some 'extremely
large' rent increases on individual estates in Cork, concluded that the more typical increases
ranged from 20 to 30 per cent which were 'well within the limits of the price and
production increments of the time'. Barbara Solow, using parliamentary papers and
agricultural statistics, calculated that rents increased by just under 30 per cent from 1850 to
1880. A study of estates by this writer found an average rental increase of 26 per cent.
Vaughan, *Landlords and tenants in mid-Victorian Ireland*, p. 48; Donnelly, *Land and people of
Cork*, pp 191–4; Solow, *The land question*, pp 66–70; Dooley, *The decline of the big house*, p. 31.
94 Dooley, *The decline of the big house*, pp 30–4.   **95** Vaughan, *Landlords and tenants in mid-
Victorian Ireland*, p. 21.   **96** See, for example, Vaughan, *Landlords and tenants in mid-Victorian
Ireland*, pp 138–60; David Fitzpatrick, 'Class, family and rural unrest in nineteenth-century
Ireland' in P.J. Drudy (ed.), *Irish studies 2, Ireland: land, people and politics* (Cambridge, 1982),
pp 37–75; Charles Townshend, *Political violence in Ireland: government and resistance since 1848*
(Oxford, 1983), pp 14–24; A.C. Murray, 'Agrarian violence and nationalism in nineteenth-
century Ireland: the myth of Ribbonism' in *Irish Economic & Social History*, xiii (1986), pp
56–73. For local agrarianism between the famine and land war see Breandán Mac Giolla
Choille, 'Fenians, Rice and Ribbonmen in Co. Monaghan, 1864–67' in *Clogher Rec.*, vi, no.
2 (1967), pp 221–52; Kevin MacMahon and Thomas McKeown, 'Agrarian disturbances

and evictions averaged only around 20 in 10,000 over most of the period, so that 'tenants enjoyed practical security of tenure on most estates, and, even when threatened with eviction, showed considerable powers of survival and resistance'.[97] Evictions waned in a climate of prosperity that was much freer from agrarian outrage than Ireland had been in the decades before the Great Famine with very few clearances after 1853;[98] of course, the fact that the cottiers and labourers, the very classes who had sustained agitation in the past, had been virtually wiped out by famine was a contributory factor. Evictions continued to be frequent during periods of temporary depression when arrears were high and agricultural output was low as in the early 1850s, early 1860s, late 1870s and early 1880s; they were less frequent when agricultural output and prosperity increased and arrears decreased as from the mid-1850s to the early 1860s and from 1865 to 1877. One of Barbara Solow's most controversial conclusions, emanating from her econometric analysis, was that the low eviction rate of around 3 per cent between 1855 and 1880 was not conducive to good estate management. She points out that 'when one considers such valid reasons for eviction as dilapidation, bad farming practices, and prevention of subdivision, not even to mention consolidation, the small number of evictions is perhaps not a subject for congratulations'.[99] This argument, however, fails to consider the social responsibility that landlords may (or may not, depending on the individual) have felt towards his tenantry that made a business-like approach to estate management often morally impossible.

Many of those who did prosper used their new-found wealth to branch into business by buying or establishing local shops, public houses and hotels,[1] or perhaps just as often, increased trade saw many shopkeepers, publicans and merchants branch into farming, as landholding was still far more socially prestigious than owning urban property. The interconnection helped consolidate links between the rural and town traders and the farming class that would have great significance from the late 1870s with the rise of the Land League.[2]

Meanwhile, landownership remained the preserve of a privileged minority. Assuming that the smallest estate entitling its owner to be considered a landlord was 500 acres, there were about 6,500 landlords in Ireland by the 1870s. However, as

---

around Crossmaglen, 1835–55' in *Seanchas Ardmhacha*, 9 (2) (1979), pp 302–32; 10 (1) (1981), pp 149–75; 10 (2) (1982), pp 380–416; J.W. Hurst, 'Disturbed Tipperary, 1831–60' in *Éire-Ireland*, ix (1974), pp 44–59. **97** Vaughan, 'Landlord and tenant relations', pp 219–20. **98** There were two notable exceptions: in September 1853, forty-two families were evicted in the townland of Kilcoosh, Co. Galway; in April 1861, forty-even families were evicted at Derryveagh in Co. Donegal. Vaughan, *Landlords and tenants in mid-Victorian Ireland*, pp 20–6; idem, *Sin, sheep and Scotsmen: John George Adair and the Derryveagh evictions, 1861* (Belfast, 1983); Dolan, *Land war and eviction in Derryveagh, 1840–65*. See also Gerard Moran, *The Mayo evictions of 1860: Patrick Lavelle and the 'war' in Partry* (Cathair na Mart, 1986). **99** Solow, *The land question*, p. 53. **1** For a classic example see the unpublished memoirs of Thomas Toal who was to become first chairman of Monaghan County Council in 1899 and hold the position for over forty years (Monaghan County Museum, Toal papers). **2** See below.

W.E. Vaughan points out: 'Most of the country was covered by much larger estates: about 48 per cent by estates of 5,000 acres and upwards, which were owned by only 700 landlords.'[3] Economically landlords remained at the apex of Irish rural society, drawing a rental of over £10 million which was distributed amongst what was, after all, a relatively small group. The most obvious manifestation of post-famine prosperity was their embarkation on what could be described as the last great phase of big house embellishment in Ireland.[4] Very few landlords built new houses in the post-famine period but there were likewise very few who did not remodel existing ones, add to their contents or further adorn their demesnes. In this respect they were greatly facilitated by the increased collateral value of Irish land that allowed them to borrow extravagantly in order to live likewise.[5]

Agents continued to manage the larger estates. Even though by the 1870s a significant proportion were still drawn directly from landed families, there was a tendency to appoint lawyers and solicitors to vacant positions (but many of these, it should be noted, were often no more than a generation removed themselves from the landed class). There was also a growth in land agency firms whereby several estates were administered from one central office in cities such as Dublin and Cork. By 1880 the firm of Hussey and Townsend, for example, collected £250,000 in annual rents from eighty-eight estates in the south of Ireland.[6] This is not to say that agents operated alone; there remained a much more complex administrative hierarchy in place on most of the larger estates involving agents, sub-agents, bailiffs, auditors and so on.[7]

After the Great Famine, the management of estates generally became much more vigorous as landlords attempted to make up lost ground by ensuring rents were paid in full and on time; they rigorously opposed subdivision and subletting; they looked less favourably on the middleman system and they became increasingly reluctant to grant long leases (by 1870 only about 20 per cent of 662,000 holdings were held on leases, most of them for terms of twenty-one or thirty-one years).[8] There was not as Pomfret had claimed a ceaseless demand for increased rents; in general landlords usually only increased their rents after the termination of a lease, the transfer of a holding to a son, the succession of an heir to the estate, or after the revaluation of an estate which might only take place every twenty years or so. In 1880 a survey of 1,300 estates (covering about one third of Irish land) carried out by the Irish Land Committee found that on 70 per cent of the acreage rents had been fixed in the 1850s or earlier and not raised thereafter. Many looked to the consolidation of farms as a means of improving estate management or retained

3 Vaughan, *Landlords and tenants in mid-Victorian Ireland*, p. 6.   4 See chapter three.
5 Dooley, *The decline of the big house*, pp 34–43; see also chapter three.   6 Donnelly, *Land and people of Cork*, pp 182–5.   7 Lindsay Proudfoot, 'The management of a great estate: patronage, income and expenditure on the duke of Devonshire's Irish property, *c.*1816–1891' in *Irish Economic & Social History*, xiii (1986), pp 37–8.   8 Donnelly, *Landlords and tenants in nineteenth-century Ireland*, p. 60; for a contemporary insight to Irish land laws see A.G. Richey, *The Irish land laws* (London, 1880).

large tracts of vacated untenanted land for themselves as they branched more and more into farming to share in what was becoming an increasingly more lucrative form of enterprise from the mid-1850s. From 1855 to 1890, William Ross Mahon of Castlegar, in County Galway, for example, appropriated over 2,000 acres from large graziers on his estate as their leases expired. Whereas, in 1850, his predecessor had farmed only 250 acres, rearing 48 heifers and 160 sheep, William Ross was rearing 1,000 cattle and 2,000 sheep on a ranch over ten times that size in 1890. His gross stock sales in 1890 were £8,200 compared to his predecessor's £170 in 1850. By the 1870s around 15 per cent of Irish land was held in demesne farms.[9]

'If', as W.E. Vaughan rightly asked, 'rents lagged behind increases in the value of agricultural output and if tenants were prosperous, why were there so many complaints about rents and why was there a growing, if somewhat erratically pursued, demand for legislation to curb the powers of the landlords?'[10] Vaughan himself offers three possible explanations: there were too often illogical increases and variations in rents which created resentment among farmers on the same estate, if not from estate to estate, who were given ample ammunition to complain about the inequity of the system; any of the statistics above should not hide the fact that increased prosperity was by no means universal: the small uneconomic holders, primarily in the west, continued to struggle against hardship; and that 'the very fact that rents lagged behind increases in the value of agricultural output gave tenants a vested interest in securing legislation which would prevent them from ever catching up'.[11] Moreover, the overall investment behaviour of landlords in their estates continued to leave a lot to be desired. Cormac Ó Gráda suggests that landlords spent no more than 3 to 5 per cent of their annual rental income on improvements from 1850 to 1875.[12]

In post-famine Ireland, the burning issue in agrarian politics was essentially the provision of the 'Three Fs': fair rents, fixity of tenure and free sale.[13] Tenant right had existed long before the 1850s. In Ulster, the tradition went back to the early plantations – therefore the alternative term 'Ulster custom' – but it had no foundation in law, being merely based on the customary co-operation of landlords and agents with their tenants.[14] The greatest problem regarding tenant right was the extreme difficulty in actually defining what it meant, how it was interpreted, used

9 Jones, *Graziers*, pp 121–3.   10 Vaughan, 'Landlords and tenant relations', p. 217.   11 Ibid.
12 Ó Gráda, 'The investment behaviour of Irish landlords', pp 151–3. On nine estates, W.E. Vaughan found that around 11 per cent was spent on improvements. However, he concludes that this was probably above the average because of the presence of large estates in his sample: 'the sort of estates where high expenditure on improvements was most likely to occur'. He estimates that the average for all estates was probably no more than 4 or 5 per cent; Vaughan, *Landlords and tenants in mid-Victorian Ireland*, pp 122–3, 277–8.   13 R.D. Collison Black, *Economic thought and the Irish question, 1817–1870* (Cambridge, 1960), p. 24; R.V. Comerford, 'Churchmen, tenants, and independent opposition, 1850–56' in Vaughan (ed.), *A new history of Ireland, v, Ireland under the union, I*, p. 397; E.D. Steele, *Irish land and British politics: tenant right and nationality, 1865–70* (Cambridge, 1974).   14 M.W. Dowling, *Tenant right and agrarian society in Ulster, 1600–1870* (Dublin, 1999).

and enforced. Contemporary lawyers Ferguson and Vance thought it 'a phantom that melts away under every attempt to define it and that, chameleon-like, appeared to assume a different aspect every time it presents itself'.[15] In its most simple form, the custom, which was more widespread than Ulster, presumed that tenants would not be evicted as long as they paid their rents, which were presumed to be fair, and that they could sell their right in their holding when giving it up. The most important F was free sale; this right to sell was extremely valuable to outgoing tenants as some got as much as twenty years' the value of the rent of their holdings (which possibly equated to the fee simple value of the farm).[16]

By the 1850s the general application of the Ulster Custom was seen as a fundamental right by tenant organizations and the demand for its universal implementation became increasingly widespread. Earlier attempts to legislate for the custom, most notably by William Sharman Crawford, MP for Rochdale, in 1847, had failed miserably but Sharman's attempts coincided with the development of a number of tenant organizations in counties such as Kilkenny and Tipperary in response to the agrarian crisis of the Great Famine. Within two years, a national organization emerged, the Irish Tenant League, officially established in Dublin in the early autumn of 1850. Led by priests and Presbyterian ministers, it drew together the many tenant protections societies that had been operating at local level and gave Catholic and Presbyterian small farmers, north and south, common cause (at least temporarily). In 1852 two years after the extension of the Irish county franchise to occupiers of land valued at £12 and over, forty of the MPs returned for Ireland were returned on the Tenant League ticket. However, they became embroiled in wider political controversies which did little to forward agrarian issues in Ireland. Then, as the economy recovered, tenant agitation became less important and went into decline.

The next significant agrarian upheaval coincided with the economic depression of the early 1860s. Historians have not been widely attracted to this particular episode which lasted from roughly 1859 to 1864.[17] A combination of major droughts in 1859 followed by the inundations of 1860–2 and another drought in 1863 contributed to massive losses in both crop and livestock agricultural produce with negative impacts on all classes from graziers down to smallholders. While the depression had regional variations – the west and north-west were the worst affected areas while the south escaped relatively unscathed – the overall effect was calamitous as the smaller tenants, at least, struggled to pay their rents. While permanent evictions increased once again, as they always tended to do during periods of economic crisis, rising to an average of 1,230 families a year between 1861 and 1864, they never reached the scale of the Great Famine.[18]

---

15 Vaughan, *Landlords and tenants in mid-Victorian Ireland*, p. 67.   16 Quoted in ibid., p. 71; for a fuller discussion on tenant-right see ibid., pp 67–102.   17 The only significant work to date is J.S. Donnelly jr., 'The Irish agricultural depression of 1859–64' in *Irish Economic & Social History*, iii (1976), pp 33–54.   18 Ibid., p. 49.

There were landlords such as Robert Dillon, third Baron Clonbrock in Galway, for whom the consolidation of farms in the post-famine period and the rise of the strong farmer on his estate – he had at least twenty tenants who were paying in excess of £100 per annum and between them accounting for 40 per cent of total rents paid – meant that he weathered the storm with little difficulty. The ability of these large farmers to pay their rents in full and on time even during the critical period of the early 1860s allowed him to grant abatements to the less well-off tenants of either a year's or a half year's rent, almost as a pre-emptive strike to any agitation.[19]

Historians have been grappling with the question as to why this economic depression did not lead to the type of mass agitation that was to accompany the outbreak of the late 1870s. One possible reason is suggested by the Clonbrock example above: rent increases had remained moderate on the estate while the prosperity of the large farmer, who had probably managed to save during the good years, subsidized the abatements granted to the smaller tenants. There were, of course, wider considerations such as the efficiency of the constabulary in keeping disorder in check, the opposition of the Roman Catholic clergy to secret societies and generally 'the complexity of the relationship between constabulary, landlords and priests, and their capacity to settle disputes'.[20] The spectre of famine was still too vivid in tenants' minds; the energy and motivation that was required for collective organization was simply not vibrant enough less than ten years after the Great Famine had ended. In the early 1860s farmers were not as fully politicized as they would be by the early 1880s, with aspirations towards a share in the running of a Home Rule Ireland.

On the other hand, by 1879, a generation later, J.S. Donnelly jr. has argued that the land war was brought about by 'rising expectations' created by prosperity: tenant farmers had become accustomed to a standard of living that they were anxious to maintain.[21] When the economic bubble burst for everybody in the late 1870s, smallholders found themselves being championed by their strong farmer neighbours (who, it should be noted, were less likely to interact with them socially) and shopkeepers, publicans and merchants in search of political status on Land League platforms and a commensurate share in the political governing of Ireland to match their new-found socio-economic status. Moreover, by the late 1870s, individually impressive and charismatic leaders such as Charles Stewart Parnell, Michael Davitt and John Devoy drew together constitutionalists, agrarian agitators and separatists in the so-called new departure.[22] These different leaders may have

---

19 Dooley, *The decline of the big house*, pp 32–3. **20** Vaughan, *Landlords and tenants in mid-Victorian Ireland*, p. 205. **21** Donnelly, *Land and people of Cork*, pp 249–50; see also below. **22** For their involvement in the land questions see Bew, *C.S. Parnell*; idem, *Charles Stewart Parnell* (Dublin, 1991); idem, 'Parnell and Davitt' in D.G. Boyce and Alan O'Day (eds), *Parnell in perspective* (London, 1991), pp 38–51; R.V. Comerford, 'The land war and the politics of distress, 1877–82' in W.E. Vaughan (ed.), *A new history of Ireland, vi: Ireland under the union, II, 1870–1921* (Oxford, 1996), pp 26–52; Michael Davitt, *The fall of feudalism: or the story of the*

had different agendas but the new departure at least recognized the inextricable link between the land and national questions and that one could be used to forward the other. The change in attitudes of the Fenian leadership epitomized this. In the 1860s the primary focus of the Fenians was national independence, not the solution of the land question, even if it did at this time give birth to the cry of 'the land for the people', and fuel the belief that a successful Irish revolution would lead to the re-division of Irish land.[23] The movement attracted only some disgruntled agricultural labourers and small farmers. By the late 1870s the leadership had more fully familiarized itself with the potential that supporting an attractive agrarian programme offered for conjuring mass appeal and the movement in turn would become important to the land war (although never popular with the graziers and large farmers whom Fenian leaders often portrayed, along with landlords, as hindrances to nationalist aspirations.) J.S. Donnelly jr. has argued:

> The new agrarian militancy of many fenians in the 1870s was predicated on the view that tenant farmers could be converted to revolutionary nationalism by enlisting them in an agitation that had peasant proprietorship as one of its main goals, a goal that would be maddeningly refused by the British parliament, thus convincing outraged tenants of the necessity of prior political revolution.[24]

In the meantime, after the hiccough of the early 1860s, rural society settled down to an extended period of relative calm during which there was considerable stability in landlord-tenant relations throughout the second half of the 1860s and much of the 1870s. However, land questions did not disappear and there continued to be grievance-driven schisms on a number of estates linked particularly to the fallout from the 1870 Land Act. This act was introduced by a Liberal government under W.E. Gladstone as part of his self-proclaimed 'mission to pacify Ireland'. It set out to tackle the burning issue of insecurity of tenure that had never been resolved and which had the potential to lead to continued agrarian problems in the future.

land league revolution (London, 1904); Terence Dooley, 'The greatest of the Fenians': *John Devoy and Ireland* (Dublin, 2003); L.M. Geary, 'Parnell and the Irish Land question' in McCartney (ed.), *Parnell: the politics of power*, pp 90–101; Carla King, *Michael Davitt* (Dundalk, 1999); Donal McCartney, 'Parnell, Davitt and the land question' in King (ed.), *Famine, land and culture in Ireland*, pp 71–82; F.S.L. Lyons, *Charles Stewart Parnell* (London, 1977); T.W. Moody, 'The new departure in Irish politics, 1878–9' in H.A. Cronne, T.W. Moody & D.B. Quinn (eds), *Essays in British and Irish history in honour of James Eadie Todd* (London, 1949), pp 303–33; idem, *Davitt and the Irish revolution*; Alan O'Day, *Charles Stewart Parnell* (Dublin, 1998); *Devoy's post bag, 1871–1928*, ed. William O'Brien & Desmond Ryan (2 vols, Dublin, 1948, 1953; reprint Dublin, 1979); Sally Warwick-Haller, 'Parnell and William O'Brien: partners and friends – from consensus to conflict in the land war' in Boyce & O'Day (eds), *Parnell in perspective*, pp 52–76. **23** R.V. Comerford, *The Fenians in context: Irish politics and society, 1848–1882* (Dublin, 1985), p. 115. **24** J.S. Donnelly jr., 'The land question in nationalist politics' in T.E. Hachey & L.J. McCaffrey (eds), *Perspectives on Irish nationalism* (Lexington, KY, 1989), pp 90, 98.

Section one legalized the tenant-right custom in Ulster. Section two legalized it where it existed elsewhere. This gave effect to compensation for disturbance, compensation for improvements carried out by tenants in the event of eviction and the right of a tenant to sell the 'goodwill' of his holding in the event of him relinquishing his claim to it.[25]

The fact that Gladstone managed to carry the act through a British parliament that still clung jealously to the sacrosanct rights of landownership was itself notable. But it did not provide the solutions that were sought for an intractable problem. The act was extremely long and complex and very difficult to interpret with the result that it led to a great deal of litigation. Tenants in arrears were excluded from compensation for disturbances, the very tenants who, of course, were most likely to require these safeguards because they were the ones most likely to be evicted. Also excluded from the terms of the act were the 135,000 leaseholders, about 25 per cent of all tenant farmers.

Of major contention was the fact that if landlords in the future were to grant leases of thirty-one years or more, they could claim immunity from claims for compensation for disturbances, a fact which arguably prompted the rush of landlords to issue leases to about 75,000 tenants in the decade following the passing of the act, many of which contained controversial covenants to protect landlords against the compensation provision. Tenants reacted by organizing themselves into tenant defence associations, usually based on the estate. Many of these were extremely successful in combating landlord intentions, most notably the one established on the Leinster estate in Kildare and the one established on the absentee Bath and semi-absentee Shirley estates in Farney, County Monaghan.[26] There has been very little research into the composition or the working of these local associations or any type of investigation as to how they related to the later Land League but certainly on the above mentioned estates, the Land League seems to have been very late in establishing itself simply because of the strength and success of the pre-existing tenant defence associations

For most of the 1870s, the land question in Ireland simmered rather than boiled. It had come to prominence in successive Conservative and Liberal governments' attempts to solve what was often termed the Irish question on the premise that Ireland could only be pacified by tackling agrarian issues, but, as Samuel Clark wrote: 'It is difficult, as a rule, to keep people interested in political agitation when times are prosperous.'[27] It was only when prosperity was threatened from 1877 that agrarianism once again became a burning national issue.

25 Isaac Butt, *A practical treatise on the new law of compensation to tenants in Ireland, and other provisions of the Landlord and Tenant Act, 1870* (Dublin, 1871); T.W. Guinnane & R.I. Miller, 'The limits to land reform: the land acts in Ireland, 1870–1909' in *Economic Development and Cultural Change*, 45 (1997), pp 591–612. **26** See Thomas Nelson, *The land war in County Kildare* (Maynooth, 1985); Peadar Livingstone, *The Monaghan story* (Enniskillen, 1980), pp 334–5. **27** Samuel Clark, 'The social composition of the Land League' in *I.H.S.*, xvii, no.

THE LAND WAR

The extended land war from the late 1870s until the first decade of the twentieth century has proved another of the great focal points for historians of nineteenth-century Ireland.[28] The composition of the various agrarian movements in late Victorian Ireland, their aims and objectives, their workings and to a lesser extent their legacy have been well documented up to now.[29] It is not, therefore, the objective of this section to revisit these areas, except in context; instead this overview concentrates on the effects of the land war on estate management.

Until the publication of J.S. Donnelly jr.'s *The land and people of nineteenth-century Cork*, the land war was, in his words, perceived as 'the product of an intolerable, rapacious land system which finally cracked under the weight of a severe agricultural crisis'.[30] Donnelly turned everything on its head by arguing that the growth of the Land League was a direct result of a 'revolution of rising expectations', in other words that contemporary farmers were determined that 'their impressive material gains [made] in the preceding quarter century could and must be preserved by a determined stand against the customary rents'.[31] But it is important not to lose sight of the fact that no matter how much the agricultural crisis of the late 1870s may have dashed the hopes of the prospering farmer class, it only added to the intolerable woes of the uneconomic holders of the west, where the agitation took root, and where it would continue long after strong farmers were at least partially satiated by the terms of land legislation from the 1880s.[32]

Townsmen who had begun to feel the financial pinch as farming incomes fell quickly threw in their lot with the Land League.[33] Their participation was possibly

68 (1971), p. 448.   **28** Comerford, 'The politics of distress, 1877–82', pp 26–52.   **29** See footnote 131.   **30** Donnelly, *Land and people of Cork*, p. 91; for the type of analysis referred to by Donnelly, see J.E. Pomfret, *The struggle for land in Ireland, 1800–1923* (Princeton, 1930). **31** Donnelly, *Land and people of Cork*, p. 6; see also Vaughan, *Landlords and tenants in mid-Victorian Ireland*, pp 208–16.   **32** See below; other major works on this subject include Bew, *Land and the national question*; idem, 'The Land League ideal: achievement and contradictions' in Drudy (ed.), *Irish studies, 2. Ireland: land, politics and people*, pp 77–92; idem, *Conflict and conciliation in Ireland, 1890–1910: Parnellites and radical agrarians* (Dublin, 1987); Bull, *Land, politics and nationalism*; J.W.H. Carter, *The land war and its leaders in Queen's County, 1879–82* (Portlaoise, 1994); W.L. Feingold, *The revolt of the tenantry: the transformation of local government in Ireland, 1872–86* (Boston, 1984); idem, 'Land League power: the Tralee poor-law election of 1881' in Clark & Donnelly (eds), *Irish peasants*, pp 285–310; Donald Jordan, *Land and popular politics in Ireland: County Mayo from the plantation to the land war* (Cambridge, 1994); R.W. Kirkpatrick, 'Origins and development of the land war in mid-Ulster' in Lyons & Hawkins (eds), *Ireland under the union*, pp 201–35; Moody, *Davitt and Irish revolution*; Gerard Moran, 'An assessment of the Land League meeting at Westport, 8 June 1879' in *Cathair na Mart*, 3 (1) (1983), pp 54–9; idem, 'Famine and the land war: Relief and distress in Mayo, 1879–81' in *Cathair na Mart*, 5 (1) (1985), pp 54–66 and 6 (1) (1986), pp 111–27; idem, 'James Daly and the rise and fall of the Land League in the west' in *I.H.S.*, xxix, no. 114 (1994), pp 189ff; D. Murphy, 'The land war in Donegal, 1879–91' in *Donegal Annual*, 32 (1980), pp 476–86; F. Thompson, 'The landed classes, the Orange Order and the anti-Land League campaign in Ulster, 1880–81' in *Éire-Ireland*, xx (spring, 1987), pp 102–21; Warwick-Haller, *William O'Brien*.   **33** Clark, 'The social

further influenced by increasingly more public accusations, in many cases well-founded, that the local landlord was of little benefit to the local shopocracy – in other words that landlords preferred to buy their goods in England or at least in Dublin – and that it was time to relay the message of the need for change. It was with this in mind that the *Connaught Telegraph* felt justified in claiming in August 1879 that 'the money that this country produces is spent out of it'.[34] While the land war was certainly about more than economics, it is difficult not to see its primary objective as 'an attempt to force a change in the allocation of seriously reduced agricultural income, to the benefit of tenants and merchants and the detriment of landed proprietors.'[35]

The Land League was certainly different to any of the movements that had preceded it for it ushered in a new era of much wider community participation as small and large farmers, shopkeepers, publicans and Roman Catholic priests organized a widespread network of local branches which drew these groups together in political activity.[36] What began as a local campaign in County Mayo soon captured the imagination of Michael Davitt, himself a Mayo man and veteran of the Fenian movement, who founded the Irish National Land League in Dublin in October 1879. Shortly afterwards, Charles Stewart Parnell, leader of the Irish parliamentary party, was elected president which meant that he simultaneously headed the land and national movements. Parnell's astuteness and good fortune allowed him to steer a path towards the organization of mass protest which enhanced his and the Irish parliamentary party's political position while at the same time avoiding the type of revolution that some of the more radical agrarianists might have wished for. Perhaps understandably for one born into the Irish landed ascendancy he initially found it difficult to balance potential against risk but the rapid spread of the Land League and the realization that the land question was not about to go away made up his mind. On the other hand, as Paul Bew rightly contends, he may have been somewhat naïve in believing that once the land war had settled the land question, the way would be prepared for landlord participation in a Home Rule Ireland.[37] That, after all, would have depended as much on landlord attitudes towards Home Rule as Nationalist attitudes towards landlord participation.

While the Land League spread quickly to most parts of Ireland, it failed to take root in the predominantly Protestant areas of Ulster. There, from at least 1881,

composition of the Land League', pp 450–1. **34** *Connaught Telegraph*, 9 Aug. 1879; quoted in Clark, 'The social composition of the Land League', p. 450. **35** Comerford, 'The politics of distress, 1877–82', p. 43. **36** Clark, *Social origins*; idem, 'The social composition of the Land League', pp 447–79; R.V. Comerford, 'Isaac Butt and the Home Rule Party, 1870–77', 'The Land War and the politics of distress' and 'The Parnell era, 1883–91' in Vaughan (ed.), *A new history of Ireland, v: Ireland under the union, I*, pp 1–80; A.W. Orridge, 'Who supported the land war? An aggregate-data analysis of Irish agrarian discontent, 1879–82' in *Economic and Social Review*, 12 (3) (Apr., 1981), pp 203–33. **37** Bew, *Land and the national question*, p. 143; idem, *C.S. Parnell*, p. 33.

landlords looked towards the Orange Order as a bulwark against the spread of agitation and a means of maintaining at least some of their political rights. Through the Orange Order they re-established themselves as the leaders of a Protestant (predominantly Presbyterian) tenantry who, despite their shared agrarian griev-ances, were gradually becoming more alienated from their Catholic neighbours because of the growing association of the Land League with the Catholic clergy and the Home Rule movement.[38]

The working of the Land League could impact in a variety of ways on an estate, if, indeed, it impacted at all. There was, as R.V. Comerford rightly contends, 'no uniformity from place to place either in the demands on landlords or in the form of agitation patronized by the league'.[39] In general terms, the crux centred on whether tenants would continue to pay their rents that Land League propaganda widely propagated as unaffordable, particularly when compared with Griffith's valuation which had been carried out between 1852 and 1865 for the purpose of local taxation and which was never intended to reflect the letting value of land.[40] By the late 1870s, the valuation was as much as 33 per cent below the real letting value of land and so it is easy to understand why tenants would clamour for rents to be reduced to its level. It is just as easy to understand why landlords would oppose calls for reductions. In general, they felt that their levels of indebtedness were such that they could not reduce their rents without bringing ruin to themselves.[41] A myriad of estate expenses,[42] family charges, and interest repayments meant that most landlords were fortunate to have around 20–30 per cent of their gross rental income available to them as disposable income at the best of times. A reduction of 20 per cent could have disastrous consequences. Lord Ormonde, for example, would have suffered a 24 per cent reduction in rental income from £21,352 to £16,359 on his Kilkenny and Tipperary estates. As his annual estate expenditure for the years 1879 to 1890 averaged £17,400, a reduction of 24 per cent in rental income would have made it impossible for him to meet his financial obligations.

If there was no uniformity in the demands on landlords, there was, likewise, no uniformity in landlord response to Land League activity. In the early stages of agricultural depression some of the more patriarchal or even more business-conscious landlords granted abatements to their tenants as a form of pre-emptive strike against the withholding of all rents. More procrastinated; others refused to

38 Dooley, *The decline of the big house*, pp 220–1; Thompson, 'The landed classes', pp 102–21. **39** Comerford, 'The politics of distress, 1877–82', p. 43.   **40** For an understanding of the background to the valuation, see W.E. Vaughan, 'Richard Griffith and the tenement valuation' in G.L.H. Davies and R.C. Mollan (eds), *Richard Griffith, 1784–1878: papers presented at the centenary symposium organised by the Royal Dublin Society, 21 and 22 September 1978* (Dublin, 1980), pp 103–22.   **41** For landlord indebtedness at this time see Curtis, 'Incumbered wealth'; Vaughan, *Landlords and tenants in mid-Victorian Ireland*, pp 130–7. **42** These often included, amongst other things, the upkeep of big house and demesne, agency fees, legal fees, rates, charitable donations, taxes, head rents, charges, interest

grant abatements without certain qualifications – in 1879, for example, Lord Digby said he would grant abatements only to those tenants who had properly cleaned and scoured their drains[43] – while still others refused reductions under any circumstances. But as L.P. Curtis jr.'s work on landlord responses to the Land League shows quite clearly not all landlords acquiesced in the demands of the Land League, but instead thousands opposed it in a number of organizations such as the Irish Land Committee, Property Defence Association and the Orange Emergency Committee, if not by active participation then by financial subscription (perhaps as much as £350,000 during the 1880s) towards the running of the same, eventually turning the land war: 'into a hard-fought contest rather than a rout'.[44]

Either in their procrastination or their active opposition landlords fuelled the growth in agrarian agitation. Initially, and with the blessing of Parnell, the ostracization of uncooperative individuals became the preferred *modus operandi* in many areas, particularly after the widespread attention paid to the campaign in the autumn of 1880 against Mayo land agent, Captain Charles Boycott of Lough Mask House, who, of course, gave his name to that particular form of moral force.[45] Physical force was regularly threatened on landlords and their employees through the ubiquitous threatening letter, and less frequently carried out in the form of assaults on them or their property. The growth in agitation during 1881 and the proliferation of rents strikes forced more and more landlords to grant temporary abatements, so that an estimated 25 per cent of all rents due between 1879 and 1882 were lost with serious consequences for many landlords.[46]

In the midst of this crisis, the government introduced the Land Law (Ireland) Act of 1881 in an attempt to restore a semblance of order to the countryside. The act gave recognition to the three Fs: fixity of tenure was given to a tenant as long as he paid his rent and observed his covenant; a tenant was allowed free sale of his interest in his holding and perhaps most crucially was the establishment of the Irish Land Commission with powers to form regional sub-commissions to adjudicate on fair rents between individual tenants and landlords.[47] Thirty-six sub-commissioners

repayments. **43** *King's County Chronicle*, 30 Oct. 1879. **44** L.P. Curtis jr., 'Landlord responses to the Irish land war, 1879–87' in *Éire-Ireland*, xxxviii (2003), pp 169, 186; at more local level, see Carter, *The land war and its leaders in Queen's County*, pp 119–22, 199–202. **45** C.A. Boycott, *Boycott: the life behind the word* (Ludlow, 1997); James McGuire, 'Boycott: the inside story' in *North Mayo Historic Journal*, 2 (3) (1989–90), pp 47–54; Gerard Moran, 'The origins and development of boycotting' in *Galway Arch. Soc. Jn.*, 40 (1985–86), pp 49–64; see also Cressida Annesley, 'The land war in west Cork: the boycott of William Bence Jones' in *Cork Hist. Soc. Jn.*, 99 (1994), pp 1–22. **46** See Dooley, *The decline of the big house*, pp 90–4. **47** Comerford, 'The politics of distress, 1877–82', p. 47; see also K.H. Connell, 'The land legislation and Irish social life' in *Economic History Review*, 2nd ser., 11 (1) (Aug. 1958), pp 1–7; C. Dewey, 'Celtic agrarian legislation and Celtic revival: historicist implications of Gladstone's Irish and Scottish Land Acts, 1870–86' in *Past & Present*, no. 64 (1974), pp 30–70; Guinnane & Miller, 'The limits to land reform'; C.F. Kolbert & T. O'Brien, *Land reform in Ireland: a legal history of the Irish land problem and its settlement* (Cambridge, 1975); R.B. McDowell, 'Administration and the public services, 1870–1921' in Vaughan (ed.), *A new history of Ireland, v, Ireland under the union, II*, pp 583–6; also of value L.P. Curtis jr., *Coercion*

were eventually appointed and empowered to fix fair rents on all yearly tenancies for a period of fifteen years, subsequently known as (first term) judicial rents. (Fair rents could also be fixed outside the courts if landlord and tenants came to an amicable agreement or if they used an arbitrator.) From when the sub-commissioners began their operations in August 1881 to the end of the first judicial term in December 1902, they dealt with 342,019 cases in which rents were fixed. The former rents of these holdings aggregated £6.93 million; the judicial rent lowered it to £5.48 million, representing a decrease of 20.8 per cent.[48] This more than anything else helped to dilute agrarian agitation and went a considerable way to ending the first phase of the land war.[49] On the other hand, the labourers had gained nothing and the small farmers of western Ireland who had begun the struggle were no better off after 1882 than they had been before. Arguably the Land League had failed both smallholders and labourers miserably.

Finally, the act was also intended to act as a mechanism for the transfer of landownership from landlords to tenants. But this was not the ultimate objective of the Land League. As far as the large farmer members of the league were concerned the lowering of rents statutorily was as much as they desired at this stage. They had no great desire to buy their lands during an economic depression particularly when rents were falling and they were guaranteed security of tenure. Arguably, tenants could not raise the necessary one fourth of the purchase price nor were they willing to meet landlords' asking price of around twenty-three years' purchase. As the bitter agrarian and political struggle of the time closed the doors of the Irish land market to all bidders except the occupying tenants, there was the inevitable gulf between what the tenants regarded as a fair price and what the landlords required, even if the large farmers had showed interest in buying, which they did not. Thus the act failed as a land purchase act – only 700 tenants purchased.[50]

Because fair rent fixing came at a time when arrears on estates were escalating and landlords were finding themselves in increasingly complicated financial difficulties, fears of the impact of the 1881 act grew, to be later compounded by the admission of leaseholders into the rent arbitration system in 1887 and the reduction of their rents by up to 25 per cent.[51] By 1896 twice as many tenants were entering

and conciliation, 1880–92: a study in Conservative Unionism (Princeton, 1963); Andrew Gailey, *Ireland and the death of kindness: the experience of constructive unionism, 1890–1905* (Cork, 1987); J.T. Sheehan, 'Land purchase policy in Ireland, 1917–23: from the Irish Convention to the 1923 Land Act' (unpublished MA thesis, St Patrick's College, Maynooth, 1993).   **48** *A return showing according to provinces and counties the number of cases in which judicial rents have been fixed by all the matters provided by the Land Law Acts for a first and second statutory term respectively to 31 December 1902 with particulars as to acreage, former rents of holdings, and percentage of reductions in rents.* HC 1903, lvii, 91; for a local study see K. Buckley, 'The fixing of fair rents by agreement in Co. Galway, 1881–5' in *I.H.S.*, vii, no. 27 (1959), pp 149–79.   **49** R.V. Comerford, 'Land Commission' in S.J. Connolly (ed.), *The Oxford companion to Irish history* (Oxford, 1998), p. 296.   **50** The amount advanced was to be paid in an annuity of 5 per cent over thirty-five years. The annuity was the tenant purchaser's annual repayment on the loan.   **51** Dooley, *The decline of the big house*, pp 94–6, 100–4.

the land courts than had been the case in the early 1880s. Bitter disillusionment became the order of the day amongst landlords. In 1897 Lord Dufferin, in a letter to Edward Carson, summed up the perceived hopelessness of the situation of Irish landlords. Referring to Gladstone's 'blundering legislation', he contended that the situation was 'irremediable':

> An enquiry into the proceedings of the Irish land courts might result in showing the blind, capricious and inconsistent way in which they work, and, perhaps that their general scale of reductions has been excessive; but I should fear that the ultimate upshot of this would not very much improve our position.[52]

Furthermore, the Arrears of Rent (Ireland) Act of 1882 resulted in £1.76 million in arrears being extinguished from landlords' rentals.[53] In real terms the loss to landlords was approximately half this figure as under the terms of the act the Land Commission could make an order for the payment of a sum equal to one half of antecedent arrears to or for the benefit of the landlord. However, the greater significance lay in the fact that it was even more demoralizing for landlords than the 1881 act, for the extinction of arrears was a form of confiscation. In the past landlords had granted abatements at a time and a level that suited them. Now the government dictated the terms and this interference possibly more than any other factor undermined confidence in landed property.

While there was a temporary economic respite in 1883 and 1884, the mid- to late 1880s saw a renewal of agricultural depression. The Land League had been suppressed in 1882 to be replaced by the less radical National League. In October 1886, a number of Land League veterans including John Dillon, William O'Brien and T.C. Harrington proposed a Plan of Campaign.[54] Under the plan tenants on an estate were expected to demand a reduction of rents as a collective body from their landlords; if these reductions were refused, the tenants were to withdraw *en masse* without paying any rents and to pool what they had offered in a plan fund to support tenants in the event of evictions. The campaign was eventually launched on just over 200 estates ranging in size from less than 100 acres to more than 100,000 acres, though its impact was probably felt on many more.[55] In most cases the landlord targeted was heavily encumbranced, the underlying belief being that

52 Marquis of Dufferin to Edward Carson, 24 Apr. 1897; quoted in Patrick Buckland, *Irish unionism, 1885–1923: a documentary history* (Belfast, 1973), p. 48. **53** 45 & 46 Vict., c.xlix (18 Aug. 1882), and *Return of payments made to landlords by the Irish Land Commission pursuant to the first and sixteenth sections of the Arrears of Rent (Ireland) Act 1882*, HC 1884, lxiv, 97. **54** F.S.L. Lyons, 'John Dillon and the plan of campaign, 1886–90' in *I.H.S.*, xiv (1965), pp 313–47; Emmet Larkin, *The Roman Catholic Church and the plan of campaign in Ireland, 1886–88* (Cork, 1978); L.M. Geary, *The plan of campaign, 1886–1891* (Cork, 1986); Ambrose Macaulay, *The Holy See, British policy and the plan of campaign in Ireland, 1885–93* (Dublin, 2002). **55** Geary, *The plan of campaign*, p.180; see also Donald Jordan, 'The Irish National League and the "unwritten law": rural protest and nation-building in Ireland, 1882–1890' in *Past &*

his indebtedness made him more susceptible to pressure and likely to acquiesce in tenant demands for rent reductions. Even on some of the previously better-managed estates arrears grew to dangerously high levels. While for the five-year period, 1875–9, Lord Cloncurry, for example, had collected aggregate rents of £17,800 on his Limerick estate, the figure fell by almost 46 per cent for a similar five-year period from 1880 to 1884. From 1885 to 1889, when the Plan of Campaign was established on the estate, aggregate rents received fell 43 per cent below the 1875–9 figure. While an aggregate of only £980 was outstanding in arrears for the years 1875–9, this figure escalated to £8,700 for the 1885–9 period.[56]

The prolonged agricultural depression marked the beginning of a long period of economic exigency for Irish landlords after which it was impossible for many of them, particularly the small and middling-sized landowners, to revive the position they held prior to the late 1870s. Landlords who had borrowed heavily during the 1850s, 1860s and early 1870s now found a higher proportion of their annual rental income going towards interest repayments.[57] Mortgagees who panicked during the land war began to call in their loans as landlords temporarily defaulted, thus distinguishing this agricultural depression from the one in the 1860s when landlords managed to extricate themselves from financial difficulties through the medium of borrowing.[58] Thus, in 1883 a deputation of Irish landlords wrote to the British Prime Minister, W.E. Gladstone: 'There are few (if any) sources for borrowing money on land in Ireland now open and … trustees, assurance societies and private lenders are steadily refusing to advance upon mortgages on Irish estates'.[59] But politicians showed little concern for the plight of Irish landlords and pleas fell on deaf ears. The fact was that British politics was beginning to undergo radical change. Politicians were increasingly becoming aware of the need to woo the expanding electorate, leading them to sympathize more with the masses than the besieged minority of Irish landlords. The only viable option for many landlords at this stage was the sale of their estates; and the only available purchasers were their own tenants.

THE BREAK-UP OF ESTATES, 1881–1914

The acts which followed during the period 1885 to 1896 were more progressive than the 1881 act in terms of land sales firstly because their terms were more conducive to sale, and, secondly, because landlord indebtedness had risen considerably through the 1880s making sales more of a necessity. The 1885 act was

---

Present, no. 158 (1998), pp 146–71.   **56** Estate rentals of Lord Cloncurry's Limerick estates, 1875–89 (NLI, Cloncurry papers, MSS 12,893–12,907).   **57** See Curtis, 'Incumbered wealth'; Dooley, *The decline of the big house*, pp 99–102; Vaughan, *Landlords and tenants in mid-Victorian Ireland*, p. 131.   **58** By 1894, for example, £850,000 of the Scottish Widows Company's estimated £1.2 million invested in Ireland had been repaid; David Cannadine, *The decline and fall of the British aristocracy* (New Haven & London, 1990), p. 95; see also Dooley, *The decline of the big house*, pp 101–2.   **59** Quoted in *Cork Examiner*, 1 Aug. 1883.

introduced by the Conservative government as part of their policy of 'killing home rule by kindness' and once again was in part a response to the renewed economic distress and attendant agrarian agitation. Under this act, the tenant could obtain the full purchase price from the Land Commission; the annuity was lowered from 5 to 4 per cent and the repayment period was extended from thirty-five to forty-nine years. The purchase money was to be paid to the landlord in cash. However, one fifth was retained as a guarantee deposit in the event of tenants defaulting on their repayments of annuities. Between 1885 and 1891, almost £10 million was advanced allowing tenants to become purchasers, emphasizing the need for landlords to secure capital. Many of these sales concerned large landowners who sold small outlying estates, representing only a percentage of their total acreage, but allowing them to meet immediate debts. The fee simple of these estates was much more valuable than their mortgagable capacity and, at any rate, as we have already seen, loans were almost impossible to secure at this time.

Sales under the 1891 Land Act followed essentially the same pattern: while many small estates came onto the market, larger landowners continued to sell off parts of their estates and with a few exceptions did not sell significant tracts. Landlords were now paid in land stock rather than cash. As land stock was subject to fluctuation it could at times be a disincentive to sell so the general pattern was that as land stock increased in value, more land came onto the market indicating that landlords were more likely to sell if the proper terms were put into place. In 1893, for example, the highest price quoted for land stock was 97.33. Only 2,391 loans were applied for that year. In 1898 a total of 6,201 loans were applied for when it reached its highest point of 114.2.[60] This act also legislated for the establishment of the Congested Districts Board, thereby acknowledging the different and more difficult circumstances of tenant farmers in the west of Ireland. Rent reductions and inducements to purchase were of little value to smallholders who could not eke out a living on their tiny holdings but who, instead, wanted either more land or at least some form of supplementary income.[61]

The land acts from 1870 to 1896 resulted in the purchase of almost 74,000 holdings on 2.5 million acres for £24.78 million.[62] This represented only about 10 per cent of Ireland's total acreage. The many landlords who had consolidated small farms from which occupiers had been evicted during the land war of the 1880s

---

60 *A return showing as far as practicable for each year the lowest and highest prices (in each calendar year) of guaranteed land stock and the number and amounts of loans under the Land Purchase (Ireland) Acts 1891 and 1896*, HC 1903, lvii (hereafter cited as *Return of land stock, 1903*). **61** W.L. Micks, *An account of the Congested Districts Board for Ireland, 1891–1923* (Dublin, 1925); a congested district was defined as one where 'more than 20 per cent of the population of a county, or in the case of Co. Cork, either riding thereof, live in electoral divisions of which the total ratable value, when divided by the number of the population, gives a sum of less than £1 10s. od. for each individual, these divisions shall for the purpose of this [1891 Land Act] be separated from the county in which they are geographically situated, and form a separate county ...' **62** *Report of the estates commissioners for the year from 1 April 1920 to 31 March 1921 and for the period from 1 November 1903 to 31 March 1921*, HC 1921, xiv.

(there were approximately 28,000 evictions during the years 1880–87[63]) and then leased them to large solvent graziers under the eleven months' system were, it seems, content to carry on. The most obvious advantage of this system to landlords was that the grazier tenants could not claim formal tenancy and so could not avail of the fair rent fixing facilities of the 1881 Land Act.

There were many more landlords willing to sell if the proper incentives were put in place. In 1887 Sir Henry Gore Booth of Lissadell, for example, claimed: 'I would be willing to sell every acre, it would be a great saving to me if I could get twenty-three years' purchase on the ordnance valuation, one fourth added.'[64] In October 1902 the Irish Landowners Convention, a landlord organization set up in 1886 because landlords felt they needed to protect their interests and property from the threat posed by the National League, the Plan of Campaign, and government legislation, adopted a resolution: 'The landowners who have not hitherto sold are, as a body, resolved not to part with their estates on terms under which, in addition to the loss already incurred, their present incomes would be substantially reduced.'[65] Landlords needed to be guaranteed 'a price which invested at 3 per cent [would] yield an income approximately equal to the present net income'.[66] There was a growing body of what could, perhaps, be termed more pragmatic landlords who were prepared to open negotiations with tenant representatives on the subject. But there was also increasing pressure coming from the bottom up, a new wave of agrarian agitation sweeping once again from the west under the United Irish League, founded by William O'Brien in 1898, and from Ulster under T.W. Russell's campaign for compulsory purchase.[67]

The arrival of George Wyndham, who had an astute awareness of the realities of Irish life and politics, in Ireland in 1900 as chief secretary (he had been in Ireland before as Arthur Balfour's private secretary) heralded a new era for the land question. The report of the Irish Land Conference of 1902–3, a meeting of landlords and tenant representatives to negotiate terms of sale acceptable to

63 Vaughan, *Landlords and tenants in mid-Victorian Ireland*, p. 231.   64 *Report of the royal commission on the Land Law (Ireland) Act, 1881, and the Purchase of Land (Ireland) Act, 1885* [C4969], HC 1887, xxvi, 1, p.473 (Earl Cowper, chairman).   65 *Return of the resolution and statement adopted by the Irish Landowners Convention on 10 Oct 1902 ...*, HC 1903, lvii, 321. 66 Ibid.   67 For studies of the UIL and the ranch war and politics of the period, see, for example Philip Bull, 'William O'Brien: problems reappraising his political career' in Oliver MacDonagh & W.F. Mandle (eds), *Ireland and Irish-Australia: studies in cultural and political history* (London, 1986), pp 49–63; Fergus Campbell, 'Irish popular politics and the making of the Wyndham Land Act, 1901–3' in *Historical Journal*, 45 (4) (2002), pp 755–73; idem, *Land and revolution*; Thomas Conal, 'The land for the people: the United Irish League and land reform in north Galway and west Mayo, 1898–1912' in *Cathair na Mart*, 19 (1999), pp 167–70; J.D. Dillon, 'The United Irish League and Baron Ashtown' in Kieran Jordan (ed.), *Kiltullagh/Killimordaly as the centuries passed: a history from 1500–1900* (2000), pp 68–85; Gailey, *Ireland and the death of kindness*; Warwick-Haller, *William O'Brien*; Jones, *Graziers*; Michael MacDonagh, *The life of William O'Brien, the Irish nationalist* (London, 1928); C.C. Murphy, 'Conflict in the west: the ranch war continues, 1911–1913, part I' in *Cathair na Mart*, 15 (1995), pp 112–39; idem, 'Conflict in the west: the ranch war continues, 1911–1912, part II'

landlords and tenants, published in January 1903, provided much of the basis for the act introduced that same year by Wyndham who was determined that this act 'should provide, not the stop-gap measure of earlier legislation, but an effective and final solution to the vexed problem of land occupancy in Ireland.'[68] To this end it became the first act to make purchase a realistic goal for tenants while simultaneously providing the inducements for landlords to sell. The entire purchase money was paid in cash to landlords who were also given a 12 per cent cash bonus on the sale of estates. The bonus was very important because regardless of the level of debts or charges on an estate, this bonus was paid to the vendor who could not be sued for any portion of it by his creditors. Moreover, the act also contained provision to allow landlords to sell their demesne and untenanted lands to the Land Commission up to a maximum value of £20,000 and to repurchase them under the same generous terms as their tenants, thereby providing landlords with what was effectively a low-interest extended term loan. During the period 1903–21, landlords repurchased 355 demesnes, embracing over 122,000 acres for £1.9 million of which £1.68 million (88 per cent) was advanced by the Land Commission.[69] From the tenants' point of view, a complicated system of arriving at the purchase price that could only be set between certain maxima and minima 'zones' guaranteed that the annuities paid by them represented a 10–30 per cent reduction on second-term judicial rents and a 20–40 per cent reduction on first-term rents.[70]

Initially the promises that new land legislation held out and the subsequent enactment of the 1903 act contributed to an abatement in agrarian agitation in Ireland between 1902 and 1904 and according to Fergus Campbell, almost 12,000 members left the UIL during this period because, he presumes, they had purchased their farms.[71] Under the Wyndham Land Act, and the 1909 amending act,[72] there was a dramatic, but by no means complete, transfer of land ownership in Ireland. By the end of March 1921, 9,459 estates comprising 270,396 holdings on 9.03 million acres had been sold for £85.9 million.[73] There were also significant land sales under the auspices of the Congested Districts Board whose powers were extended under the 1903 and 1909 acts making more money available and conferring authority upon it to acquire land compulsorily for the relief of congestion. By the time the board was dissolved in 1923 it had purchased 874

---

in *Cathair na Mart*, 16 (1997), pp 112–39. **68** Philip Bull, 'The significance of the nationalist response to the Irish land act of 1903' in *I.H.S.*, xxviii, no. 111 (1993), p. 283; see also Earl of Dunraven, *Past times and pastimes* (2 vols, London, 1922), ii, 3–11. **69** *Report of estates commissioners … to 31 March 1921* [Cmd 1150], HC, 1921, xiv, 661. **70** For a fuller discussion on the workings of the 1903 Land Act see L. Paul-Dubois, *Contemporary Ireland* (English translation, London, 1908), pp 282–9. **71** Campbell, *Land and revolution*, p. 87. **72** The 1909 Land Act reverted to the old system of payment by land stock; for the experience of Co. Cavan landowner, Col. Edward Saunderson, see Alvin Jackson, *Col. Edward Saunderson: land and loyalty in Victorian Ireland* (Oxford, 1995). **73** *Report of the estates commissioners for the year from 1 April 1920 to 31 March 1921 and for the period from 1 November 1903 to 31 March 1921*, HC, 1921, xiv.

estates totaling 1.77 million acres for £8.9 million.[74] On the other hand, there remained approximately 114,000 unpurchased holdings comprising some 3 million acres as well as over 2 million acres of untenanted lands in landlords' hands.[75]

FROM THE RANCH WAR TO THE GREAT WAR, 1907–14

Given the importance of the Wyndham Land Act, remarkably little has been written about it by historians.[76] In fact, until quite recently, land issues post-1903 were almost completely ignored by historians, the reason being that it was believed there was no land question after 1903 essentially because the rather dramatic transfer of landownership post-1903 took away the *raison d'être* for agrarianism. This orthodoxy was summed up by Philip Bull in 1989 when he concluded that the Wyndham Act 'brought about a revolution in land tenure in Ireland, the end of landlordism as an institution, and the effective removal of the basis on which the land question had assumed its political importance'.[77] However, more recent work by this author and others including Fergus Campbell and David Seth Jones has suggested the need to reappraise this whole area, and, indeed, the land question in Ireland for decades after independence.[78]

The central reason for the continuation of the land question post-1903 was that its main legacy (and that of the earlier acts) was the creation of a mass of small farmers who did not have enough land to make their holdings economically viable and so purchase had done little to alleviate their day-to-day struggle for survival. By 1917 there were an estimated 296,566 occupiers of one to thirty acres in Ireland (in addition to 112,787 occupiers of less than one acre.) A significant proportion of these, just over 28 per cent, were situated in the defined congested areas (the Connaught counties of Sligo, Leitrim, Roscommon, Mayo and Galway, Donegal in Ulster, Kerry and six rural districts of Clare and four of Cork in Munster). However, there were also very high levels of uneconomic holdings elsewhere; by 1921 an average of around 65 per cent of all agricultural holdings in each of the nineteen counties outside the designated congested areas came under the definition of 'uneconomic' as set out by the Land Commission at that particular time, that is

74 *Irish Land Commission report for the period from 1 April 1923 to 31 March 1928*, p. 20. 75 *Return of untenanted lands in rural districts, distinguishing demesnes on which there is a mansion, showing: rural districts and electoral divisions; townland; area in statute acres; poor law valuation; names of occupiers as in valuation lists*, HC, 1906, c.177.   76 Bull, 'The significance of the nationalist response'.   77 Bull, *Land, politics and nationalism*, p. 3; for similar conclusions see Paul Bew, Ellen Hazelkorn & Henry Patterson, *The dynamics of Irish politics* (London, 1989), p. 20. 78 Terence Dooley, 'Land and politics in independent Ireland, 1923–48: the case for reappraisal' in *I.H.S.*, xxxiv, no. 134 (2004), pp 175–97; idem, '*The land for the people*'; Campbell, *Land and revolution*; David Seth Jones, 'Land reform legislation and security of tenure in Ireland after independence' in *Éire-Ireland*, xxxii–xxxiii (1997–8), pp 116–43; idem, 'Divisions within the Irish government over land distribution policy, 1940–70' in *Éire-Ireland*, xxxvi (2001), pp 83–109.

below £10 valuation or roughly 20 acres of 'reasonable' land.[79] Post-1903 many of the purchased smallholdings did not generate the income to make annuity repayments to the state (via the Land Commission) any more than they had generated the income to make rental payments to landlords in the past. Many new proprietors found themselves faced with resumption orders, which were no less daunting than eviction notices had previously been. The Land Commission, as a bureaucratic state body, did not grant any of the assistance formerly available from benevolent landlords, however scarce or plentiful they may have been. It did not, for example, take a particularly bad harvest into consideration when assessing farmers' needs for annuity abatements.[80] Thus, in Tipperary, Dan Breen could recall the 1903 Land Act bringing 'great joy to the farmers' which was soon dissipated by the realization that annuities were no easier to pay than the former rents.[81]

The United Irish League that had declined in support as a result of the anticipation of miracles by the Wyndham Land Act was rejuvenated as the frustration of smallholders increased within about three to four years of its enactment. This frustration was conditioned by two factors: firstly, smallholders who purchased soon began to demand access to more land, and, secondly, as early as 1904 it had become clear that applications for sales under the Wyndham Act were greater than the government's ability to deal with them either logistically or financially. It seems that a handful of very large estates including the massive Leinster estate in Kildare, one of the very first to be sold in November 1903 (the chief trustee of which was a lay land commissioner and kinsman of George Wyndham), ate very quickly into the purchase and bonus funds. As late as 1923 there were still 432 estates, totaling almost 500,000 acres, awaiting advances of almost £4 million under the 1903 and 1909 acts.[82]

In the meantime, the UIL organized rural malcontents to focus their attention upon the owners of untenanted lands in another attempt to redress their socio-economic grievances. The former were drawn from a variety of social groups including smallholders, evicted tenants and the landless while the latter were mainly traditional landlords (who, as noted above, retained an aggregated total of approximately 2.5 million untenanted acres by 1922) or large graziers predominantly, though not exclusively, located in the eastern and midland counties of Meath, Kildare, Westmeath and Offaly as well as the western counties of Galway, Roscommon and parts of Mayo. Ironically, graziers were often shopkeepers, publicans and the occasional priest, members of the very groups who had stood shoulder to shoulder with the farmers in the Land League and who now were prominent in the UIL more for political gain than socio-economic loss. The agitation that followed from 1906 to around 1912 was significant enough to be seen

79 *Report of the estates commissioners for the year from 1 April 1920 to 31 March 1921*, p. vi. **80** This significant change was not lost on contemporaries; see M.J. Bonn (translated by T.W. Rolleston), *Modern Ireland and her agrarian problem* (London, 1906), p. 101. **81** Dan Breen, *My fight for Irish freedom* (Dublin, 1924; Dublin, 1981 ed.), p. 8. **82** *Irish Land Commission report, 1923–28*, p. 14.

in terms of a 'ranch war'.[83] There were some notable successes, the case of the Clonbrock estate in Galway being particularly instructive.

In a letter to the *Morning Post* in February 1903, Lord Clonbrock argued that he was too sentimentally attached to his Galway estate to want to sell it. As his was a well-managed estate, the elderly Clonbrock was hesitant to shift from a rental income to an income derived from investment and so he advocated that there should be 'no moral obligation on landowners to sell'.[84] (Most landlords had absolutely no experience of the City – such business transactions had been regarded as being rather vulgar in the past, when land was the great provider of economic and social status, which, in turn, bestowed political status.) However, his tenantry, who up to now had involved themselves very little in any of the earlier agrarian outbreaks, soon relegated his patriarchal reputation firmly to the past – he was now represented in the local nationalist press as 'a fossilised bigot' in opposition to the public will[85] – once the enticing terms of the 1903 Land Act indicated they could be owners with annuities lower than former rents. They organized themselves under the UIL and from 1903 to 1907 the estate was engulfed in extreme agitation. By 1907 Clonbrock's rental had fallen by around 15 per cent while arrears rose at an unprecedented rate to £6,400 in 1907. Clonbrock was faced with no option but to sell and by 1915 all he had of his original 20,000-acre estate was six townlands comprised of forty-four tenants paying an aggregate of only £240 in rents.[86]

The introduction of the 1909 Land Act in an attempt to deal with the bureaucratic nightmare and to address the agrarian crisis only highlighted the fact that the British government had underestimated what the Wyndham Act would cost them. Under the 1909 act, the government reverted to the payment of landlords in government stock instead of cash and the level of bonus was decreased with the result that there was a marked decline in the number of estates sold per annum. The ranch war fizzled out by around 1912, not because the UIL had succeeded but rather because for a variety of reasons it failed to achieve its objectives. Notably, the ending of the war coincided with the beginning of the third Home Rule campaign and the growing perception that the land question might be addressed in the near future in an Irish nationalist dominated parliament.[87]

---

83 Jones, *Graziers*; for a very good local study, see J.N. McEvoy, 'A study of the United Irish League in King's County, 1899–1918' (unpublished MA thesis, St Patrick's College, Maynooth, 1990). **84** *Morning Post*, 17 Feb. 1903. **85** *Connaught Leader*, 2 July 1904. **86** See Dooley, *The decline of the big house*, p. 117. **87** For the politics of this period see, for example, Paul Bew, *Conflict and conciliation in Ireland, 1890–1910* (Oxford, 1987); Bull, *Land, politics and nationalism*; David Fitzpatrick, *Politics and Irish life, 1913–21: provincial experience of war and revolution* (Dublin, 1986); Marie Coleman, *County Longford and the Irish revolution, 1910–1923* (Dublin, 2003); J.J. Lee, *Ireland, 1912–85* (Cambridge, 1989); Patrick Maume, *The long gestation: Irish nationalist life, 1891–1918* (Dublin, 1999); Senia Paseta, *Before the revolution: nationalism, social change and Ireland's Catholic élite, 1879–1922* (Cork, 1999).

A NEW LAND WAR, 1917–23

The years of the Great War, 1914–18, proved yet another watershed in landed estate life, as it would in big house life.[88] Firstly, the virtual closure of emigration outlets during the Great War meant that a higher proportion of young, energetic rural malcontents were housed in Ireland than had been the case for generations. Secondly, the war stopped land purchase when the British Treasury curtailed advances, directing their funds instead to the war effort. By 1921 there were 1,248 estates encompassing 46,000 holdings on 1.5 million acres that sales to the value of £10.7 million had been agreed upon but for which advances had not yet been made. At the same time, many landlords continued to hold on to huge tracts of lands: Lord Farnham in County Cavan, for example, retained close to 20,000 acres; John Leslie retained over 12,000 acres in County Monaghan; the earl of Courtown retained almost 13,000 acres in Wexford. Thirdly, the war forced the postponement of the Congested District Board's acquisition of almost 270,000 acres, impacting negatively once again on the western congests who were most in need of assistance.[89]

When the war reinvigorated the long depressed agricultural economy it was the landlords, the graziers and the strong farmers who benefited most. As the price of conacre soared to unprecedented levels only the prospering farmer could hope to secure more lands to make greater profits. Then, in 1917 a genuine fear of a food shortage led to a popular demand for increased tillage in Britain and Ireland and to this end the government introduced a compulsory tillage order requiring all occupiers of ten or more acres of arable land to cultivate 10 per cent more of it than they had done the previous year. The idea of compulsory tillage appealed to the smallholders and landless labourers: it meant that large graziers would have to set aside lands for tillage and employ more men to work them or else let portions of their lands in conacre that would allow for more freedom of access, provided that the price of conacre was affordable. As graziers procrastinated, demands for the break up of lands became more intense. From the spring of 1917 the last significant phase of popular agrarian revolt was orchestrated in the west by alleged Sinn Féiners and in February 1918, after months of isolated agrarian disturbances, Eamon de Valera encouraged every Sinn Féin club in County Clare to form a company of the Irish Volunteers 'to help divide the land evenly'. Sinn Féin was now promoting the idea that the 'true remedy for the land problem' was the 'exclusive control of our own resources which sovereign independence alone can win'.[90] By exploiting the land question in order to promote political change, Sinn Féin leaders ensured that the merging of the land and the national question (the latter moving away from constitutionalism towards separatism) would once more become inevitable. The party could attract the support of rural malcontents in the same way

88 For the latter see chapter three.   **89** For a more detailed study of this period see Dooley, *'The land for the people'*, pp 26–56.   **90** Labhras MacFhionnghail [Laurence Ginnell], *The land question* (Dublin, n.d.), pp 18–19.

that the nationalist party had benefited from its association with the land question during the 1880s.

Throughout 1918, in the western and midland counties of Sligo, Roscommon, Leitrim, Galway, Clare, Mayo, Limerick, King's County, Queen's County and Westmeath, large bodies of men with ploughs, bands and Sinn Féin flags marched to grazing farms and forcibly took possession of lands. Land agitation became linked to revolutionary activity.[91] Historians have been slow to acknowledge the social dimension to the revolution[92] but agrarian issues undoubtedly played a significant rôle in motivating at least some young men to join the Volunteers, later the IRA, which of course, is not to deny the simultaneous existence of other more patriotic reasons for after all the land question and the struggle for independence had been so closely connected in previous generations that patriots and land agitators were regarded as one and the same.[93] In the localities, leaders such as Michael Brennan in Clare claimed that he 'hadn't the slightest interest in the land agitation, but I had every interest in using it as a means to an end ... to get these fellows into the Volunteers'.[94] In fact, the British government recognized the attractiveness of the proposal around the same time when in June 1918 Lord Lieutenant French issued a proclamation aimed at replenishing the Irish Divisions at the front by 50,000 men before 1 October. One particular inducement made a potent appeal to young Irishmen and was possibly borrowed from Sinn Féin – the promise of landownership. According to the proclamation: 'Steps are, therefore, being taken to ensure, as far as possible, that land shall be available for men who have fought for their country'.[95] Significantly, the appeal was aimed 'almost entirely' at young men in urban areas – shop assistants, publicans' assistants and so on – who were 'mostly transplanted countrymen, the sons of small farmers'.[96] In December 1919, as a follow-up to the proclamation, the British government introduced an act to facilitate the provision of land in Ireland for Irish men who had served in the British army, navy or air forces during the course of World War I.[97] Up to March

91 Paul Bew, 'Sinn Fein , agrarian radicalism and the War of Independence' in D.G. Boyce (ed.), The revolution in Ireland, 1879–1923 (Dublin, 1988), p. 223; Dooley, 'The land for the people', pp 33–9; Townshend, Political violence in Ireland, p. 339.   92 See Joost Augusteijn, From public defiance to guerrilla warfare: the experience of ordinary volunteers in the Irish War of Independence, 1916–21 (Dublin, 1996). A more recent collection of essays on the Irish revolution, The Irish Revolution, 1913–1923 (Basingstoke, 2002), edited by Joost Augusteijn, has little more to say about the land question. See Peter Hart, 'Definition: defining the Irish revolution' in Augusteijn, The Irish Revolution, p. 27; J.M. Regan, The Irish counter-revolution, 1921–36 (Dublin, 1999), p. 377.   93 See Terence Dooley, 'IRA veterans and land division in independent Ireland, 1923–48' in Fearghal McGarry (ed.), Republicanism in modern Ireland (Dublin, 2003), pp 86–107; for suggestions as to why young men joined the IRA, see Fitzpatrick, 'The geography of Irish nationalism, 1910–1921', pp 113–37; Tom Garvin, The evolution of Irish nationalist politics (Dublin, 1981); Peter Hart, 'The geography of revolution in Ireland, 1917–1923' in Past and Present, no. 155 (1997), pp 142–73; Erhard Rumpf and A.C. Hepburn, Nationalism and socialism in twentieth-century Ireland (Dublin, 1977).   94 Quoted in Michael Hopkinson, Green against green: the Irish Civil War (Dublin, 1988), p. 45.   95 Quoted in Irish Times, 4 June 1918.   96 Ibid.   97 Irish Land (Provision for Soldiers and Sailors) Act 1919

1921 the commissioners had purchased 5,046 acres of untenanted land under the act for £125,000 and were in negotiations to purchase a further 10,600 acres to accommodate former soldiers and sailors. By then, 134 ex-servicemen had been given possession of holdings comprising 2,700 acres (or a respectable average of just over twenty acres each).[98] Their history would make for an interesting study.

By early 1920 the War of Independence was in its embryonic stages but agrarianism, particularly in the west, was endemic. Big house burnings were just one aspect of intimidation directed against landowners (landlords as well as their former tenants) as social revolution thrived amidst political revolution. The IRA action directed against the forces of law and order created the chaotic conditions that allowed agrarian agitators (many of whom were local IRA members) free rein to give physical outlet to the social and emotional frustration that had been gathering and festering since the late 1870s. Estate employees were intimidated, demesne walls and gates were broken, cattle were driven, all in a bid to drive out landlords and have their lands divided.[99] In his memoirs published in 1922, the Duc de Stacpoole, a Galway landowner, wrote that conditions in his county were worse than at any time during the land war of 1879–82:

> Even demesnes and land immediately round the owner's house, and already farmed by him may be considered suitable for division. In many cases the landlord has been compelled to give up farming altogether, owing to threats from those who consider that he is in possession of too much land, while others have not sufficient.[1]

When in the spring-summer of 1920 agrarian agitation 'spread with the fury of a prairie fire over Connacht',[2] Dáil Éireann found it necessary to attempt to repress it through the establishment of arbitration courts and the deployment of the IRA to the most disaffected areas, the main objective being to channel energy back into the political revolution.[3] But neither judicial nor military endeavour managed to eradicate social discontent. If anything, the social revolution assumed a life of its own and was carried on independently of the political revolution (although, of course, this is complicated by the fact that in many local areas agrarian agitators continued to use the guise of the IRA to give more authority to their threats). This was particularly true during the Civil War when large areas of the country became anarchical in the absence of any effective law enforcement body.[4] The number of

[9 & 10 Geo.V, ch. 82] (23 Dec. 1919).   **98** *Report of estates commissioners for the year from 1 April 1920 to 31 March 1921*, pp x–xi; Minutes of meeting of Provisional Government, 1 Feb. 1922 (National Archives of Ireland [hereinafter NAI], A, G1/1).   **99** See chapter three; also Dooley, *The decline of the big house*, pp 128–29.   **1** Duc de Stacpoole, *Irish and other memories* (London, 1922), p. 255.   **2** Kevin O'Shiel in *Irish Times*, 11 Nov. 1966.   **3** [Erskine Childers], *The constructive work of Dáil Éireann: no. 1* (Dublin, 1921), p. 10; Bew, 'Sinn Fein, agrarian radicalism and the War of Independence', p. 234.   **4** Patrick Hogan, 'Memorandum on land seizures, 22 Dec. 1922' (hereinafter Hogan memo., 22 Dec. 1922) (Military Archives, Cathal Brugha Barracks (hereinafter Mil. Arch.), A/7869); William Rochfort to secretary of

big houses burned tripled with mansions such as Tubberdaly in King's County and Currygrane in Longford falling to agrarian agitators, some landlords were viciously assaulted, cattle were driven or stolen, and land grabbing remained endemic.[5] As the anti-Treatyites lost support, Patrick Hogan, the influential Minister for Agriculture, felt they attempted to make up lost ground by becoming involved in this widespread land grabbing: 'it would have the advantage of being much more popular, in fact quite in the best traditions. The "land for the people" is almost as respectable an objective as the "republic" and would make a much wider appeal'.[6]

Landowners began to seek protection from the Free State government, but the attitude was not always sympathetic, nor was action immediate, if it followed at all.[7] But as land committees, evicted tenants associations and landless associations began to spring up throughout the country, the Provisional Government realized by December 1922 that the combined activities of these groups was no longer a concern of the Department of Home Affairs or the civil courts; the situation was so ungovernable that it was now a matter for the army to take 'immediate and drastic action against people who [had] seized other people's land' and so in February 1923 the Minister for Defence, acting on Patrick Hogan's suggestion, established a Special Infantry Corps specifically to tackle agrarian disorder.[8]

Almost simultaneously and more significantly, after six months of Civil War, it was recognized within government circles that the final settling of the land question through legislation was a necessary step towards the restoration of law and order.[9] Given the historical precedents since the 1880s of defusing agrarianism with land legislation, this response was rather inevitable in light of the dramatic growth in agrarian crime that was, rightly or wrongly, predominantly associated with the activities of the anti-Treatyite faction who, as noted above, were accused of rallying support in the localities by exploiting traditionally emotive agrarian grievances. In January 1923 the first tentative steps were taken towards the formulation of a new land bill as a matter of 'importance and urgency.'[10] In the aftermath of the Land Purchase and Arrears Conference of 10–11 April that had been established in an attempt to negotiate common ground between landlords and tenants, Hogan proclaimed the mood of a significant proportion of the electorate to the government:

> They [the tenant representatives] informed the landlords in all moods and
> tenses that a great change had come; that they were now in a small minority,
> and an unpopular minority; that they could take the land from them for

Minister for Home Affairs, 7 Apr. 1923 (NAI, Dept. of Justice files, H5/56); Patrick Hogan to W.T. Cosgrave, 7 Apr. 1923 (NAI, Dept. of the Taoiseach files, S3192).   **5** Dooley, *The decline of the big house*, pp 187–92.   **6** Hogan memo., 22 Dec. 1922; see also 'Public notice issued by Kyleavallagh and Kyleoughan Land Committee, April 1922' (NAI, Dept. of Justice files, H5/123); Report compiled by Arthur Blennerhassett, Ballyseedy, Co. Kerry, 7 Mar. 1922 (NAI, Dept. of Justice files, H5/57).   **7** Dooley, *The decline of the big house*, pp 130–1. **8** Hogan memo., 22 Dec. 1922 (NAI, Dept. of the Taoiseach files, S1943); also ministry of defence memo., 1 Feb. 1923 (Mil. Arch., A/7869).   **9** *Dáil debates*, vol. 2, 5 Jan. 1923, 592. **10** Ibid.

nothing if they wished; that the people meant to have the land cheaply, and that if the present government did not meet the wishes of the people in this respect, they would put in a government the next time who would.[11]

It seems that the socio-political climate of the time dictated that the land bill would have to be pushed through before the impending general election on 27 August 1923. The formal introduction of the bill to the Dáil in May 1923 coincided with the ending of the Civil War and may very well have significantly contributed to the decline in support for the anti-Treatyites' agrarian campaign. In a powerful speech, Kevin O'Higgins, the Minister for Home Affairs, warned against recalcitrancy:

> Within the last year, under cover of activities against the Government, men have gone out in an entirely selfish, wilful and criminal spirit to seize land by the strong hand, or by the hand which they thought was strong … [I will urge] on the Minister for Agriculture from my department, that the people who go out in that spirit, who go out in the defiance of the law and in defiance of the Parliament to press their claims by their own violence and their own illegalities be placed definitely outside the benefits of this Bill.[12]

And on 8 August 1923 President W.T. Cosgrave introduced a special resolution to both houses of the Oireachtas:

> … during the last two or three years a good deal of dislocation of the ordinary administration has been attributable to the land agitation … This is a Bill on which the maximum amount of agreement has been brought to bear by all the parties to it … But I think the general consensus of opinion in the Oireachtas and in the country is that the measure is one that will go far towards making for much more peaceful conditions and much more ordered conditions and for greater security and greater stability than perhaps any other measure we have had under consideration here. We consider that the public peace is ensured by the passing of this Bill.[13]

The bill passed into law on the following day.[14] In the long term this act and those which followed would redesign the social structure of Irish rural society; in the short term it contributed to the return to more peaceful ways in the Irish countryside at least as much as any other legislative measure introduced by the Free State government in the first eight months of 1923 had done.

11 Patrick Hogan, 'Report on the Land Purchase and Arrears Conference of 10–11 April 1923', 17 Apr. 1923 (University College Dublin Archives, Blythe papers, P24/174). 12 *Dáil debates*, vol. 3, 28 May 1923, 1161–62. 13 *Dáil debates*, vol. 1, 8 Aug. 1923, 1983–5. 14 *An act to amend the law relating to the occupation and ownership of land and for other purposes relating thereto* (no. 42 of 1923).

THE END OF THE GREAT ESTATES

The 1923 Land Act has primarily been associated with the completion of land purchase that had been begun by the British land purchase acts.[15] It was, however, much more significant than a mere facilitator of the completion of land purchase. In its very ambitious attempt to solve the land question once and for all, it gave the newly constituted Land Commission[16] powers to compulsorily acquire and redistribute lands. It recognized that the completion of land purchase was only one stage in the solving of the land question; the other stage, which was much more complex and would remain intractable, was the relief of congestion.[17]

The completion of land purchase and division under the act cost considerably more than was anticipated; David Seth Jones has provisionally set the figure at £58 million, a truly colossal figure for the implementation of any social policy, and this was really only the proverbial tip of the iceberg because subsequent land legislation cost considerably more.[18] The funding came from a huge loan from Britain; Hogan defended the provenance of the same by arguing that it was necessary to stabilize the countryside and thereby attract future long-term investment,[19] but this social engineering scheme undoubtedly constrained the political ambitions of Cumann na nGaedheal and, indeed, their expenditure in other areas of social policy.

But it was in the realm of acquisition and division that the 1923 and later Free State/Irish Republic land acts impacted most upon landlords and subsequently their big houses. It was largely with confiscation in mind that the terms of the act were formulated:

> All tenanted land wherever situated and all untenanted land situated in any congested districts county and such untenanted land situated elsewhere as the Land Commission shall before the appointed day, declare to be required for the purpose of relieving congestion or of facilitating the resale of tenanted land, shall by virtue of this act vest in the Land Commission on the appointed day.

There were limited exceptions such as home farms[20] and demesnes. The act made two further significant exceptions: untenanted lands which were stud farms and 'untenanted land which is intermingled with woodland ... the acquisition of which would be detrimental to the preservation of woodland and to the interests

15 See, for example, F.S.L. Lyons, *Ireland since the famine* (London, 1973 ed.), p. 606; J.A. Murphy, *Ireland in the twentieth century* (Dublin, n.d.), p. 65; Ronan Fanning, *Independent Ireland* (Dublin, 1983), p. 73; Jackson, *Ireland, 1798–1998*, p. 283.   16 *Land Law (Commission) Act, 1923: an Act to amend the law relating to the Irish Land Commission and to dissolve the Congested Districts Board for Ireland and transfer its functions to the Irish Land Commission and for other purposes connected therewith*, no. 27 of 1923 (24 July 1923).   17 Dooley, 'The land for the people', pp 57–98.   18 I would like to thank Professor David Seth Jones for sharing this information with me.   19 *Dáil debates*, vol. 3, 28 May 1923, 1150–1.   20 These were defined as farms 'used for the convenience of the owner's residence ... and not merely as an ordinary farm for the purpose of profit'.

of forestry' could not be acquired.[21] Few of the great houses in Ireland did not have demesnes which had untenanted lands intermingled with woodland. Regarding stud farms, this exception was understandable at the time for the equine industry and the whole horseracing industry was growing in importance and the government was well aware of the need to continue to promote it. But this exclusion also offered an opportunity to many of the great landowners of the past to continue to hold on to untenanted lands by establishing stud farms. In some cases these stud farms operated in name only; in other cases they were quite successful. By the late 1920s Lord Dunraven's Fort Union Stud at Adare was highly successful, as was Charles Moore's stud at Mooresfort in Tipperary; the Marchioness Conyngham established a stud at Slane; Sir Gilbert Greenall continued breeding horses and pedigree cattle at Kilmallock in Limerick and Lord Mayo established an extensive stud farm at Palmerstown.[22]

But all exceptions, other than public authority or municipal lands, could be disregarded by the Land Commission if it declared any estate to be important in the relief of congestion. An automatic method of fixing the price payable to the landlord for tenanted land was provided which was commonly referred to as the 'standard price'. Landlords were entitled to the equivalent of fifteen years' purchase on rents.[23] The advances were paid to landlords in 4.5 per cent land bonds. Effectively, this meant that landlords who were compelled to sell under this act and succeeding acts were much worse off than those who had sold under the 1903–9 acts. Landlords had to accept the standard rate of fifteen years' purchase compared to the average of 25.4 years' purchase available under the 1903 act up to 1908. And in the post-war economy of the 1920s and 1930s, payment in land bonds did not represent a very good return for the loss of an important socio-economic asset.

The transfer of tenanted holdings under the 1923 act was slow and unsatisfactory from the government's point of view and was hampered by legal constraints. The 1931 Land Act was intended to speed up the process. This act enabled the vesting of holdings in the Land Commission to be accomplished by means of the publication of lists of vested holdings in the *Iris Oifigiúil* subject to the correction of errors and omissions that might be found necessary. Every tenant of a holding included in the published list was deemed to have entered into an agreement for the purchase of his holding on the appointed day at the standard price. However, loopholes continued to be exploited. Frank Aiken, speaking in the Dáil in July 1933 on the new land bill of that year, summarized these difficulties. He claimed that 'very few realize the legal and other difficulties which the Land Commission have

---

21 *Irish Land Act 1923.* **22** Dooley, *The decline of the big house*, pp 267–8; F.F. MacCabe & T.E. Healey, 'Racing, steeplechasing and breeding in Ireland' in Charles Richardson (ed.), *British steeplechasing* (London, 1927), pp 294–6. **23** A purchase annuity set at 65 per cent of rent and capitalized at 4.75 per cent left the landlord with 13.68 years' purchase and an annual income of £61 12s. per £100 rent. From a tenant's point of view the new standard purchase annuity amounted to a reduction of 35 per cent of a first term judicial rent or 30 per cent on a second term judicial rent. The government provided a contribution of 10 per cent of the price bringing the landlord's total to 15.05 years' purchase or £67 15s. per £100 rent.

to surmount before they can divide even a single estate' and that 'the safeguards given to home farms and demesne lands have operated to impede the work of the Land Commission in the relief of congestion'.[24] The 1933 Land Act introduced by Fianna Fáil was intended to expedite the compulsory acquisition and redistribution of lands; it empowered the Land Commission to redistribute any property it found suitable with the exception of ordinary owner-occupied farms. This prevented landowners from laying claim to outlying farms as they had done in the past for it empowered the Land Commission to acquire property of landowners who did not reside in its immediate vicinity or who did not use this property 'in the same manner as an ordinary farmer in accordance with proper methods of husbandry'.[25] Practically all agricultural lands were, therefore, bought out from former landlords. By the late 1930s the Free State land acts had succeeded in transferring the bulk of the 114,000 unpurchased holdings on three million acres for £20.8 million.[26] The largest estates vested in the Land Commission from 1923 to the mid-1930s included for example, over 11,000 acres of the marquis of Waterford; 12,000 acres of Viscount Powerscourt in Wicklow; 11,000 acres of Dame B.F.E. Carew in Tipperary; 11,000 acres of the duke of Devonshire in Waterford; 11,000 acres of Lady Edith Windham in Monaghan; and 20,000 acres of Lord Farnham in Cavan.

CONCLUSION

The period from 1903 to the outbreak of World War I was perhaps the most catalytic in terms of the break up of landed estates in Ireland and, indeed, the decline of the big house. The economic crash and prolonged agricultural depression which followed the Great War in themselves would have had disastrous consequences for landed estates but when compounded by a political revolution, a social revolution in the form of a new land war, a campaign of big house burnings (as much for agrarian as political reasons), a land act aimed at the final completion of land purchase and the compulsory acquisition of all untenanted land to ease congestion, as well as a rise in taxation and rates, and the economic war of the 1920s and 1930s, meant that the break-up of estates became all but inevitable. As many houses were gradually stripped of their great demesnes through compulsory state acquisition, they became anachronisms in the Irish countryside. From 1923 to the late 1930s, thousands of acres were taken from the demesnes, for example, at Woodlawn in Galway, Lyons in Kildare, Dunsany in Meath, Kilboy in Tipperary and Frenchpark in Roscommon to name but a few. Within thirty years all of the big houses centred on these demesnes had been sold by the original families.

24 *Dáil debates*, vol. 48, 13 July 1933, 2378–95.   25 *Irish Land Act 1933, no. 38 of 1933,* section (29). Under previous acts residential property was exempted from their scope which meant landowners could claim untenanted land was residential even if only a derelict ruin stood on it.   26 Kolbert & O'Brien, *Land reform in Ireland,* p. 55.

CHAPTER 2

Sources for the study of Irish landed estates

The aim of this chapter is to introduce the reader to the most important primary sources which are available for the study of a local landed estate in Ireland. Essentially what is offered is the ideal in that it describes all that could be available in the perfect situation. Unfortunately, as for example in the case of estate records, this ideal is not always attainable. Nonetheless with the variety of sources discussed below, the researcher should be able to gain an insight into various aspects of the layout, topography, management, and rise and decline of an individual estate. The discussion which follows analyses the strengths and weaknesses of the relevant sources and directs the researcher to where they are located. As pointed out in the introduction to this guide, the sources are not arranged in any hierarchical order of importance. If they were, estate records would take precedence. It has been decided instead to begin with works of reference, directories and gazetteers because these help to geographically locate an estate and they often offer a freeze-frame introduction to the area in which it was situated.

WORKS OF REFERENCE, DIRECTORIES AND GAZETTEERS

There are a number of reference works available, particularly for the second half of the nineteenth century, which will enable the local historian to determine the geographical location of the estate being studied (at least on a county basis), to ascertain its acreage and to estimate its valuation. The most important of these are John Bateman, *The great landowners of Great Britain and Ireland* (reprinted with an introduction by David Spring, Leicester, 1971) and V.H. Hussey de Burgh, *The landowners of Ireland: an alphabetical list of the owners of estates of 500 acres or £500 valuation and upwards in Ireland* (Dublin, 1881). These works also offer incidental information on the sitting landlord regarding his education, army career (if any), and the club(s) to which he belonged. Unlike De Burgh, Bateman indicates if landlords with property in Ireland also owned property in Britain.

For the nineteenth century a variety of directories[1] and gazetteers[2] are available which feature some information on landowners in an area. The most useful

---

1 Also known as trade or commercial directories, these were essentially printed lists of local businessmen, professionals and so on. In addition, they provided lists of 'principal inhabitants' and public officials who, in rural areas, were predominantly local landlords. *Thom's* lists of local justices of the peace in the nineteenth century is a fair indicator of the number of resident gentry in a county. 2 These were books containing geographical and topographical

gazetteer for pre-famine Ireland is Samuel Lewis, *A topographical dictionary for Ireland*
(2 volumes & atlas, London, 1837). It is organized on a county basis and parishes
within each county are arranged in alphabetical order.[3] An overview is given for
each county which provides some information on the range in size of estates there
or the average size of farm holdings. One is alerted to the variations in agricultural
practice within an area or variations in the quality of land, information which may
be useful when examining, for example, the rental capacity of farm holdings.[4]
Whereas for the first half of the nineteenth century, one has Lewis's *Topographical
dictionary* and the three-volume *Parliamentary gazetteer of Ireland,* published in 1846,
there is no other comparable gazetteer available for the later nineteenth century.

Directories such as *Thom's almanac and official directory of the United Kingdom and
Ireland* (1845–), *Pigot's City of Dublin & Hibernian Provincial Directory*, and *Slater's
national commercial directory of Ireland* (published occasionally, 1846–94) are collections
of information on a wide variety of topics and while they are arguably of more
benefit to urban historians, such directories do provide some useful, if limited, detail
on estates.[5] For example, from the mid–1870s, the size of most estates in Ireland can
be found in *Thom's directory*. In the 1846 edition of *Slater's directory* one finds that
the town of Castleblayney in County Monaghan took its name from the Blayney
family, the most prominent landowners in the area, one of whom, Sir Edward
Blayney, built a castle there during the reign of James I (1566–1625). The demesne
of Lord Blayney's castle embraced 'the whole of Lough Muckno, its pretty islets and
soft swelling boundaries; and the rich foliage which now mantles the latter adds
much to the splendor of the scenery. The plantations also clothe many of the
surrounding heights, and while they increase the beauty of Lord Blayney's
residence, they add to the appearance and comfort of this respectable town'.[6] We
are also told that Lord Blayney promoted the linen industry in the area at the end
of the eighteenth century by establishing a market in the town and encouraging his
tenants to grow flax on their holdings. In the 1870 edition of *Slater's directory*, one
finds the Blayney family no longer associated with the town and that the demesne
and castle were by then owned by the widow of the late Thomas Hope. *Slater's
directory* also features lists of the prominent nobility and gentry families in each area.
An indication of local landlord patronage can be gauged from their association with
various local schools.[7]

information alphabetically arranged.   **3** Most of the information contained in this gazetteer
was supplied by local landlords.   **4** For example, Samuel Lewis points out that there was a
wide variation of soil type in south County Monaghan where 'even in several parts of the
same field [the soil] is seen sometimes to vary extremely, being deep and agrillaceous at one
spot, a gravelly grit at another, exhibiting at a third a stiff clay, and at a fourth a partly-
coloured mixture of red and greenish gravel'. See Samuel Lewis, *A topographical dictionary of
Ireland* (2 vols & atlas, London, 1837) (Lewis, *Topog. dict. Ire.* hereinafter), ii, 380.   **5** These
directories can be found in the NLI or NAI. They may also be found in county libraries or
some editions can be accessed online at, for example, www.failteromhat.com/slater.htm and
www.failteromhat.com/pigot.htm.   **6** *Slater's directory, 1846.*   **7** Information of this type can
also be taken from Lewis's *Topographical dictionary*. For example, Lewis remarks that the

There are other directories that deal specifically with individual counties. These may have been once-off or occasional publications. These works can be located by examining the subject volumes of the printed books catalogues in the National Library of Ireland [NLI] under the name of the county[8] or by consulting the guide to Irish directories produced by Rosemary ffoliott and Donal Begley in 1981 which lists all the Dublin and provincial directories in chronological order.[9]

The beginning of the nineteenth century also saw the publication of a number of important statistical surveys, carried out by the Royal Dublin Society, which, like the works above, can provide the historian with at least some information on the topographical, social and economic life of the area in which the estate is located. For example, James McParland's *Statistical survey of Co. Mayo, with observations on the means of improvement* (Dublin, 1802) offers a fairly detailed physical description of each of Mayo's nine baronies; farm sizes and agricultural practices in the county; fairs and agricultural prices. It also contains a list of the principal landlords in Mayo at that time classifying them as resident or absentee. The same author's *Statistical survey of Co. Leitrim with observations on the means of improvement* (Dublin, 1802) offers information on the nature of tenures, rents, leases and their typical covenants in that county as well as providing a list of its most prominent landlords, categorizing around twenty of them (including Lord Leitrim, Lord Southwell and Lord Granard) as absentees. Unfortunately no surveys were carried out for counties Carlow, Fermanagh, Limerick, Kerry, Westmeath, Louth, Longford or Waterford.[10] For a valuable contemporary insight into the practice of estate management, Thomas De Moleyn's *The landlords and agents practical guide* (various editions, Dublin, 1860–77) is a useful starting point.

ESTATE RECORDS

The most important sources available to anybody undertaking the study of a landed estate are contained in its estate records. Surprisingly such records were not extensively used in the past by historians concerned with the land question or the

---

Roman Catholic church in Monasterevin, Co. Kildare, was built by the marquess of Drogheda 'in lieu of one which was originally situated within their demesne.' The parochial school 'for which a good school house, with apartments for the master and mistress, was erected on an acre of ground given by the Rev. H. Moore, with £300 presented by the trustees of the marquess of Drogheda's estate, is supported by the incumbent, by a bequest of the late Viscountess Ely, and by a grant of £30 per annum from the marquess of Drogheda who also gave £300 towards the national school and allows £30 per annum to the master and mistress'. See Lewis, *Topog. dict. Ire.*, ii, 386.   **8** Works acquired after 1968 are listed in a separate card catalogue in the NLI.   **9** R. ffolliott & D.F. Begley, 'Guide to Irish directories' in D.F. Begley (ed.), *Irish genealogy: a record finder* (Dublin, 1981), pp 75–106.   **10** Some other statistical surveys include, Sir Charles Coote, *Statistical survey of the King's County* (Dublin, 1801); J. Dubourdieu, *Statistical survey of the County of Down* (Dublin, 1802); idem, *Statistical survey of the County of Antrim* (Dublin, 1812); W. Tighe, *Statistical observations*

agrarian economy. However, since the 1970s, studies by historians such as J.S. Donnelly jr., W.E.Vaughan and this author amongst others have shown the value and necessity of using these sources. Estate records reveal the reality of estate life as opposed to the myth which has often been handed down in oral history or, indeed, in biased history texts that perpetuated the stereotype of the rackrenting, capricious and alien landlord.

The first step for the researcher is actually finding out if records survive for an estate and if so where they are located. This can be done in a number of ways. An important starting point is still Richard Hayes' *Manuscript sources for the history of Irish civilisation* (11 vols, Boston, MA, 1966) and *Manuscript sources for the history of Irish civilization. First supplement, 1965–75* (3 vols, Boston, MA, 1979). For the student of the landed estate the most relevant volumes are 1–4 dealing with persons, and 7–8 dealing with place. In these volumes one should look up the name of the landlord under study or the name of the area(s) where the estate was located. Usually, the same entry will be found repeated in each of these sections where appropriate, but one may find the occasional manuscript that has not been repeated.[11] One will find a brief description of the manuscript, the manuscript number if available in the NLI or, if not, the name of the repository where the manuscript is stored.[12] For example, looking under the name of Cloncurry, one finds the following: 'MSS 5661–5664: Cloncurry papers: Domestic farm and workmen's accounts relating to Lord Cloncurry's estates in Kildare and Limerick, c.1830–1899 (discontinuous, with rentals and accounts, 1860–99)'. There are some manuscripts, the originals of which are stored outside the NLI, but copies of which may be available in the library on microfilm. These will have a number such as N104 P33 at the end of the entry. Occasionally one may also come across a reference number such as P.C. 4180. 'P.C.' stands for 'packing case' which means that these papers are in the NLI but have not yet been catalogued and are, therefore, not on open access. However, access may in some cases be granted after having written to the keeper of manuscripts in the NLI seeking permission to consult the collection.

In the National Library, the card catalogue in the manuscript reading room should also be consulted as these cards contain information on more recently acquired estate papers not to be found in Hayes' *Manuscript sources*. There are also 'special lists' available on family or estate collections in the NLI which have only recently been sorted by the library staff. 'Special list A' is an index to these

relative to the County of Kilkenny (Dublin, 1802); H. Townsend, *General and statistical survey of County Cork* (2 vols, Dublin, 1815). See also Wakefield, *An account of Ireland, statistical and political*.   **11** Similarly it may be of benefit to consult the subjects volumes under, for example, such headings as 'evictions'.   **12** Some of the abbreviations in Hayes's *Manuscript sources* are now out of date, for instance the S[tate] P[aper] O[ffice] and the P[ublic] R[ecord] O[ffice] have been amalgamated to form the National Archives of Ireland. Occasionally one may find a reference such as F 59 (1–24). These usually refer to manuscript maps, or valuation surveys with maps which are kept on microfilm in the NLI, for instance, F 59 (1–24) is the reference for 'Maps of the estate of Lord Cloncurry in the barony of Owneybeg, Co. Limerick, by John Washington, James Quinn, Thomas Lynch, James Serry,

collections. It gives the number of the list in which a collection is catalogued and this list can be consulted in the manuscript reading room.[13] Indexes to recently sorted collections are now available online and can be consulted in pdf format at www.nli.ie by clicking on 'Lists of manuscripts and special collections'.

One should also consult the periodic reports of the Irish Manuscript Commission and National Library of Ireland on estate collections in private hands. These reports, based on the work of Sir John Ainsworth, give a summary of the material that was available in private collections around the 1950s. Some of these collections may subsequently have been transferred to various repositories or may even, unfortunately, have been destroyed but the summaries can in themselves be informative.

The NLI is, of course, not the only repository that contains a comprehensive collection of Irish estate papers. There is also a very comprehensive collection in the Public Record Office Northern Ireland [PRONI]. At least seventy of these collections could be described as being very extensive. Information on estate records there can be found in PRONI, *Guide to estate collections* (Belfast, 1994), or on website http://proni.gov.uk/records/landed.htm.

The National Archives, Bishop Street, Dublin [NAI] also houses some estate collections. While there is no printed guide to these, indexes to them can be found on the shelves in the reading room. Estate collections may also be found in other Irish repositories such as Trinity College Library, or British repositories such as the National Archives, Kew. Information on Irish estate papers housed in various repositories throughout the United Kingdom may also be obtained from the National Register of Archives website at http://www.hmc.gov.uk/nra/indexes.htm. Here one can search under personal and family name or place name. Looking under the place name of County Monaghan, for example, one finds twenty-five listings of which eighteen are estate records of landed families in that county. Of these one finds that estate records of the Shirley family of Lough Fea, for example, are to be found in PRONI and Warwickshire County Record Office. To find the records of peerage families one should enter the peerage title under 'descriptive term' if the records do not show up under family name. It is important to realize that some estate collections have been scattered across a number of repositories. This is particularly true of those belonging to absentee or semi-absentee landowners who had estates in Ireland and Britain or, indeed, in different parts of Ireland.[14]

University libraries should also be consulted. To take but one example, NUI Galway's library holds a number of important collections.[15] These include the

and others. 24 maps, some coloured, with names of tenants, 1743–1835'.   **13** For example, 'special list A' shows that the Headfort papers are to be found indexed in catalogue 'A3'. This index gives a brief description of each manuscript in the Headfort collection as well as the relevant manuscript numbers.   **14** There is a collection of Cloncurry estate records in the NLI. There is also a collection of records for the years 1880–1909 housed in Glenstal Abbey, Murroe, Co. Limerick, and more are in private hands. Quite a few surviving estate records for individual estates are divided between the NLI and PRONI. While, for example, the greater part of the Leinster papers are in PRONI, there are a few valuable records in the NLI.   **15** See www.library.nuigalway.ie/resources/archives/guidetoholdings.html.

account book of John Carson, agent for Lord Crofton in County Roscommon which covers the important pre-Famine period, 1833–40. There are four boxes of material relating to the Daly family of Dunsandle which enlighten on land sales in Tipperary and Galway in the nineteenth and twentieth centuries. The Blake of Ballyglunin collection supplements (or is supplemented by) the collections belonging to the same family in the NLI and the much smaller collection in the NAI.

Throughout the country, various local libraries and museums and historical society offices have accumulated (parts of) local collections down through the years. For those in Sligo County Library, for example, see J.C. McTernan, *Sligo: sources of local history* (Sligo, 1988). The Offaly Historical and Archaeological Society office at Bury Quay in Tullamore has important collections of estate archives belonging to the Charleville and Digby estates in the county, while Monaghan County Museum has a number of important map collections belonging to estates such as the Lucas Scudamore estate at Castleshane.

If no records pertaining to a particular estate can be traced to a major repository, it is worth finding out if an estate's solicitors are still in business as they may still have family papers or know of their whereabouts.[16] Solicitors may be able to put one in contact with descendants of the landed family who may still retain at least some of the estate records.[17] Descendants may also be traced by using the most recent editions of *Burke's landed gentry of Ireland* or *Burke's peerage, baronetage and knightage*. Finally, local libraries, heritage centres and local archives now house some estate collections and are also worth checking with.[18]

A number of very significant collections remain in the guardianship of the original families who continue to reside in their country houses. There are important collections, for example, in Birr Castle in County Offaly (Lord Rosse); Kilruddery in County Meath (Lord Meath); Killadoon in County Kildare (Clements family); Barmeath in County Louth (Bellew family); and Borris in County Carlow (Kavanagh family). It must be remembered that these are not public repositories, so access to private collections may be facilitated by appointment only.

Having located an estate collection, what can one hope to find in them? It is perhaps best to answer this question by reference to what one could hope to find in a complete collection. Title deeds and conveyances[19] are essential to an under-

---

16 One possible means of identifying the estate's solicitors is consultation of the Land Commission papers pertaining to the estate. However, these are not always easily accessed (see section below on Irish Land Commission papers).   **17** The estate office archives in Birr Castle, Co. Offaly, for example, houses the Rosse papers from the early seventeenth century to the present day; most of the Meath papers are still housed in Kilruddery in Bray (a catalogue of these is available in the NAI); Strokestown House has a considerable collection of the Pakenham-Mahon estate records.   **18** For example, a considerable amount of papers belonging to the Digby and Charleville estates are to be found in the offices of the Offaly Historical Society in Tullamore, Co. Offaly; Sligo County Library has rentals belonging to the Palmerston estate; Monaghan County Museum houses papers not only pertaining to estates in that county but also to estates in Dublin and Meath.   **19** See also section below on Irish Land Commission.

standing of the acquisition, administration, maintenance and sale of estates in Ireland. Conveyances detail the transfer of lands from one owner to the next, giving dates of the same, and usually valuable information on location, acreage, and sometimes valuation and rental capacity. They inform on the various stages at which landlords acquired and sold properties, when they sold outlying estates in order to purchase neighbouring lands or to meet charges and debts.

In order to comprehend the intricacies of estate administration, the above records should be used in conjunction with administrative records such as leases, mortgages (often detailing how dependent Irish landowning families were upon each other to raise finances to purchase new lands or settle debts and charges), rentals, accounts, the correspondence of the estate's agents and so on. Not only will these sources inform on the administration of an estate, they will also elucidate agricultural practices, the nature of landholding and tenurial arrangements, land values, rents, soil type and a myriad of other related aspects of estate life. Furthermore, they illustrate the legal minefield in which Irish landlords operated. Some estate collections contain dozens of legal papers relating to searches concerning titles to lands, lawyers' opinions and bills of costs. There are documents relating to legal disputes with neighbouring landlords or tenants (including documentation concerning legal actions proposed or taken for the recovery of rents or the carrying out of evictions).

Estate rentals are particularly valuable especially when extant in annual or semi-annual series for the duration of the period under study (for extended periods, a full run of rentals is quite rare). They detail rents due, rents paid, and the extent of arrears indicating how successful a landlord was in collecting his rental income. They enable a study of the effects of periods of crises such as the famine of the 1840s or the land war of the 1880s on estate rents. When available in a long unbroken series with uniform headings, rentals allow one to calculate the size of rent increases on individual holdings or on the estate as a whole, and to compare rent increases on individual holdings. In analyzing rent movements on an estate, one should consider agricultural incomes as the level of agricultural incomes determined the tenants' capacity to pay the asking rent. It should also be remembered that estate rentals and accounts do not, as a rule, contain any information on sources of non-landed income such as income from political office or commercial investment, so they will not necessarily provide a true statement of disposable income.

The Clonbrock estate in County Galway was divided into seven administrative units – Doone, Castlegar, Ballydonelan, Dalyston, Quansbury, Lecarrow and Pallas. The rental ledgers for each year are divided according to these seven administrative units. The names of tenants in each estate are listed according to the townland in which they lived. Their arrears for the previous two gale days are specified, as are the half year's rent due, the rent and arrears received and the remaining arrears due thereafter. These details are followed by a summary of the rental accounts for each administrative unit giving totals of rents received, rent and arrears due and so on.

Finally, there is a summary of rental accounts for the estate as a whole. The rentals which are available for the pre-1827 period are mainly in the form of loose sheets. After that year, they appear in bound volumes.

Rent books were kept by landlords or their agents to provide an accurate account of their dealings with individual tenants. They recorded the tenant's name, the gale days on which his or her rent was due, the amount paid on the last gale day and the amount outstanding in arrears. They may also record any change in tenancies due, for example, to the falling in of leases. Comments columns in such ledgers can be useful. They sometimes record the landlord's or the agent's observations on tenants, offering reasons why a tenant is unable to meet his/her full rental obligation. The comments' columns in the Clonbrock rent ledger for 1881, a time when the landlord was having difficulties in collecting rents due to agricultural depression, shows that individual tenants were 'very poor, unable to pay'; 'wife has lambs to sell, he [her husband] is gone to America to make rent'; that the tenant was now 'dead. House pulled down' or the tenant had been 'ejected. Arrears lost. Land relet'.[20] In some collections there are also separate lists of tenants who were in arrears.

Several types of estate account books exist. Some comprehensive collections have account books which detail day-to-day expenditure on an estate. The Clonbrock estate account books for the second half of the nineteenth century provide a daily record of expenses incurred in the maintenance of the big house, demesne, farm, gardens, stables, and labour. These account books also record any income received including even the sum of £4 3s. 11d. received in 1868 for 'dripping' sold from the house.[21] Fortunately, for the researcher interested only in end of year accounts, the collection also contains account books where all expenses are totaled and balanced against all income received. Income was primarily made up of rents received from tenants but accounts show that some landlords received additional income from a variety of other sources as diverse as the selling of wood to the leasing of the big house ballroom (which Lord Headfort did in the late nineteenth century). Landlords also drew income from investments, demesne farming, and turbary. Some landlords drew urban as well as agricultural rents.[22] Agents' and stewards' account books give detail of the services performed by them

20 Clonbrock estate rent ledger, 1881 (NLI, Clonbrock papers, MS 19,634). 21 Clonbrock estate account book, 1868 (NLI, Clonbrock papers, MS 19,511). 22 The headings used vary greatly from one estate to the next. The areas of expenditure specified in the Clonbrock estate accounts in the 1880s were as follows: insurances, head rents, interest, rent charges, church fund, quit rent, income tax, poor rates, county cess, mill account, Clonbrock school, Killisalen school, charity, pensions, Dalyston woods, Clonbrock estate, Ballydonelan estate, Luansbury estate, Doone, estate, Castlegar estate, Dalyston estate, salaries, nursery, (assisted) emigration, seed potatoes, abatements, bills, stamps, and agency fees. Remittances to the landlord and his family were also listed as expenses. Income headings included rents received, monies received for meal sold at the estate mill, timber and bark sold, the tolls received for Cappataggle fair, and the interest received on loans. Illuminating comments are sometimes added to the end of year accounts specifying, for example, to whom interest is

and the expenses incurred in running the estate. They usually detail expenditure on drainage, fencing, pension lists, expenses incurred in assisted emigration, pension schemes, tenant housing and so on. In this respect, the agents' (and other) accounts indicate the role of the estate in the wider community. They shed some light on the benevolence (or lack of it) of landlords, their interest in estate improvements, and the importance of the estate as a source of employment. They provide unwitting testimony regarding tenant housing, the extent of poverty (by detailing poor rates) and the registration of freeholders. They elucidate the levels of employment on the estate during the various seasons, detailing the numbers of labourers employed and their wages. Most particularly they give a good indication of the wealth or indebtedness of a landlord in the nineteenth century. In using such accounts, a working knowledge of double entry book-keeping is essential. Worth noting is the fact that expenditure accounts usually include remittances paid to the landlord and his dependents which should be considered when balancing income against the cost of maintaining the actual estate.

An estate collection may also include demesne farm account books recording farm profits and losses on an annual basis, as well as the stock on hand at the end of each accounting year. For the Ormonde estate, for example, there are farm account books of Dunmore farm which provide day to day accounts of the income and expenditure on the farm, indicating the livestock bought and sold, the prices received or given, labour expenses, manuring practices, and the profit or loss at the end of each year. There is also an inventory and valuation of stock and plant at hand on the farm at the end of each year, all of which helps to increase our understanding of the significance of demesne farming to landlords in the nineteenth and twentieth centuries.[23]

Much rarer are investment books detailing the investment behaviour of Irish landlords after the sale of their landed estates from the 1880s, but particularly after 1903 when the bulk of Irish landlords sold their estates to the occupying tenants. The investments books that exist suggest that Irish landlords invested globally in places such as Russia (Europe's fastest growing economy in the pre-1914 era), North America, South Africa, Australia and so on. Very little was invested in Ireland. As the Russian economy went into turmoil in 1917 and a prolonged worldwide depression struck after the end of the Great War, Irish landlords found their once impressive share portfolios decimated with severe consequences for their ability to retain their big houses or maintain their accustomed lifestyles.

Lease books are important for what they reveal about the management of an estate and the agricultural practices thereon. The purpose of the lease was primarily to devise letting conditions likely to enhance the value of an estate. A typical lease gave details of its duration, the landlord and tenant names, the amount of land being leased, the annual rent or consideration charged, and any special clauses or covenants. In March 1842, for example, Henry Bruen of Oak Park in County

payable and on what amount of loan. **23** Dunmore farm account books, 1883–94 (NLI, Ormonde papers, MS 23,833).

Carlow, entered into a lease with two of his tenants Thomas Booth senior and Thomas Booth junior for a holding of eighty-seven acres at £1 4s. 8d. per acre per year for the duration of the lives of those named in the lease. The lease described the location of the lands, and reserved all game, fishing, mines, minerals, coals, limestone, timber and turf rights to the landlord. It contained covenants regarding the payment of rent and the right to distrain for rent in the event of non-payment, further covenants making the lessee responsible for planting ditches with white thorn quick and building fences. Penalties were specified for failing to do so. There were covenants for keeping land and premises in repair and free from trespass; forbidding the lessee from sub-letting or sub-dividing; cutting turf or building houses without the landlord's consent.[24]

A lease book or collection of leases can offer insights into the nature of land tenure on an estate, the levels of rent, and often dates and reasons for evictions. From 1870 many leases show the lengths which landlords went to in order to evade the payment of compensation under the terms of the 1870 Land Act. One of the most controversial leases drawn up at this time was by the duke of Leinster. Most of the clauses were aimed at good estate management and were very similar to those which appeared in the Bruen lease referred to above.[25] The duke's tenantry objected vehemently to the clause which stipulated that 'the said lessee, his executors, administrators or assigns or any of them shall not make any claim for compensation in respect of disturbance or improvements (except with improvements made with the written consent of the lessor, his heirs or assigns) or for compensation in any other respect under any of the clauses or provisions' of the 1870 Land Act.[26]

For the management and day-to-day running of an estate, agents' letter books are a very revealing source. These contain copies of outgoing and incoming correspondence between agent and landlord, or agent and tenants on a daily basis. This correspondence features important information on various aspects of estate business including agricultural practice; information on the level of rents; difficulties caused by agitation or agricultural depression; employment practices; changing market conditions; and the need to adopt different strategies in the management of the estate. A perusal of the vast collection of correspondence for the Ormonde estate for the early years of the 1880s reveals much about an agent's difficulties of collecting rents at that time. A study of this type of correspondence may be enlightening, not only in relation to estate management, but also, for example,

---

24 For an excellent discussion of leases see Dickson, *Old world colony*, pp 181–90.   **25** The usual description of land and tenements were made, reserving to the landlord all mineral, woods, game and fishing rights. The lease enjoined the maintenance and repair of buildings and fences. It imposed additional yearly rents for all permanent grass broken up for tillage and all arable land overcropped or used 'contrary to an approved course of husbandry'. It prohibited sub-letting, assigning and con-acre; it forbade the erection of unsuitable buildings, and made provision for breach of covenant in the event of tenant bankruptcy. The lease was to be bequeathed to one person only.   **26** *Irish Times*, 28 Dec. 1880.

regarding the different type of relationships which may have existed between a landlord and his large tenants and a landlord and his smaller tenants.

The correspondence of stewards and legal advisers can be equally illuminating. This material can shed valuable light on the transfer of properties, the renewal of leases, their changes in estate management policy, the fixing of rents, and the general running of the estate, demesne and farm. Because all of the above were affected at different times by political change, economic crisis, agrarianism and so on, letters of stewards and solicitors can often point to the reasons for change and how it has been effected. They can point to the effects of changes in the economic climate upon the running of estates, pointing to when landlords, for example, sold off parcels of their lands in order to remain solvent or purchased more lands when circumstances improved. Estates were by no means static; they were continuously evolving and changing territorial shape.

Estate correspondence is one of the few sources available which offer an insight into the world of the tenantry and a landlord's or his agent's policy towards them. Take, for instance, the Farnham estate correspondence for the late-nineteenth century. In the main, tenants seem to have written directly to Lord Farnham who, in turn, having read their letters, passed them on to his agent, T.R. Blackley, with any queries or suggestions he may have had. In September 1898, a tenant, Rose Cahill, wrote to Farnham: 'I beg to let your lordship know that I lost a good cow from a broken back last November crossing a ditch. Shortly after that I lost a yearling calf from blackleg. And another calf this year in February from redwater … I have never entered courts and I hope you will consider my distress and allow me a little on account of the unavoidable death of my cattle.' Farnham passed the letter to Blackley who wrote a note back to him stating that: 'I had to take proceedings at the quarter sessions against Rose Cahill. I do not know whether her statement is true, but I would not recommend any gratuity.'[27] Blackley's comment is in itself a warning to the historian to be discerning when approaching such correspondence and to guard against the cute Irish tenant so often caricatured by the likes of Somerville and Ross in their novels and short stories.[28]

Ejectment books are unfortunately a rarer source. Amongst the most valuable of those in existence are two such books of Earl Fitzwilliam's estate in Wicklow and Wexford for the years 1845 to 1881. These books record the notices to quit served annually between these years and in many cases the reasons for their service. They reveal a good deal about the eviction process: tenants were not just ejected for non-

---

27 Farnham estate correspondence, 1898 (NLI, Farnham papers, MS 18,618). An even more unlikely reason for not having to pay his rent was offered by another of Farnham's tenants, William Jackson. He wrote to Lord Farnham: 'For the past 47 years I have sold yearly at Farnham a quantity of carrots always at the same price which enabled me to pay my rent. This year I applied to your lordship's steward as usual to take them but he refused'. Farnham noted that this was 'certainly an unofficial way of paying rent', while Blackley wrote: 'A respectable old man but I would find serious fault if your land steward did not grow as good carrots as Jackson'; ibid. **28** Edith Somerville & Martin Ross, *Some experiences of an Irish R.M.* (London, 1899); idem, *Further experiences of an Irish R.M.* (London, 1908).

payment of rents or accumulated arrears (although this was the most common reason); notices to quit were served for sub-letting, bad husbandry (or farming practices), and admitting lodgers.[29] Serving a notice to quit did not necessarily lead to actual eviction. In the Fitzwilliam ejectment books comments such as 'settled' or 'postponed' indicate that tenants and landlord came to some sort of amicable arrangement regarding the payment of rents. Similarly, the fact that the same names appear time and time again in these books suggests that the notice to quit was used as a warning rather than as a sanction.

In a work of this length, it is not possible to go into all the various types of records which may be available in an estate collection. What have been described above are the most important sources for the study of estate management. A comprehensive archive such as that of Ormonde estate on deposit in the NLI also contains items which may be of value to those interested in more specialized areas. For example, this collection contains a register of petitions to the agent from tenants for the years 1845–62 which offers a great deal of information on the effects of the famine and aftermath on the estate. For those interested in landlord improvements the collection contains a list of houses built on the estate from 1854 to 1880. (Patrick Duffy's work on the Shirley estate in County Monaghan bears testimony to the amount of invaluable information to be gleaned from 'Estate improvement books' which allowed him to focus on landlords as agents of change in south Monaghan in the 1840s as they constructed tenant houses, cleared lands of the stones and planted rows of quick thorn hedges as a means of enclosing the patchwork of small fields still evident on the local landscape.)[30] In the Ormonde collection there is a register showing the amounts advanced to tenants in the post-famine period in order to improve their holdings with details of the improvements carried out. The collection also includes a register of tenants relating to judicial rent agreements granted in the Land Commission courts between 1884 and 1905 (an important indicator of the effects which government legislation had on the decline of landlord rents from the enactment of the 1881 Land Act); an account book of tenants who were constituted as caretakers from 1887 to 1897 (these were mainly occupying tenants who had been evicted for non-payment of rent but who were subsequently readmitted as caretakers later on); and a set of tenants' notebooks for the years 1885–1923. There are copies of proposals for the sale of holdings to tenants (both judicial and non-judicial) on the estate in 1904, the year after the passing of the Wyndham Land Act when most of the Ormonde estate was sold off. A number of important lists of people are featured in the collection including one of people to be invited to balls at Kilkenny castle (which provides an insight to the narrow social circles in which the landed class moved); an alphabetical list of landowners in Kilkenny and the south-east compiled sometime between 1900 and

29 Fitzwilliam ejectment books, 1845–60, 1861–86 (NLI, Fitzwilliam papers, MSS 4972, 4992). 30 Duffy, 'Management problems on a large estate'; idem, 'The nuts and bolts of making landscape in the mid-nineteenth century' in *Group for the Study of Irish Historic Settlement Newsletter*, viii (1997), pp 13–16.

1916; and an alphabetical list of the tenants on the estate for the years 1880–85, essentially the period of the land war.[31]

Similarly, the Headfort papers contain, for example, a remarkable series of inventories of trees from 1820 to 1830 and two woodrangers' report books, 1839–60, in which details of the duties of woodrangers and the rules they had to obey are set out by the marquis of Headfort. Woodland was, of course, a major source of income for landlords, which is often overlooked. When landlord fortunes suffered setbacks, the sale of woodland came to the rescue of many. This and other collections contain records of game reared on the estate for hunting purposes, garden and demesne accounts, wills and marriage settlements (more details of which will be discussed under the records available in the registry of deeds), records of loans between landlords and the Board of Public Works, all of which can contribute in some measure to an understanding of the day to day running of a landed estate.

Estate records, it should be emphasized, are hugely important in understanding the much wider changes that affected rural Ireland outside the demesne walls. This can be seen in correspondence of landlords with various public bodies such as the Commissioners of Public Works regarding drainage works carried out under the various drainage acts. The Clonbrock papers contain information of reports on the proposed drainage of the River Suck in the late-nineteenth century, surveys of the River Shannon, correspondence with Galway County Council after 1899 regarding the payment of rates and so on. They detail the role of the Dillon family in the establishment and running of several national schools on the estate between 1870 and 1920. Amongst these records are correspondence with Dr Gillooly, bishop of Elphin, and Patrick Healy of the Royal Commission of Primary Education concerning the setting up of a national school on the estate at Killosolan, County Galway.[32]

Finally, estate maps and surveys are also valuable sources and local historians would be advised to take a look at all the maps they can find in order to locate and reconstruct the layout of the estate under study.[33] The reader's attention is directed to Jacinta Prunty's extremely comprehensive *Maps and map-making in local history* (Dublin, 2004), published as part of the Maynooth Research Guides for Local History series, for a more detailed discussion of the importance of maps, how to access them and use them. What follows here is a basic introduction to estate maps.

During the seventeenth century, plantation surveys undertaken by the state had resulted in the mapping of large parts of the country. The last and most comprehensive of these surveys was that carried out by Sir William Petty in the 1690s, better known as the Down Survey.[34]

---

31 This list, as is the case with many other estate records, may be an invaluable source to genealogists.   32 Stephen Ball, 'Collection list no. 54: Clonbrock estate papers' (NLI), p. 50. 33 See Paul Ferguson, *Irish map history: a select bibliography of secondary works, 1850–1983, on the history of cartography in Ireland* (Dublin, 1983); J.H. Andrews, *Plantation acres: an historical study of the Irish land surveyor and his maps* (Belfast, 1985); idem, *Shapes of Ireland: maps and their makers, 1564–1839* (Dublin, 1997); idem, *History in the Ordnance map: an introduction for Irish readers* (Dublin, 1974); A. Bonar Law, *The printed maps of Ireland* (Dublin, 1998).   34 See P.J.

Prior to the Ordnance Survey of the 1830s (see below), cartography, surveying and landscape map production depended largely on the interest of landlords in these disciplines. In the late-eighteenth and early-nineteenth centuries many landlords, particularly larger ones, employed surveyors to provide an overview of their estates and cartographers to produce maps of their property as their prosperity increased.[35] The eighteenth century saw an explosion in privately commissioned estate mapping. This was the golden age of cartography when maps were often produced as much for ornamental purposes (the elaborate works of the French cartographer, John Rocque (1705–62), being a case in mind) as for functional purposes. Estate maps were often works of art, stylishly drawn and embellished and beautifully bound or often framed for ornamental purposes for as J.H. Andrews has concluded: 'The map of a man's land met the same psychological need as a picture of his house or a portrait of his wife and children'.[36]

Private surveys were undertaken for a variety of reasons, but usually on the sale of property, the succession of a new heir to an estate, the introduction of new management policies or to settle disputes. The surveys set out the boundaries of a property, measuring it in acres, delineating individual holdings, often giving their valuation and rental, identifying demesne lands, plantations, roadways and so on. Surveys provide a good deal of information on tenants, their holdings and the rents they paid. A survey of Lord Cloncurry's Kildare estate in 1838, for example, is divided according to townland. The name of the occupier of each holding is specified with a description of the lot such as 'steep, rockey [sic], arable, very shallow, furzy'; 'fine soil for tillage. Medium quality rather coarse pasture'. The quantity of land held by occupiers is given in both Irish and English acres along with the rent per acre and the poor law valuation of the holding.[37]

Surveys accompanied by detailed maps gave the landlord an overview of his tenants and provided him with the information to decide what possibilities there existed for increasing future income on individual holdings.[38] In the early 1830s, James Edward Vaughan carried out a detailed survey of Lord Clonbrock's estate in County Galway. He produced a general map to the scale of 3 inches to 1 mile. This map outlines the main features of the estate such as roads, waterways, bogs and woods. It marks out field divisions and there is an index which records the names of the tenant who held each field. It features information on the quality of the land demarcating arable and upland pasture, improved cut bog, inferior boggy pasture, improved mountain, bog and waste.[39] Geographical denominations equated to townlands on the estate, although some maps cover a number of small townlands.

Duffy, 'Eighteenth-century estate maps' in *History Ireland*, 5 (1) (spring, 1994), pp 20–4. **35** Amongst the most famous cartographers of the time was John Rocque who was employed by great landowners such as the duke of Leinster; see J.H. Andrews, 'The French school of Dublin land surveyors' in *Ir. Geography*, v (4) (1967), pp 275–92. **36** J.H. Andrews, *Plantation acres: an historical study of the Irish land surveyor and his maps* (Belfast, 1985), p. 152. **37** Survey of Lord Cloncurry's Kildare estate, 1838 (NLI, Cloncurry papers, MS 5,667). **38** Jacinta Prunty, 'Estate records' in William Nolan & Anngret Simms (eds), *Irish towns: a guide to sources* (Dublin, 1998), p. 123. **39** James Edward Vaughan's surveys of Lord

There is a valuable collection of estate maps in the NLI which were drawn up by William Longfield in the late eighteenth and early nineteenth centuries. The index to this collection is available in the manuscript reading room. It is divided according to county. There are maps available for estates in all thirty-two counties although there are substantially more maps available for the Leinster counties (maps for County Kildare alone account for twenty-seven pages of the index).[40]

The representative nature of estate maps may be questionable, and one must keep this in mind; however, such maps, in the absence of other source material, have added considerably to our understanding of pre-famine economic and social development. They allow one to study the physical characteristics of the landscape which in turn offers suggestions as to the social and economic conditions of the landlord who owned it. They may provide information on the extent and nature of enclosures; changes in settlement patterns; the development of road networks; the nature of outoffices on an estate and the extent of the demesne.

At this juncture, it is appropriate to discuss the Ordnance Survey maps. The Ordnance Survey was established in the Phoenix Park, Dublin, in 1824, when a parliamentary committee of that year advised that the whole of the country should be mapped in detail on the scale of six inches to the mile as a necessary prerequisite for valuing property and assessing tax liability. By 1846 this task had been completed and 1,906 sheets on the recommended scale had been compiled. These maps were subsequently used by Sir Richard Griffith in his primary valuation and later by the Irish Land Commission and the Congested Districts Board as they proceeded to break up Irish landed estates from the 1880s. J.H. Andrews points out that as the number of six inch sheets per county ranged from 25 to 153 (in the case of Cork), there was a need for separate index diagrams which became important maps in their own right and these: 'gave a surprisingly full if somewhat congested picture of roads, rivers, towns, villages, large houses and demesnes'.[41] Moreover, because they marked out demesnes, it is much easier for the historian to pinpoint their actual location than it would be to take this information from the six-inch maps. As the early Ordnance Survey maps were compiled in the pre-famine period they offer an insight to farming and settlement patterns not always available elsewhere.

Post-1922, a separate Ordnance Survey office for the six counties was established in Belfast and the existing records for the six counties were transferred there. The Ordnance Survey offices in the Phoenix Park, Dublin and Stranmillis Court, Belfast continue to house a significant collection of records. Besides their maps, the records include some information relevant to the sale and break-up of estates such as

Clonbrock's estate, 1832 (NLI, Clonbrock papers, MSS 22,008–09). **40** There is also an index of maps available in the NLI that can be consulted in the reading room. It is to be found in bay number 1. Many of these maps are of estates in the nineteenth century: for example, there are maps of the Blake estate in Co. Mayo for 1859; of the DeLapp estate in Co. Cavan, 1858; a set for the Balfour estate, 1692–1893; another set for the Dillon estates in Mayo and Roscommon, 1842–75. However, 'for urgent conservation reasons' some of these maps may not be available for consultation. **41** See Andrews, *History in the Ordnance map*, p. 22.

rentals, statements of conditions of sale and descriptions of properties which may sometimes include a photograph of the big house on the estate.

Estate records are undoubtedly the most valuable and important sources available to the historian attempting to trace the rise, development, and fall of an Irish estate. Rentals, accounts, surveys or valuations, letter books, maps and leases all help in the overall reconstruction of estate life. Information on rent movements may be gleaned from parliamentary papers or even newspapers but it is really only rentals that reveal the true picture. They do not exaggerate low rents as a landlord or his representative might do before a commission of enquiry; nor do they exaggerate high rents as a tenant might do to the same enquiry. Except where a land agent was fraudulent (and some did exist), estate rentals and accounts were not falsified as this served no purpose since they were prepared for the landlord's information rather than any intention of being made public.

Unfortunately, however, estate records are not without their weaknesses. Firstly, only a relatively small percentage of estate records has survived. Larger estates and Ulster estates are generally better represented than small estates or estates in the other three provinces of Leinster, Connaught and Munster. Furthermore, much fewer estate records have survived for the pre-famine than for the post-famine period. There are a number of reasons for this low survival rate. It is probable that a great deal of landlords, particularly smaller ones, were not as likely to store estate records over generations as were larger landowners such as the Downshires, Ormondes or Clonbrocks. Indeed, proper accounts may not have been kept at all on some estates if there was not a large degree of organization and a dutiful agent. If a landlord doubled as his own agent, as many smaller landlords were apt to do, he did not need the same amount of records. Nor would agent letter books exist from such an estate. A standard form of rental only really became popular in the post-famine period; prior to that estate records were often kept by agents on loose sheets of paper, which down through the years were much less likely to survive.

J.S. Donnelly jr., in his search for estate records pertaining to County Cork, found that havoc had been wreaked upon estate records by wastepaper collections. This was particularly true of those in the possession of family solicitors or land agency firms. Donnelly points out that 'one church-sponsored paper drive in Cork city in the late 1950s claimed an enormous collection of documents from the South Mall firm of Hussey and Townsend, probably the largest land-agency concern in all of Ireland during the 1880s, with some ninety estates under its management'.[42] Similarly, many estate collections were undoubtedly destroyed during the revolutionary period in Ireland when around 300 big houses were burned. Families were sometimes given a short time to remove valuables: estate records were probably the last thing on their minds. From the 1920s onwards those who bought big houses, including the Land Commission, or even many of those

---

42 Of the thirty-one sets of estate records found by Donnelly relating to Co. Cork, only nine were in public repositories; Donnelly, *Land and people of Cork*, pp 386–7.

who inherited them saw little of value in cumbersome ledgers. Some were destroyed *in situ*; some found their way to local archives and local libraries; some were retained by interested relatives or friends; and some were taken for curiosity value and subsequently hidden away in attics or outoffices.[43]

Those now in private keeping are largely of a fragmentary nature and this brings related problems.[44] Ideally, for the study of the economics of a landed estate, for instance, a series of estate ledgers and accounts should be available for the entire period under study. Furthermore, they should be legible and organized in a systematic manner as to give such information as the changes of rent from year to year. Unfortunately, this ideal is too often unattainable – many series of estate rentals are broken. Finally, when studying the economics of an estate, one has to come to terms with the accounting system. As W.E. Vaughan points out: 'more difficult perhaps is the propriety of counting certain items as proper charges against the receipts on a particular estate … Some improvements were made on the demesne farms and ideally should be counted not just against rent receipts but against farm income'.[45]

On the other hand, all fragments are crucial in creating the history of an estate. As Donnelly concluded regarding his hunt for existing collections: 'After exhaustive searches in public and private archives in England and Ireland as well as attics, cellars, stables and barns throughout County Cork, enough has been discovered to furnish a solid basis upon which to reconstruct the framework of estate administration and to measure its impact on the rural economy and the land question'.[46]

TITHE APPLOTMENT BOOKS

Tithe applotment (or composition) books were compiled between 1823 and 1837 to assess the monetary tithes which were payable to the Church of Ireland under the Irish Tithe Composition Acts.[47] During this period holdings in each civil parish

43 For example the estate records of Shanbally, Co. Tipperary. When the Land Commission purchased the demesne in the 1950s, some of the estate records were destroyed *in situ*. Many more ended up in a waste-paper factory. Two trunks of records were saved by a local historian. Excellent use has been made of the existing records by W.J. Smyth to trace the making of the estate landscape; W.J. Smyth, 'Estate records and the making of the Irish landscape: an example from Co. Tipperary' in *Ir. Geography*, ix (1976), pp 29–49.   **44** There are few estate collections as comprehensive in scope for the nineteenth century and early twentieth century as the Ormonde or Clonbrock collections in the NLI or the Downshire collection in PRONI.   **45** Vaughan, *Landlords and tenants in mid-Victorian Ireland*, p. 277. Similarly, estate accounts will not necessarily reveal the full extent of a landlord's indebtedness. Lord Ormonde's personal overdraft for the 1890s does not appear in estate accounts but his auditor's reports refer to its dangerously high level on a number of occasions (NLI, Ormonde papers, MSS 23,725–6).   **46** Donnelly, *Land and people of Cork*, p. 8.   **47** See J.H. Johnson, 'The Irish tithe composition applotment books as a geographical source' in *Ir. Geography*, xi (1958), pp 254–61; R.C. Simington, 'The tithe composition applotment books' in *Analecta Hibernica* (hereinafter *Anal. Hib.*) no. 10 (1941), pp 295–8.

were valued with the value of land being based on the average price of wheat and
oats in the parish during the seven years preceding 1 November 1821. Around
2,500 of these parish returns are available for consultation in the NAI. These are the
surviving originals for the twenty-six counties, although copies of those pertaining
to the six counties are also available. The original books relating to the latter are
available in PRONI. The NLI has copies of the books on microfilm, while most
county libraries and other local repositories hold copies pertaining to local areas.

To use the tithe applotment books, one needs to know the civil parishes in
which an estate was located. Indexes available in the main repositories make it easy
to locate the books pertaining to these parishes.[48] The townlands within the parish
are divided alphabetically. There was no central authority supervising the valuation,
so the same information is not available for each parish. For most holdings one can
find the name of occupier, area of holding, valuation and tithe payable. There are
some books which merely state the amount of tithe payable by each holding. On
the other hand, there are books for some parishes which give a great deal more
information than was required. The latter books often provide an insight into topics
such as pre-famine land divisions, rents per acre paid by tenants, whether the
rundale system was prevalent in an area, and the type of crops grown by individual
tenant farmers.

Tithe applotment books do not exist for every parish.[49] They contain no
information about the landless who were exempt from the payment of tithes. Nor,
as stated earlier, are they always illuminating. Unfortunately, unlike a similar source
which exists for England, there are no accompanying maps to show land division
on a field-by-field basis. Furthermore, the researcher will find difficulties in actually
interpreting the quality of the land described, for example, as 'marsh and arable'.

PRIMARY (GRIFFITH'S) VALUATION

If one is in any doubt about the identity of a landlord in a particular area during
the mid-nineteenth century, one can consult the government valuation. The *general
valuation of rateable property in Ireland*, commonly referred to as Griffith's valuation as
it was carried out under the supervision of Sir Richard Griffith, is important not
only in identifying landlords but in its own right as a source for the study of the
landed estate in Ireland.[50] The valuation was published between 1847 and 1865 and

48 The NLI index to tithe applotment books (available at the counter in the reading room
or in bay number 1) is divided into counties and parishes within each county are then listed
alphabetically. The parish name, diocese, county, date of valuation, tithe applotment book
reference, and microfilm number is given.   **49** There are no books for fifteen parishes in
the twenty-six counties, eleven of these being Dublin parishes.   **50** W.A. Smyth,
'Distinguishing between Griffith's valuation and the "poor Law valuation" – more than just
semantics' in *Irish Genealogist*, xi, no. 3 (2004), pp 205–8; for the setting up of the valuation
and the relationship of the valuation to the real letting value of land see Solow, *The land
question*, pp 59–67; also W.E. Vaughan, 'Richard Griffith and the tenement valuation' in G.L.

estimated the valuation of every farm in the country as a basis for local taxation.[51] The printed valuation runs to more than 200 volumes and contains more than one million entries documenting the names of every occupier of land or buildings in the country as well as the name of the immediate lessor (normally the landlord) by townland, parish and poor law union. It is the only assessment of its type for the nineteenth century.

The source material of the valuation can be divided into three parts. Valuation manuscripts were the notebooks of the valuers who had been carefully trained by Griffith to investigate each holding. They consist of house books which give the names of occupiers and description of houses regarding their quality, length, breadth, height, number of measures, rate per measure and amount; tenure books detailing the contents of farms, rent, tenurial arrangements and general obser-vations; and field books giving the amount of land, a description of the holding, quality of holding (taking into consideration such things as the quality of topsoil and subsoil, fertility, climate and proximity to markets) and value per statute acre. The books for the twenty-six counties of the present Irish Republic are available for consultation in the NAI while those for the six counties of Northern Ireland are in PRONI.

The printed valuation is based on the valuers' notebooks. A full collection can be found in the NLI and the library of the Irish Genealogical Research Society.[52] All county libraries hold the volumes relevant to their county. Griffith's valuation is also available on-line at http://www.irishorigins.com on a pay-per-view basis.

If the names of the parishes and townlands comprising the estate are known, consult the typed index to the primary valuation in the reading room in the NLI or the *Index to Griffith's valuation* published on microfilm by the All-Ireland Heritage Inc. in 1987. Counties are arranged alphabetically as are parishes within the county. A fiche reference for the parish is given, for example 14.E.2 The fiche reference for any individual parish indicates only the first exposure referring to the parish. The list of householders for any one parish will usually run over a number of pages. W.A. Smyth notes the controversy regarding Griffith's adoption of townland names, pointing to the fact that 'in the case of country houses, the name submitted by the landlord was accepted without question and the demesnes attached to these country houses were usually treated as townlands in their own right, marked with distinctive shading on all maps from 1834'.[53]

The valuation sheets are divided into a number of columns. Column 1 lists map references which are the keys to the 6 inches to 1 mile Ordnance Survey maps. These references point the researcher towards the appropriate sheet of the six-inch map and to the number assigned by the valuators to each tenement within a townland. The Valuation Office holds the most extensive collection of these maps,

Herries Davies & R. Charles Mollan (ed.), *Richard Griffith, 1784–1847* (Dublin, 1980), pp 103–22.   **51** Land and buildings were valued separately. Land came to £9.1 million while buildings connected with agricultural land were valued at about £1 million in the 1870s. **52** The call number is Ir 3335 g10.   **53** Smyth, 'Griffith's valuation', p. 206.

which have now been digitized. The same tenement numbers appear on them as on the printed valuation, having been annotated in red ink. By using both the printed valuation and the annotated maps together, one can get a comprehensive picture of what the tenurial geography of the mid-nineteenth century must have been like.[54] Column 2 records the name of the townland and occupiers. Column 3 gives the name of the immediate lessor or landlord. Column 4, headed 'description of tenement', describes the tenant farmer's holding with reference to houses, offices and lands. A distinction is drawn between tenements which consisted of land only and tenements which had a house or other buildings located on them. Columns 5–8 detail the area of land held, the valuation of the land, the valuation of buildings and the total valuation of the holding.

Cancelled books are especially important in tracing the changes in landownership in Ireland from the 1850s onwards. The Valuation Office kept a record of all changes in occupancy which took place from the completion of the valuation by retaining the manuscript copies of the original valuation and updating changes which took place by using different coloured inks. The cancelled books are organized in the same format as the printed valuation with the addition of an extra column at the end headed 'observations'. In this latter column, one may be occasionally lucky to find observations on the rent being paid for a holding, the existence and terms of a lease, the dimensions of a house or outoffices on the holding, or one may find a line drawn through the ratable valuation of a house with the observation that the house is 'down'. It is also worth checking the inside covers of each bound volume for additional information about a prominent landlord in the District Electoral Division [DED] to which the volume pertains. From the various coloured inks, one is able to see the changes in lessor, occupier, area or valuation of holdings that took place over time. Where the lessor changes following purchase under the various land acts, a stamp appears with the initials 'L.A.P.' signifying Land Purchase Act. These books are arranged by DED, so when one knows the townlands comprising an estate, one can check in the townlands index to find the relevant DED volumes which need to be consulted. Townlands are arranged alphabetically within the volumes.

The books which pertain to the twenty-six counties of the Irish Republic are to be found in the Valuation Office and may be consulted on the payment of a prescribed fee (from which students are exempt). The books for the six counties of Northern Ireland are available in PRONI. While black & white photocopies of relevant pages are available, they are useless as the key to the changes in landownership are the different colours of ink used. It is, therefore, preferable to record relevant information while in the repository. As this may be time consuming one should be as well prepared as possible before consulting these books. Before going to the Valuation Office it would be beneficial to have the name of the landlord you are interested in, with the names of relevant townlands, parishes,

---

54 It must be remembered that partnership farms held on the rundale system did not have holdings separately measured.

baronies and DEDs. Bring four coloured pens to record the changes of ownership as they appear in the books. The sheets of paper one uses to record one's findings should be divided into columns as found in Griffith's valuation with an additional column included at the end and headed 'observations'.

Griffith's valuation has some drawbacks. For example, not all tenants names are recorded. Partnership farms held on the rundale system[55] had their individual parcels bracketed together without being separately measured thereby excluding certain tenant names. One must also be careful in interpreting Griffith's ratable valuation as being an indicator of the real letting value of land or as being an indicator of the rental income drawn by a landlord from his property. By the mid-1860s, with increased agricultural prosperity, Griffith's valuation was around 15 per cent below the real letting value of land and by the 1870s at least 25–30 per cent below.[56] A survey of 1,300 estates carried out by the Irish Land Committee in 1880 showed that only 7 per cent of land was let at Griffith's valuation; 46 per cent was let at up to 40 per cent above it; 7 per cent at more than 40 per cent above it; and 16 per cent was let below it.[57] Estate rentals are the only truly reliable source in this respect. Despite these drawbacks, a systematic examination of the valuation (in conjunction with Ordnances Survey maps) can reveal a great deal about settlement patterns in post-famine Ireland as is evident from the works of scholars such as Jack Burtchaell and Geraldine Stout.[58]

PARLIAMENTARY PAPERS

The term 'parliamentary paper' applies to bills, all papers printed by order of the House of Commons or House of Lords, and to papers presented to either or both houses by royal command.[59] From the point of view of this work, the most relevant publications are reports of select committees and royal commissions, as well as the series of returns which parliament required of various departments in the course of its work. The fact that there are thousands of volumes of parliamentary papers makes it a most imposing, if not intimidating source. But the researcher should not be put off by this; the initial problems associated with sorting through indexes will invariably lead to some detailed information either on place or subject.

---

55 In certain parts of Ireland, particularly in the west, the letting of land in communal partnership was still in existence by the time the valuation was carried out. This system, known as rundale, gave each family in a community a share of the communal property. See Donnelly, *Landlords and tenants in nineteenth-century Ireland*, pp 9–10. **56** See appendix 10, 'The tenement valuation' of Vaughan, *Landlords and tenants in mid-Victorian Ireland*, pp 251–5. **57** *Report of her majesty's commission of inquiry into the working of the landlord and tenant (Ireland) Ac, 1870, and the Acts amending the same* [C2779], HC 1881, ... *Minutes of evidence, pt. ii*, p. 1289 (hereinafter *Bessborough Commission*). **58** Jack Burtchaell, 'A typology of settlement and society in County Waterford' in Nolan, Power & Cowman, *Waterford: history and society*, pp 541–78; Geraldine Stout, *Newgrange and the bend of the Boyne* (Cork, 2002). **59** Hugh Shearman, 'The citation of British and Irish parliamentary papers of the nineteenth and

Obviously in a work of this nature, it is only possible to discuss a very limited number of relevant and informative papers. It will be necessary for the student of a landed estate to spend some time searching the various indexes to find other papers which may contain information pertaining to their area of study. Chapter 13 of volume iv of Peter Cockton's *Subject catalogue of the House of Commons parliamentary papers, 1801–1900* (Cambridge, 1988) is a listing of papers relevant to Ireland. The most relevant sub-section in Cockton's catalogue is the one dealing with 'agriculture and the land'. Full references are given to each paper, including session, paper number, volume and page number and the filing number of the Chadwyck-Healey complimentary microfiche edition.[60] With regard to the latter one should also consult Peter Cockton's *House of Commons parliamentary papers, 1801–1900: guide to the Chadwyck-Healey microfiche edition* (Cambridge, 1991). The CD-ROM, Introduction to the index to the House of Commons parliamentary papers, is a cumulative index of all the House of Commons parliamentary papers published from 1801 to the 1990s drawing together material from Chadwyck-Healey's *Subject catalogue of the House of Commons parliamentary papers, 1801–1900*, the House of Commons decennial indexes covering the period 1900–79, and data from the Parliamentary Online Information Service database. To search for papers relevant to an area one can enter the name of the area under 'keyword' and if the name of the area appears in the title of one or more parliamentary papers, a listing will be given along with the reference to the parliamentary paper volume in which it can be located or the Chadwyck-Healey microfiche number. The problem is, however, that if the name of an area does not appear in the title of the paper, these indexes are of little value. Another recommended starting point are the bibliographies of secondary works relating to the Irish land question, some of which contain very comprehensive lists of parliamentary papers.[61]

The most significant development in recent years with regard to accessing parliamentary papers relating to Ireland has been the setting up of the Enhanced British Parliamentary Papers on Ireland, 1801–1922 [EPPI] project in 2003 under the directorship of Dr Peter Gray. The project aims to catalogue electronically, with full-text digitization, almost 14,000 documents (365,000 pages) from Southampton University's *Ford collection of official publications*. It features a searchable database of

twentieth centuries' in *I.H.S.*, iv, no. 13 (1944), p. 33.   **60** See also P. & G. Ford's *A guide to parliamentary papers: what they are, how to find them, how to use them* (Oxford, 1955); A. & J. Maltby, *Ireland in the nineteenth century: a breviate of official publications* (Oxford, 1979); P. & G. Ford, *Select list of British parliamentary papers, 1833–1899* (Oxford, 1953, reprinted Shannon, 1969); P. & G. Ford, *A breviate of parliamentary papers, 1900–1916* (Oxford, 1957); P. & G. Ford, *A breviate of parliamentary papers, 1917–39* (Oxford, 1951). For the post–1922 period, see P. & G. Ford, *A select list of reports and inquiries of the Irish Dáil and Senate, 1922–72* (Dublin, 1974); A. Maltby & B. McKenna, *Irish official publications: a guide to Republic of Ireland papers with a breviate of reports, 1922–72* (Oxford, 1979); A. Maltby, *The government of Northern Ireland, 1922–72: a catalogue and breviate of parliamentary papers* (Dublin, 1974).   **61** See for example the excellent lists of parliamentary papers in Donnelly, *Land and people of Cork*, pp 393–404; Vaughan, *Landlords and tenants in mid-Victorian Ireland*, pp 294–309.

papers relating to Ireland that can be accessed at http://www.eppi.ac.uk. Full text digitized records have been added on a monthly basis since 2003.

Barbara Solow showed in the early 1970s how parliamentary papers could be used to offer a new and valuable insight into the land question.[62] Using them she estimated the movement of rents, questioned many of the traditional views that saw landlords as capricious evictors, estimated the value of agricultural output and encouraged a new generation of historians to examine again the vicissitudes of landlords and tenants in nineteenth-century Ireland.

Solow drew much of her information from evidence presented to inquiries. A royal commission of inquiry was a group of persons appointed by the crown to inquire into the subject named by a royal warrant. It was composed of persons who were deemed to be experts in the subject to be investigated or who were experienced in public affairs. They held sittings in a variety of locations throughout the country and interviewed scores of witnesses from different backgrounds. Findings and conclusions were presented in report form along with the minutes of evidence taken by the commission. Select committees were members of the House of Commons or members of the House of Lords selected to conduct investigations into particular subjects.[63] The reports of select committees are made up of the report on the subject investigated as well as a day-to-day record of the committees proceedings and minutes of evidence taken by the committee. The local historian can sometimes be fortunate to find quite an amount of material of a local nature in the minutes of evidence. As Solow argues: 'When the English parliament failed to grant the Irish any measure of Home Rule in the nineteenth century, it bestowed upon her instead an abundance of commissions and inquiries and statistics and debates so illuminating and so complete that the modern researcher may perhaps be excused for wondering if it were not really worthwhile missing Home Rule altogether.'[64]

In 1843 Sir Robert Peel agreed to appoint a royal commission to enquire into the occupation of land in Ireland. Officially titled a *Report from her majesty's commissioners of inquiry into the state of law and practice in respect of the occupation of land in Ireland*,[65] it took its abbreviated title, as was the norm, from its chairman, becoming better known as the Devon commission. The commission received evidence from 1,100 witnesses including landlords, tenants, agents and land surveyors from all parts of Ireland. The end product was three massive volumes of evidence from which information can be culled on rent movements, valuation, the con-acre system, sub-letting, tenurial agreements, middlemen and absenteeism in

---

62 See chapter one. **63** The life of a select committee usually lasted just one parliamentary session; a commission had usually a much longer period of time to carry out its inquiry. **64** Solow, *The land question*, p.131. **65** *Report from her majesty's commissioners of inquiry into the state of the law and practice in respect to the occupation of land in Ireland* [605], HC 1845, xix, 1; *Minutes of evidence, pt. i* [606], HC 1845, xix, 57; *Minutes of evidence, pt. ii* [616], HC 1845, xx, 1; *Minutes of evidence, pt. iii* [657], HC 1845, xxi, 1; *Appendix to minutes of evidence, pt. iv* [672], HC 1845, xxii, 1; *Index to minutes of evidence, pt. v* [673], HC 1845, xxii, 225.

pre-famine Ireland. If one is interested in studying a particular estate in the years before the famine, it is worth finding out if the landlord, agent, tenants, or all three gave evidence to this commission.

In 1881 the report and evidence of the Bessborough commission was presented to parliament.[66] It had been appointed to enquire ostensibly into the 1870 Land Act and amending acts but really to deal with the crisis of the land war. It held sixty-five sittings from September 1880 to January 1881 throughout the country and heard evidence from around 80 landlords, 70 agents, 500 tenants and a variety of land agents, land surveyors, valuers, agricultural experts, MPs, clergymen, solicitors, barristers and an assortment of other officials. Again, the evidence ranged over a wide diversity of landed estate related topics, covering much of the post-famine period from the 1850s to the early days of Land Leagueism and the land war. Similarly, in 1886, the Cowper commission[67] was appointed to enquire into the 1881 and 1885 land acts. Over 300 witnesses from all over Ireland, with similar backgrounds to those who had given evidence to the Bessborough commission, were examined. The evidence of this commission is particularly valuable for the light it sheds on contemporaries' perceptions of the changes wrought by the agricultural depression from the late 1870s, the growth of agrarian agitation, declining rent levels, and increasing landlord indebtedness.

There are many more valuable reports which shed light on Irish landed estates in the nineteenth and early twentieth centuries. Some deal with other land acts;[68] others deal, for example, with evictions in a particular area such as the notorious evictions at Kilrush in County Clare between 1847 and 1850 when 2,700 families were cleared from their holdings;[69] the conditions of the poor in pre-famine Ireland;[70] agriculture;[71] and congestion in Ireland at the beginning of the twentieth century.[72]

66 *Report of her majesty's commission of enquiry into the working of the Landlord and Tenant (Ireland) Act 1870 and the Acts amending the same* [C2779], HC 1881, xviii; *Minutes of evidence, part I* [C2779], HC 1881, xviii, 73; *Minutes of evidence and appendices, part ii* [C2779], HC 1881, xix, I; *Index to minutes of evidence and appendices* [C2779], HC 1881, xix, 825.   **67** *Report of the royal commission on the Land Law (Ireland) Act 1881 and the Purchase of Land (Ireland) Act 1885* [C4969], HC 1887, xxvi, I; *Minutes of evidence and appendices* [C4969], HC 1887, xxvi, 25; *Index to evidence and appendices* [C4969], HC 1887, xxvi, 1109.   **68** For example *Report from the select committee on Irish Land Act 1870; together with the proceedings of the committee, minutes of evidence, appendix and index* HC 1877 (388), xii, I (George Shaw Lefevre, chairman). **69** Besides the report and minutes of evidence of the enquiry into these evictions, the names of the tenants evicted were also published in a parliamentary paper. *Report from the select committee on Kilrush Union; together with proceedings of the committee, minutes of evidence, appendix and index*, HC 1850 (613), xi, 529; *Report and returns relating to evictions in the Kilrush Union* [1089], HC 1849, xlix, 315.   **70** *First report from his majesty's commissioners for enquiring into the condition of the poorer classes in Ireland, with appendix (A) and supplement*, HC 1835 (369), xxxii, pt. I, I; *Second report of the commissioners for enquiring into the condition of the poorer classes in Ireland* [68], HC 1837, xxxi, 587.   **71** *Preliminary report from her majesty's commissioners on agriculture* [C2778], HC 1881, xv, I; *Minutes of evidence, pt.1*, HC 1881, xv, I; *Digest and appendix to minutes of evidence, pt. I, with reports of assistant commissioners* [C2778–II], HC 1881, xvi, I; *Minutes of evidence, pt. ii* [C3069], HC 1881, xvii, I; *Minutes of evidence, pt. iii* [C3309–I],

One should approach the evidence of commissions and committees with a degree of scepticism (but not with cynicism). Solow's book has been criticized, for example, by V.G. Kiernan who claimed that 'a good deal of her evidence is culled from the answers to commissions of inquiry by land agents and others with an interest in saying what landowners wanted said'. Kiernan wondered 'what became of tenants who said all they wanted to say'.[73] It is certainly true that landlords and their agents were disproportionately represented at inquiries. It is also true that those questioned gave their evidence to make a point and it is hardly an exaggeration to claim that many had a stated or implied grievance to air. W.E. Vaughan concludes regarding the nature of questioning at inquiries that resulted in the documented evidence: 'All suffered from the weakness of any inquiry that proceeded by asking direct questions: not only was there a risk of receiving misleading answers, but the questions themselves imposed a rigid simplicity on complicated matters.'[74] Furthermore, the very adversarial nature of this type of evidence is that different historians could use it to prove opposite arguments.

However, one should not lose sight of the fact that the minutes of evidence gathered by the various committees and commissions can be used to probe how contemporaries interpreted what was happening, and what their fears and aspirations were. Reference to other primary sources will help to eliminate bias and provide a corrective to any information of a statistical nature. For example, one may rightly be sceptical of the evidence collected by enquiries regarding rents, much of which appears in the Devon, Bessborough and Cowper commissions. Claims by individual landlords regarding rent movements on their estates need to be verified by reference to estate rentals if such are still in existence. If not, then at least the evidence to the enquiry has offered some approximation as to what they probably were. Moreover, it is arguable that the information offered by tenants in the post-1881 period, after the principle of dual ownership had been enshrined in law, was much less clouded by apprehension than it might have been in the past.

Returns were papers which parliament required of the various departments in the course of its work. A particularly useful return for the student of the landed estate is the *Return of owners of land of an acre and upwards, in the several counties, counties of cities, and counties of towns in Ireland* [C1492], HC 1876, lxxx, 61. This lists alphabetically every owner of one acre of land and upwards in Ireland, giving their address, the size of their holding and the valuation of their land. Also of use in this

HC 1882, xiv, 45; *Digest and appendix to minutes of evidence, pts ii and iiii*, ibid. [C3309–II], 493; *Preliminary report of the assistant commissioners for Ireland* [C2951], HC 1881, xvi, 841; *Final report from her majesty's commissioners on agriculture* [C3309], HC 1882, xiv, 1.   **72** In total there were eleven reports between 1906 and 1908. The reference for the first report is as follows: *First report of the royal commission appointed to enquire into and report upon the operation of the acts dealing with congestion in Ireland* [Cd 3266], HC 1906, xxxii, 617; *Evidence and documents* [Cd 3267], HC 1906, xxii, 621.   **73** V.G. Kiernan, 'The emergence of a nation' in C.H.E. Philpin (ed.), *Nationalism and popular protest in Ireland* (Cambridge, 1987), p. 30.   **74** Vaughan, *Landlords and tenants in mid-Victorian Ireland*, p. 44.

respect is the *Return for 1870 of landed proprietors in each county, classed according to residence, showing extent and value of property held by each class – , and similar return of number of landed proprietors in each province,* HC 1872, (167), xlvii. A return for 1906 gives a good indication of the size of demesnes in Ireland and the amount of untenanted land in the possession of landlords in rural districts at that time. The poor law valuation of this land is also given; thus one can determine whether the untenanted land held by a landlord was held for grazing or farming purposes or was of little economic benefit being mainly wasteland.[75] There are also a number of important returns relating to, for example, the sales of estates under the Encumbered Estates Act;[76] the Arrears of Rent Act;[77] the estates purchased by the Congested Districts Board;[78] and the average number of years purchase on rents received for estates under the various land purchase acts from 1870 to 1903.[79]

With regard to the sale of Irish landed estates, the most important returns are what were termed 'returns of advances'. Essentially these were returns of the advances made to tenants by the Irish Land Commission under the various land acts from 1881 to enable them to purchase their holdings.[80] Unfortunately, under the earlier land acts (1881, 1885 and 1891), there are no general indexes of estates sold that would save the researcher much searching. The relevant volumes which one needs to consult for the 1881, 1885 and 1891 land acts are, therefore, footnoted

75 *Return of untenanted lands in rural districts, distinguishing demesnes on which there is a mansion, showing: rural district and electoral divisions; townland; area in statute acres; poor law valuation; names of occupiers as in valuation lists,* HC 1906, c.177.   76 *Number of estates offered for sale, and withdrawn for want of purchasers, in the court of the commissioners of Incumbered Estates in Ireland, stating owners, counties, denominations of land, rental and price offered; and number of estates sold, stating rental, amount, and date of sale and payment, date of distribution of money to creditors, and interest borne thereon, if not distributed,* HC 1850 (757), li, 491; *Estates in Ireland on which the quit and crown rents were purchased by the commissioners for the sale of Incumbered Estates in Ireland; specifying the rate of purchase of such quit rents; and also the number of years purchase at which such estates were sold, calculated on the rental of estates when held by proprietors; and the charges subject to which such estates were sold up to 22 July 1851,* HC 1851 (602), l, 875; see also *Report of the commissioners for the sale of Incumbered Estates as to their progress etc.,* HC [1268], xxv, 55 and HC 1851 (258), xxiv, 35.   77 *Return of payments made to landlords by the Irish Land Commission, pursuant to the 1st and 16th sections of the [Arrears of Rent] Act; and also a return of rent charges cancelled pursuant to the 15th section of the act* [C4059], HC 1884, lxiv, 97.   78 *Return of estates purchased by the Congested Districts Board for Ireland in respect of the period of six months ended 30 April 1904, for the purpose of resale to tenants and the enlargement of holdings,* HC 1904, lxxx, 525. 79 *Return showing by counties the average number of years' purchase under the different Land Purchase Acts or clauses from 1870 to 1903, with the average percentage of reductions, the number and acreage of holdings purchased under each act and the amount of interest and sinking fund payable by the tenant purchasers … up to 1 November 1908,* HC 1908, xc, 1413.   80 Details of sales and purchases under earlier acts are also available in parliamentary papers. See *Return of holdings purchased by tenants, and by other than occupying tenants, from the Church Temporalities (Ireland) Commissioners, specifying name of purchaser; benefice and denomination of land sold; county and barony; date of sale; acreage; valuation; annual rent; purchase money; gross amount; paid in cash; similar return of holdings purchased by tenants under the Land Acts 1870 and 1872 (excluding Church Temporalities land); of arrears due on above advances and on land not yet sold by the Church Commissioners,* HC 1880 (408), lvi, 707.

below for the researcher's convenience.[81] In the early returns, estates sold are listed according to counties. Obviously, if a landlord had property in a number of counties, sales in all these counties should be consulted. The volumes to be consulted for the 1903 and 1909 land acts are much too numerous to be cited here. However, a full listing of these can be found using the aforementioned indexes.[82] The estates sold under these acts from 1907 to 1921 are indexed in parliamentary papers which will save the researcher much time.[83] For the sale of estates after 1921, the researcher should consult the *Iris Oifigiúil* which is available in the NLI. This source deals in particular with estates sold under the Free State land acts from 1923. It does not offer the same detail as the return of advances but one can still estimate the amount of land sold by a landowner, its location and how much he was paid.

The value of the returns of advances can perhaps be best illustrated by reference to what exactly they contain. Taking at random the *Return of advances made under the Irish Land Purchase Acts during the months of July, August and October 1919* HC 1921 [cmd 1298], xviii, one finds the following: first there is an index listing alphabetically the names of the landowners whose estates feature in this paper. If the researcher's subject is listed here he/she need simply go to the relevant page(s). The index is followed by a 'summary of advances made during the months … by the Estates Commissioners'. This summary is comprised of twelve columns. Column 1 gives the date on which the advance was made; column 2 the name of the estate; column 3 the Land Commission record number; column 4 the name of the county; column 5 the number of purchasers on that estate; column 6 specifies the area purchased; column 7 the current rent of the holdings sold; column 8 the price paid; column 9 the amount of advance; column 10 the amount of payment in cash; column 11 the number of years' purchase of rent; and column 12 was reserved for observations.[84] Where more specific details are required one goes to the relevant pages as specified in the index. Here details are given regarding the name of the

81 *Return of proceedings under the Land Law (Ireland) Act 1881 as to advances to occupiers …*, HC 1883, lvii; HC 1884, lxiv; HC 1884–85, lxiv. See also *Return giving the name of landowners the purchase of whose properties under the Land Purchase (Ireland) Act 1885 has been sanctioned by the Irish Land Commission, showing area of the property; county; rental; valuation; purchase money and number of holdings on the estate*, HC 1889, lxi, 685; HC 1890, lx, 115 and *Return of advances under the Purchase of Land (Ireland) Act up to … specifying the situation, size, rateable value, rent, vendor, purchaser, purchase-money, advance and guarantee deposit of each holding*, HC 1892, lxv; HC 1893–94, lxxv; HC 1894, lxxii; HC 1895, lxxxii; HC 1896, lxix; HC 1898 lxxiv; HC 1899, lxxix; HC 1900, lxix; HC 1901, lxi; HC 1903, lxxxiv; HC 1903, lvii; HC 1904, lxxx; HC 1904, lxxx; HC 1905, lxv. **82** See, for example, *General index to the bills, reports and papers printed by order of the House of Commons and to the reports and papers presented by command 1900–49*, p. 400. **83** A listing of these indexes can be found in ibid., p. 401. **84** Under different land acts, these columns varied. While all gave the names of landlord and purchasers, location of property, the acreage sold, the amount paid, and the rental of the holding sold the returns under the 1903 Land Act, for example, specified the amount of the bonus paid to the landlord, while under the 1885 act the amount of guaranteed deposit retained by the Land Commission is specified.

purchasers, the acreage they bought and its townland location, along with its tenement valuation, rent and whether the rent was judicial or non-judicial (that is whether it had been fixed or not under the fair rent fixing terms of the 1881 Land Act). The price paid for the holding is specified as is the amount of the advance and/or the amount paid in cash by the purchaser and the number of years purchase on current rents which the purchase price represented.

With this type of information available so much is possible, especially if used in conjunction with estate records. One can obviously trace the sale of an estate under the various land acts. It is interesting to see when landlords sold their properties. Did some smaller sales of outlying properties by large landowners, for example, take place under the 1881 and 1885 land acts (or the equally important Settled Land Act of 1882 that relaxed the law of settlement to allow landlords to sell outlying properties) and were these sales determined by the agricultural crisis and agitation and subsequent rise in landlord indebtedness which characterized the early 1880s? Did landlords who were reluctant to sell under the early land acts rush on to the market when the Wyndham Act of 1903 offered them a 12 per cent bonus for the sale of estates? Did a landlord who did not sell in the years directly following 1903 do so after it became obvious in 1908 that the terms under the act which was to follow in 1909 would not be as generous? How much of an estate did a landlord retain in demesne and untenanted land to continue as a substantial farmer? If information on estate charges are available in estate records, it may be possible to estimate how much capital was left to a landlord from sales after charges were redeemed.

Another set of important returns are those dealing with the judicial rents fixed by the Irish Land Commission under the terms of the 1881 Land Act. Again, these returns can be located by reference to the indexes named above. They were compiled on a monthly basis and they offer the following information: firstly, each paper begins with a useful index to the counties in which cases were determined. There is then a summary, showing according to counties and provinces, the number of cases in which judicial rents were fixed during the month, the acreage, tenement valuation, former rents and new judicial rents. For each county, the information is divided into ten columns: column 1 gives the names of the sub-commissioners who heard the case; column 2 the Irish Land Commission number of the case; column 3 the name of the tenant; column 4 the name of the landlord; column 5 the name of the townland; column 6 the size of the holding in statute acres; column 7 the tenement valuation; column 8 the former rent of the holding; column 9 the judicial rent; and column 10 was reserved for observations (which included, for example, the dates of when previous rent changes had taken place).

The information in such returns can be supplemented by reports of various government bodies published as parliamentary papers such as the annual reports of the Congested District Board from 1892 to 1921 and the annual reports of the Irish Land Commission and the Estates Commissioners. Parliament also published a range of accounts and statistics annually. The material in these was usually presented on a local basis rendering it a valuable source for local historians. From 1847, for example, the annual returns of agricultural produce in Ireland were presented on a county-by-county basis. Counties were then broken down into poor law unions and further broken down into electoral districts. These statistics give information on crops and livestock, number and size of farms and the output from a range of different farm sizes thereby facilitating the reconstruction of a local economy from one year to the next.

As stated earlier, parliamentary papers present an imposing volume of possible research material. A considerable amount of time will need to be spent searching through relevant indexes and search engines to source the papers that will be of most value to the local historian. However, much of the tedium formerly associated with such searching has now been alleviated by EPPI.

The NLI houses an almost complete collection of parliamentary papers and indexes can be consulted at the desk or on CD-ROM in the reading room. The Chadwyck-Healey microfiche set has enhanced the availability of parliamentary papers. To access an original paper in the NLI, one needs to know the date of the parliamentary session and the volume number. For example, the title and reference number of one parliamentary paper footnoted below reads as follows: *Return of estates purchased by the Congested Districts Board for Ireland in respect of the period of six months ended 30 April 1904, for the purpose of resale to tenants and the enlargement of holdings,* HC 1904, lxxx, 525; 1904 is the session number; lxxx is the bound volume number; and 525 is the page number.

THE RECORDS OF THE IRISH LAND COMMISSION AND CONGESTED DISTRICTS BOARD

The Land Commission was set up in 1881 under the land act of that year. It became primarily responsible for the fixing of fair rents from 1881 and the advancement of monies to tenants to enable them to purchase their holdings under the various land acts from 1881 to 1909 (and then as a reconstituted body post-1923). The records of the Irish Land Commission are probably one of the richest sources of information on Irish estates.[85] From the mass of records that survive one could possibly survey the economic history of an estate from the early-1880s onwards.

The records in the Land Commission Records Branch office (located in the NAI building on Bishop Street, Dublin) can be divided into three main areas – those dealing with land purchase; those concerned with the fixing of fair rents; and those belonging to the Congested Districts Board. These records pertain to the twenty-six counties; most of the records for Northern Ireland are in PRONI including originating affidavits of sale, final schedules, maps, schedules of areas. While these have not been scrutinized as yet in any great detail, it seems that

---

85 See K.L. Buckley, 'The Irish Land Commission as a source of historical evidence' in *I.H.S.*, viii (1952), pp 28–36.

material on earlier land sales (under the Land Acts 1881–95) is incomplete but the body of material relating to sales under the Wyndham Act is enormous with up to twenty boxes of documents for the sale of any individual large estate.[86]

Land purchase records are arranged conveniently according to estates. Edward Keane catalogued the documents available for individual estates in the Land Commission and this catalogue is available for consultation in the NLI.[87] This is an important starting point for anybody wishing to consult the Land Commission records. The card index file in the reading room of the NLI is arranged by estate name and county. Each card contains a reference number (or numbers) which leads the researcher to the series of green volumes, also in the reading room, in which there are corresponding summaries of what is contained in each set of estate records in the Land Commission offices. For example, looking up the Clonbrock estate in the card index, one firstly finds the name of the sitting landlord at the time of the sale of the estate and the names of the baronies in which the estate was located. The number 'E.C. 7159' refers to the green volumes and 'box no. 3436' to the Land Commission reference. In the green volume one finds that 'box 3436' should contain such records as deeds for 1803 to 1907; a rental for 1909; the Land Commission inspector's report; records relating to conveyances in the nineteenth century; maps of the estate; and copies of the original wills of former owners of the estate.

The commission had to be secure in the knowledge that tenants would be able to afford to repay their annuities on their advances which necessitated inspectors making detailed studies of even the smallest holdings. Inspectors' reports are, therefore, of great value in determining the quality of holdings, tenurial arrangements, rental capacity and tenants' ability to pay their rents. As the introduction to Edward Keane's catalogues point out, this, therefore, is one of the few sources which is illuminative regarding the socio-economic life of the tenantry. Here one finds details on the type of agriculture practiced on a holding – whether grazing, tillage or mixed – the conditions of the farm; details of what improvements were carried out and whether by landlord, tenant or both; the customary rights tenants had to mountain grazing or turbary; the proximity to local markets; and the quality of house and outoffices occupied and used by tenants. (It sometimes happened that the Land Commission refused to advance loans to tenants even after sales had been agreed between them and their landlord because of the poor quality of the holdings which the commission deemed incapable of sustaining the annual repayment of advances.) Most estate files in the Land Commission office contain all the records of the various stages leading to the completion of the sale of an estate during the late nineteenth and early twentieth centuries. However, there are no originating statements or final schedule of incumbrances (see below) for sales under the 1881 Land Act in existence.

86 My sincere thanks to Olwen Purdue for bringing this information to my notice. **87** Mr Keane's survey deals with the records accumulated by the Land Commission under the land acts from 1881 to 1909 inclusive. 8,447 boxes containing records relating to 9,343 estates were examined. However, it was really only the documents relating to title that were the principal subject of the survey.

Accompanying surveyors' reports outlined any problems associated with sub-letting, joint tenancies or fragmentation and how these might be solved. K.L. Buckley emphasizes that 'evidence as to sub-tenants is particularly important, and their existence was a constant source of trouble to tenants attempting to obtain an advance from the Land Commission to purchase their holdings: it is noteworthy how quickly their sub-tenants, when noted on an inspector's report on a holding, tend to become transformed into grazing tenants, holding under caretaker or conacre agreements – and, therefore, no longer technically tenants – once the would be purchasing tenants realized that their presence as sub-tenants was a barrier to his plans'.[88] A schedule of tenancies for each estate records the names of occupying tenants at the time of purchase which is illuminated by an accompanying reference map on the scale of 6 inches to 1 mile.[89]

A particularly important source is the final schedule of incumbrance pertaining to each estate, some of which can run up to thirty pages in length. These detail the charges on an estate at the time of sale recording mortgages, family charges, jointures, and superior interest such as quit rent, head rent and tithe-rent charges. From these, as L.P. Curtis has shown, one can begin to assess the indebtedness of a landlord and to estimate the capital left to him from sales after these charges had been met.

For any researcher interested in the fixing of fair rents from 1881, the Land Commission records contain files on nearly half a million cases. These show the level of reductions granted either by the Land Commission, the Civil Bill Court, or upon agreement between landlord and tenant in the case of first, second and third term rents.[90] There are, fortunately, registers available in the Land Commission Records Branch which are indexed with the names of landlords and usually tenants. For all cases after 1896, when second term rents were fixed, there are valuers' reports on holdings which contain much the same information as the aforementioned inspectors' reports.[91]

The point has already been made in chapter one that the land question remained central to both Irish politics and Irish social life long after independence. From 1923, the reconstituted Land Commission became the most important facilitator of social engineering in Ireland as it implemented the land policy reform of successive governments, acquiring lands and redistributing them amongst a

---

88 Buckley, 'Land Commission records', p. 35. **89** It should be noted here that the return of advances gives the relevant information regarding the poor law valuation of a holding, rent, and purchase price. **90** The latter two methods of fixing fair rents were quite common but once fixed, the agreement was registered with the Land Commission. **91** Here again Buckley makes the interesting point that there seems to have been an inter-relationship between rent-fixing and land purchase. He uses the example of A.R. Costello, a landlord with property in Mayo and Roscommon, who was the only landlord in Ireland to have sold more than twenty-five holdings under the terms of the 1881 Land Act. In 1883 sixty-six of his tenants made application to the courts to have fair rents fixed. The following year, Costello agreed to sell 281 holdings. Buckley claims that Costello 'thought it more profitable' to do so 'than to have judicial rents fixed on them'; Buckley, 'Land Commission records', p. 31.

hierarchy of allottees. Therefore in its capacity as a land reform agency its various branches generated a mass of documentation. The revesting branch was responsible for the transfer of ownership of lands to allottees who were drawn from a particular hierarchy of congests and uneconomic holders, ex-estate employees, evicted tenants or their representatives, the landless and former members of the IRA who had fought in the revolutionary period. It is hoped that when these records are eventually opened to the public they will inform on who got land at local level and why.

The survey and mapping branch mapped and certified estates and holdings. The accounts branch placed the purchase monies of estates to credit following the completion of acquisition, purchase and resumption proceedings and dealt with all annuity payments to the commission. The purchase branch calculated the purchase monies to be paid to owners of estates and the annuities to be paid by new purchasers. After 1923, this branch vested 114,000 holdings comprising some three million acres in the Land Commission for resale to their tenants. The acquisition branch was responsible for the compulsory take over of lands under the 1923 and later land acts. It obviously generated a great deal of documentation as a result of objections and appeals. The resales branch processed resale schemes prepared by the commission's inspectors and lodged these schemes in head office for approval. Again, its records generated massive documentation, with some individual files running to 1,000 pages. The secretariat prepared annual estimates and ministers' speeches, produced annual statistics, drafted the Irish Land Commission annual reports (later published and now available in the NLI), dealt with the large volume of inter-departmental correspondence relating to the post-independence land question, drafted replies to parliamentary questions and dealt with correspondence from the general public. It has been estimated that during the 1930s, the secretariat was receiving an average of 400,000 letters per annum. (However, there is a question mark over the volume of Land Commission correspondence that has survived. Seemingly some of it was pulped around 1946.[92] Furthermore P.J. Sammon, a former member of the Land Commission staff, claims that further pruning of estate files was authorized in the late 1960s in order to conserve storage space.[93] Whether that has happened since remains to be seen.) The personnel branch dealt with the appointment of staff. Again there may very well be interesting documentation in its files, relating to wider issues than the land question. It is known for example that in the 1930s the then Minister for Lands, Senator Joseph Connolly, considered women unsuitable as Land Commission inspectors on physical and moral grounds; they were, he argued, unsuited to the physical exertions demanded by the job of carrying spades and jumping across drains and argued that

92 Buckley, 'Land Commission records', p. 30. Documents for each estate have letters prefixed to denote the act under which the estate was purchased. 'L.C.' denotes 1881 Land Act; 'E.C.' denotes the 1903 and 1909 Land Acts; 'S' denotes the 1923 Land Act; 'C.D.B.' denotes that the sale took place under the auspices of the Congested Districts Board. **93** P.J. Sammon's *In the Land Commission: a memoir, 1933–1978* (Dublin, 1997) remains the only published memoirs of a Land Commission official.

it would 'be readily understood that serious objection could be raised to male and female officers working together in those conditions [that is, sharing the same hotel] after normal hours, particularly in remote parts of the country'.[94]

In the early 1940s, the residual functions of the Quit Rent Office, that originally had been responsible for the collection of quit rents and other land revenues of the crown, the management of crown property and other related matters, were transferred to the Irish Land Commission.[95] The archives of the office include material on the seventeenth century surveys and forfeitures of land including certified copies of the civil survey of 1654–6, the originals of which were destroyed in the calamitous Four Courts fire of 1922. There are two complete sets of the Book of Survey and Distribution in which the landownership changes of the seventeenth century are summarized. There is a crown rental of 1706, including 83 original Down Survey baronial maps. There are numerous series of letter books, account books correspondence and memoranda covering the period from roughly 1689 to 1942, as well as numerous boxes containing deeds (originals and copies), patents and other records dating as far back as the fourteenth century.

While the Land Commission records are among the most important archival collections available for any study of a landed estate in Ireland from the late nineteenth century onwards, they are, unfortunately, not easily accessible. This author's views on the inaccessibility of these records have already been expressed elsewhere.[96] The increased frustration amongst researchers is more generally known. With the exception of records such as schedules of tenancies it is virtually impossible to gain access to records such as inspectors' reports for any estate. The argument put forward is that some of these records remain of a sensitive and confidential nature. In light of the fact that many other historical documents of a similar 'sensitive' nature are freely available, this seems rather strange to say the least. Furthermore, many of the documents which are on deposit in the Land Commission records are already available in some estate collections (in the Clonbrock collection in the NLI, for example, there are records relating to judicial rents, correspondence from tenants wanting to purchase their holdings under the 1903 Land Act, and correspondence and accounts detailing the sale of parts of the estate to the Land Commission and the allocation of purchase funds) and as noted above there is a significant collection of Land Commission records in PRONI.[97]

There is also a difficulty with regard to access to the papers relating to the Congested Districts Board also on deposit in the Land Commission Records Branch. Their inaccessibility can be somewhat offset by the availability of the baseline reports of the board's local inspectors which are available on microfilm in

---

94 NAI, Dept. of the Taoiseach files, S6664. **95** See Eilis Ellis, 'State-aided emigration schemes from crown estates in Ireland' in *Anal. Hib.*, no. 22 (1969), pp 329–94; Geraldine Tallon, 'Books of Survey and Distribution, Co. Westmeath: a comparative survey' in *Anal. Hib.*, no. 238 (1978), pp 103–15. **96** Dooley, *'The land for the people'*, pp 22–5. **97** See, for example, the Bruen papers in the NLI, and Dartrey papers in PRONI.

the NLI. Again these offer a good deal of information on landlords and tenants particularly along the western seaboard where, in some areas, even by the late nineteenth century, rundale was practiced. They sometimes offer information on the size of estates, the number and quality of holdings thereon, and their rental. They offer a picture of the socio-economic environment of a locality by describing markets, fairs, postal and telegraph facilities. They describe in detail how farmers cultivated their lands and how they disposed of their farm produce. Effectively they provide an insight into the hardship of a tenantry who were at subsistence level on most western estates. Information may be found on the type of employment available to tenants on a landlord's estate: the inspector's report for Pontoon in County Mayo pointed out that 'there is a small amount of employment given by the few resident gentry in the district; the usual wages are 8s[hillings] per week'. In Belmullet, one finds that local landlords levied a royalty of 33 per cent on all kelp made on their respective properties. There is also documentary evidence of the board's policy of promoting migration from these congested areas, a policy which was continued by the Land Commission from the 1920s when it settled migrants from congested areas in counties such as Meath and Kildare.[98]

Furthermore, one should be aware that much valuable information, statistical and otherwise, can be gleaned from the annual *Reports of the Congested Districts Board*, a listing of which can be found in the indexes to parliamentary papers.[99] Also of great importance are the dozen or so reports of the royal commission appointed to enquire into congestion in Ireland at the beginning of the twentieth century. Again reference to these can be found in indexes to parliamentary papers.[1]

REGISTRY OF DEEDS

The Registry of Deeds was set up by the Registry of Deeds Act of 1707 'to secure purchasers and prevent forgeries and fraudulent gifts and conveyances of land, tenements and hereditaments,[2] which have been frequently practised in this kingdom, especially by Papists to the great prejudice of the Protestant interest thereof'. A central office was established in Dublin in which all transactions concerning land such as leases and mortgages were to be registered. Historians have largely shied away from using the voluminous information available in the Registry of Deeds located on Henrietta Street, Dublin. Over 4,000,000 memorials[3] dealing

98 The NLI reference number for these reports of inspectors is P8383. See also Congested Districts Board, *Instructions and suggestions for the guidance of parish committees* (Dublin, 1911); idem, *List of electoral divisions that are congested in accordance with sect. 36 of the statute 54 & 55 Vict., c.48.* 15 (Dublin, 1892). The minutes of the board are also available in the NLI. **99** See, for instance, *First annual report of the Congested Districts Board for Ireland for 1892* [Cd 6908] HC 1893–94, lxxxi, 25. **1** For example, *First report of the royal commission appointed to enquire into and report upon the operation of the acts dealing with congestion in Ireland* [Cd 3266] HC 1906, xxxii, 617: *Evidence and documents* [Cd 3267] HC 1906, xxii, 621. **2** Property which, on the death intestate of the owner, devolved on the heir. **3** See below.

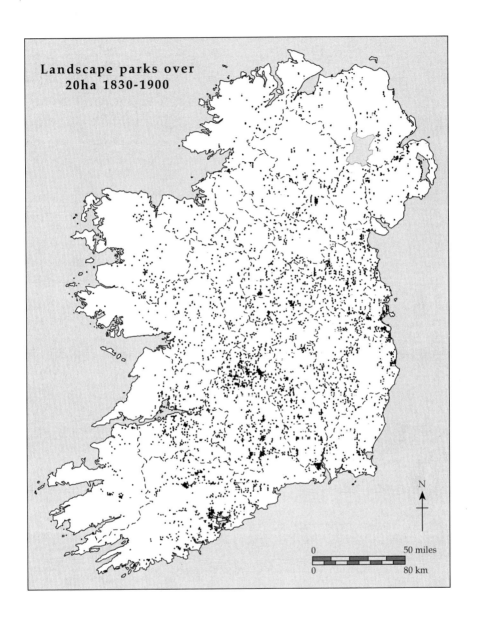

Landscape parks over
20ha 1830-1900

N

0   50 miles

0   80 km

1 Landscape parks of over 20 hectares 1830–1900, an indicator of the distribution of big
houses in Ireland in the nineteenth century (courtesy of Dr Matthew Stout).

2 Castlehyde: one of the many Irish big houses to be sold with their estates
under the Encumbered Estates Act of 1849.

3 Very little of the medieval architecture now survives as part of an existing house except for
the medieval core of castles such as Malahide (courtesy of Fingal County Council).

4 Beaulieu House, County Louth: after the Williamite wars the settlers became confident enough to begin building defenceless houses. The construction of houses such as Beaulieu reflected peace and prosperity.

5 Bellamont Forest, County Cavan, designed by Edward Lovett Pearce and according to Maurice Craig: 'a very perfect and complete example of a Palladian villa'.

6 Carton House: Richard Castle favoured the Palladian plan of a central block joined to subordinate wings by straight or curving links.

7 Page from the marquis of Kildare's household book, 1758. 'Rules for the Marquis of Kildare's butler'.

3

Rules for the Marquis of Kildare's

—— Butler ——

He must be very careful to keep all the Groceries locked up and when any wanting to go himself for them —

He must be very particular in having the Sugar and Salt in good Order and when put to dry to take care the Dust of the Fire don't get in —

He must have the Wines decanted, Water for the Table, Ale and Beer drawn and Bread cut as short a time before Dinner as possible —

He must take care to have a stale Loaf and Rowls for my Lord and Lady's use —

The Bread, Ale and Beer, Sallads &c that are left after my Lord or Lady has dined must be carried to the 2nd Table :—

The Bread and Butter that is left from the day before must be sent to the Clerk of the Kitchen next Morning

8 Ceiling of gold saloon at Carton: known as 'The courtship of the gods', this richly
figurative Baroque design bore testimony to the craftsmanship of the LaFranchini
brothers and to the wealth and social standing of the FitzGerald family.

9 The existing architectural wholeness of a house such as Bantry in County Cork
is important in understanding the architectural evolution of Irish big houses as they
were adapted according to changing aesthetic tastes and social fashions.

10 Curraghmore, County Waterford, before its Victorian remodelling (courtesy of William Laffan).

11 Emo Court, County Laois: the 1780s and 1790s witnessed the construction of some of Ireland's most imposing mansions. Lavish expenditure on Emo Court almost broke the Portarlington family.

12 Ledwithstown, Ballymahon, County Longford, a very important middling house of the eighteenth century, probably designed by Richard Castle and now the home of the Feeney family. Its architectural importance was recognised by Steven Parissien in his book *Palladian style* (London, 1994) as it was the only Irish house to be included in his study.

13 Van der Hagen's painting of Carton *c.*1738.

14 Thomas Roberts' painting of the Carton Landscape *1776*: the formal gardens and avenues evident in the earlier Van der Hagen painting have been swept away to be replaced with an idealised conception of natural landscape.

15 Castle Bernard prior to its destruction in 1921 (courtesy of Irish Architectural Archives).

16 Almost 300 big houses were burned in Ireland during the War of Independence and Civil War, 1919–23. The photograph shows Mary Gaussen, niece of Lord Bandon, amidst the ruins of Castle Bernard, burned in 1921. She recorded in her diary: 'The ruin is absolute and all one can do is to wander across the masses of debris in those precious rooms' (courtesy of Irish Architectural Archives).

17 IRA training camp at Lough Bawn House, County Monaghan, during the Civil War (courtesy of Monaghan County Museum).

18 Luke Gerald Dillon, Baron Clonbrock, and Lady Augusta Dillon, *c.* 1904 (courtesy of National Library of Ireland).

19 Clonbrock House, Ahascragh, County Galway, c.1890
(courtesy of National Library of Ireland).

20 Wedding party in front of Clonbrock House, 1905, with Lord and Lady Clonbrock at
centre/back (courtesy of National Library of Ireland).

21 Two servants at Clonbrock, 25 April 1881, identified as Pat Dolan's daughters
(courtesy of National Library of Ireland).

22 Avondale, ancestral home of Irish nationalist leader Charles Stewart Parnell (1846–91), one of the few Irish country houses to be protected by the state in the decades after independence (courtesy of Coillte).

23 Thomastown House *c.*1958. The entrance front is in the process of demolition. Taken from The Knight of Glin, D. J. Griffin and N. K. Robinson, *Vanishing country houses of Ireland* (Dublin, 1988), p. 124, original in Irish Architectural Archives.

ON THE PREMISES

Clonbrock

Ahascragh, Ballinasloe, Co. Galway

The Property of

MR. AND MRS. LUKE DILLON-MAHON

Comprising:

**PICTURES, DRAWINGS AND PRINTS,
IRISH AND ENGLISH FURNITURE,
WORKS OF ART AND FURNISHINGS,
ENGLISH, CONTINENTAL AND ORIENTAL CERAMICS,
OBJECTS OF ART, SILVER AND PLATE**

which will be sold at Auction by

CHRISTIE, MANSON & WOODS LTD.

J. A. FLOYD, A. G. GRIMWADE, GUY HANNEN, M.C., THE HON. PATRICK LINDSAY, JOHN HERBERT, A. J. H. DU BOULAY, THE HON. DAVID BATHURST, W. A. COLERIDGE, J. M. BROADBENT, W. A. SPOWERS, ROBSON LOWE, THE HON. CHARLES ALLSOPP, NOEL ANNESLEY, HUGO MORLEY-FLETCHER, ALBERT MIDDLEMISS, WILLIAM MOSTYN-OWEN, T. E. V. CRAIG, PAUL WHITFIELD, T. MILNES GASKELL, GREGORY MARTIN, JOHN LUMLEY, PETER HAWKINS, C. R. PONTER, ALAN TAYLOR-RESTELL, HERMIONE WATERFIELD, SIR JOHN FIGGESS, K. B. E., C. M. G., JONATHAN M. PRICE, A. C. A., DR. GEZA VON HABSBURG (SWISS), MICHAEL CLAYTON, S. C. DICKINSON

I. O. CHANCE, C.B.E. (*Consultant*)

8 King Street, St. James's, London, SW1Y 6QT

Telephone: 01-839 9060.   Telex: 916429.   Telegrams: Christiart, London, S.W.1

and LISNEY AND SON

23/24 St. Stephen's Green, Dublin 2

Telephone: Dublin 76 44 71   Telex 5804

CHRISTIE'S AGENT IN IRELAND
Desmond Fitz-Gerald, The Knight of Glin, Glin Castle, Glin, Co. Limerick
Tel: GLIN 44

On Monday, November 1, 1976

at 10.30 a.m. and 2 p.m. precisely

and two following days

MAY BE VIEWED THURSDAY, FRIDAY AND SATURDAY PRECEDING
9.30 a.m. - 4.30 p.m.

Illustrated Catalogue (34 Plates) Price £3 (£3.50 postage paid)

Plain Catalogue Price £2 (£2.50 postage paid)
Book Catalogue (Part II—5 Plates, 1 in colour) Price £2 (£2.50 postage paid)

**In sending Commissions or making enquiries, this sale should be referred to as
CLONBROCK**

---

24 Auction catalogue for Clonbrock, 1976: from the 1920s heirlooms, furniture, silver and works of art were sold in order to help house owners survive.

25 Clonbrock in 2005.

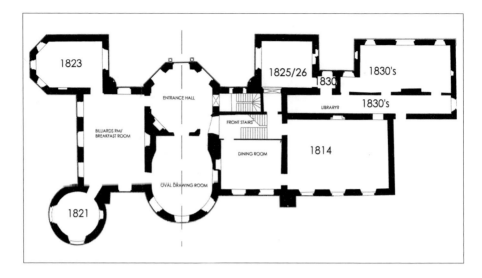

26 Killua, County Westmeath: this architectural plan (supplied by Mr Mattie Shinnors) shows the conversion of Killua from a plain Georgian house of the 1780s to a Gothic Castle by the 1830s.

27 Killua Castle before restoration work began on it in 2003 (courtesy of Mattie Shinnors and Allen and Lorena Sanginés-Krause).

with property in Ireland from 1708 are stored there. These are more often than not sufficiently detailed to substitute for the original documents which may no longer be in existence.[4]

For the landed class, marriage settlements were important. Dowries were a prime consideration in any marriage involving a member of a landlord's family, but particularly an eldest son who had the responsibility of passing on the family estate, big house and heirlooms to the next generation. Estates were kept intact by primogeniture. Therefore, a strict settlement was drawn up when the eldest son reached his majority or when he planned to marry that entailed the estate on the eldest grandson (usually not yet born), and made the immediate heir merely tenant for life. In pre-marriage settlements (which were business based and as such took the form of a business arrangement between the two families concerned), it was usually settled that a bride would receive an annual allowance, known as pin money, while her husband was alive, and that she would bring with her a dowry, which was often used to alleviate the financial burden of the family into which she married, or else it provided the basis for her jointure (effectively a widow's allowance) in the event of her husband pre-deceasing her. When, for example, Charles William Fitzgerald, marquis of Kildare, and heir to the duke of Leinster, married Caroline, daughter of the duke of Sutherland, in 1847, the marriage settlement drawn up between both families firstly specified the rental of the Leinster estate which stood at around £24,000. The incumbrances on the various estates were then outlined with a stipulation that 'Lady Caroline's fortune should be paid to the duke whose intention is to discharge with it incumbrances affecting his estate'. There was reference to sums to be invested, although not specified, which would 'secure to the marquis of Kildare during the joint lives of himself and the duke, £4,000 per annum, payable quarterly'. There was provision for £600 per annum to Lady Caroline 'during the joint lives of herself and the marquis by way of pin money'; £2,500 to her during the joint lives of herself and the duke if the marquis died during the lifetime of the duke, and £4,000 per annum by way of a jointure if Lady Caroline was to survive the marquis and the duke.

The example above gives an indication of the type of information one can accumulate regarding an estate from the information in the Registry of Deeds: one may be able to find the rental income of an estate; estimate the level of indebtedness of a landlord; see how marriage arrangements were used to alleviate some burdens; see how the same arrangements could, in fact, add to the burden especially if a widow was to survive a husband by a number of years; and indicate how a marriage settlement allowed wives of landlords much greater liberty and equality than wives in the classes below them because of the pin money and jointures guaranteed to them.

During the eighteenth and nineteenth centuries few landlords could raise the capital necessary for the payment of jointures without recourse to borrowing on

---

4 For introduction to the registry of deeds see Peter Roebuck, 'The Irish Registry of Deeds: a comparative study' in *I.H.S.*, xviii, no. 69 (1972), pp 61–73.

mortgage. Therefore, mortgages, by showing the amount of principal, the interest rate and the length of a loan, reveal a great deal about a landlord's financial position at a given time. Indentures of conveyance give prices of land sold and the terms of sale.[5] Leases, as discussed earlier, specify the position and quality of the property involved and give an insight into tenurial arrangements, rents and terms of their payment.

Notice is provided of the registration of a deed through the memorials and indexes which are available for inspection in the Registry of Deeds on payment of a prescribed fee. The memorial is a summary of the deed recording the date of it, the names of the parties and witnesses to the deeds, and a description of the property and its location. Some memorials have incidental information such as references to previous deeds. Up to 1832, all memorials (almost 600,000 of them) were numbered consecutively. From 1833 memorials were filed in books of 300. To reference an individual memorial one needs to know the year in which it was registered. Researchers are advised to begin with the transcript books into which memorials were transcribed up to 1960 and which are available for consultation for the years 1708–1960 (excluding 1951–6). The information in these books is more accessible and legible than in the original memorials. They are numbered in the same way as the memorials. They should be used in tandem with the names index books which record all grantors since 1708. Prior to 1833 the names index contained the names of all grantors (but only the surname of the first grantee), a reference to the book in which the transcript is contained, the page number in the book and the memorial number. There is unfortunately no county reference. From 1833 the names index also gives the Christian name of the first grantee, the county in which the land is situated and the full reference to the memorial (which is the same for the transcript.) There are also three special names index books which deal solely with memorials filed by the Encumbered Estates Court for the years 1850–58. The difficulty for researchers interested in the pre-1833 period is that one gets very little information and so must continuously refer to the transcripts which can be time consuming. Because the name of county is given post-1833, the amount of cross-checking is reduced greatly.

There are also land index books for 1708–1946 which are available for inspection. For 1708 to 1832, the index of lands is indexed by reference to county, townland and corporate town. A large number of years are covered in single books e.g. the first book in the series deals with the period 1708–38. The indexing is not altogether satisfactory. The arrangement of townlands in alphabetical order extends to the first letter only. One must also be wary of local variations in townland names

5 This is a deed recording a transfer of property. A deed is the legal valid record of proof of sale. They record the names of grantor (a person who grants an interest in land to another), the grantee (the person to whom an interest in land is granted), the lands and other property subject to contract. An indenture was originally a document written on paper and cut in two in a wavy line so that the authenticity of the indenture could be proven by fitting the two parts together.

and spellings as there was no obligation on parties to use standardized names. Additional references were often put at the end of books, so this should not be overlooked. From 1833 the lands index is compiled by the county, barony and townland (again in alphabetical order, although not a strict one) and corporate towns. These books are kept in five-year volumes and give details of the first grantor, first grantee, barony, townland, and registry reference of the memorial and transcript. Some entries are cramped into small spaces and may be difficult to read; a magnifying glass might be a useful tool for the researcher in this case. Copies of both the names index and the lands index are available on microfilm in the National Library of Ireland. Once one has located the relevant entry in either index, one will then find a corresponding number which will match the transcript book to be consulted in the Registry of Deeds.

When one visits the Registry of Deeds for the first time one must be prepared to give oneself plenty of time due to the very nature of the searching that is involved. One must also consider the fact that the act establishing the Registry of Deeds had its origin in the penal laws. From 1704 no Catholic could purchase a lease for more than thirty-one years nor could a Catholic invest in mortgages. This remained the case until the 1780s and while this is essentially a guide for the nineteenth and twentieth centuries it might be worth noting that even if the penal laws were rarely applied to their full extent, they must surely have greatly reduced the number of transactions concerning Catholic available in the Registry of Deeds from its establishment to their repeal. There is also little doubting the fact that large landowners in general were lethargic about officially registering leases with their tenants, particularly those on smallholdings. The socio-economic relationship between the two groups put very little onus on the landlord to do so and those leases which are registered are predominantly between more equal parties such as a small landowner and a prosperous tenant or a landlord and a head landlord. If one is interested in landlord policy regarding the granting of leases, and such information is not available from estate records, one would be advised to consult the tenure books of Griffith's valuation to ascertain whether tenants were described as 'tenants at will' in which case there is no need to go searching for leases in the registry of deeds.

ENCUMBERED ESTATES

As we have seen in the previous chapter, the (second) Encumbered Estates Act of 1849 was intended to facilitate the sale of insolvent estates. It led to the establishment of the Encumbered Estates Court. This court had the power to sell an estate without a landowner's consent if the estate was in receivership or if the level of debt on the estate was greater than half of the annual rental income. As a result of government legislation in 1858 and 1859, this court was replaced by a new body, the Landed Estates Court, which was wound-up in 1879.[6] There are five

6 In the Landed Estates Court, unencumbered or marginally encumbered estates could be sold.

sequences of rentals which have survived pertaining to these courts – two sequences are to be found in the NLI, two in the NAI, and one in PRONI.[7] The most complete sequence is the one referred to as the O'Brien rentals stored in the NAI consisting of almost 150 volumes.[8] There is a considerable amount of overlapping in the five sequences, but there are indexes available in the various repositories which will guide researchers to the landed estate under study if it was sold through the Encumbered Estates or Landed Estate Court.

It is probably fair to say that the term 'rental' is something of a misnomer as these volumes contain a much greater wealth of information than simply the rental of an estate. The information pertaining to each estate usually includes, for example, an advertisement of sale of an estate naming the owner and petitioner, stating where the sale was to take place, the date and the number of lots in which the estate was to be sold. There are accompanying coloured maps of the property to be sold; each lot distinguished by a different colour. A map may also distinguish a landlord's residence and demesne. Up to 1862, these maps were usually the work of valuators, but after that date they were official Ordnance Survey maps. The rentals of individual properties offered for sale are not uniform in content but all are divided into a series of columns which offer such information as the size of individual holdings in statute acres, the name of the townland in which it was located, the name of occupier, Griffith's valuation, poor law valuation, rents paid by tenants, gale days, tenurial arrangements of individual tenants, dates and lengths of leases where applicable, and probable rent charges. This is then followed by descriptive particulars of the individual lots such as: 'The principal part of the lands of this lot is good tillage soil; there is a large extent of bog attached.'

More unwitting information can be extracted from other details given. In the case of J.C. Burke's Tyoquin estate in County Galway, sold in October 1851, one learns that 'the entire of the property is situate in a circle, in perhaps the most agreeable and improving portion of the County Galway, immediately in the neighbourhood of Colemanstown, the Model Farm of the Society of Friends, which provides a very useful example of agricultural skill and success in this hitherto comparatively neglected section of the country, and a large field of profitable employment for the poorer classes of the locality'. The Galway railway was within four miles of the demesne; the market and post towns of Monivea and Athenry were within three miles. A note attached states that a receiver had been appointed over the property in January 1851. Since that time he had been successful in collecting £1,433 in rents and arrears from property that yielded £1,415 in rental income per annum.

These rentals and accompanying documents are extremely valuable in recreating a picture of estate life in the mid-nineteenth century. Besides giving information

7 In PRONI, there is a very valuable index to the Encumbered Estates Court sales. The reference number is MIC. 80/2.   8 These were originally stored in the Public Record Office of Ireland, Four Courts, Dublin, in 1881 on the instruction of Peter O'Brien, later lord chief justice of Ireland.

on an estate's location and its hinterland, they offer information on the size and rental of individual holdings and tenurial arrangements showing whether tenants held 'at will' or by lease. They help to illustrate the extent of landlord indebtedness as a result of the famine or indeed the effects which large-scale mortgaging to facilitate the building of big houses or the maintenance of a grand lifestyle had on estates.[9] Rentals suggest the state of neglect that some landlords had allowed their estates to fall into before the famine as a result of mismanagement or the detrimental effects of long leases for ninety-nine years granted in the eighteenth century; others show that quite a few landlords became insolvent as a result of their efforts to relieve their tenants' destitution during the famine. Unfortunately, the rentals tell nothing of the new proprietors. This is an area that has still to be adequately examined. However, one should consider that because the rentals give the dates of the auctions, it is often possible to follow up in the local newspapers who bought individual estates. The use of these rentals in conjunction with the cancelled books in the Valuation Office might be another way of beginning to tackle the transfer of landownership post-1849.

There are also a number of parliamentary papers that are worth consulting in conjunction with encumbered estates rentals. These include *Return of net value of each lot set up for sale in the Landed Estates Court, Ireland, 1865–66; number of petitions for sale presented to court, 1863–66*, HC 1867, vol. lix, 249 which gives the estate name, the number of lots in which it was sold, the acreage sold in each lot, the annual value per lot and the county; *Incumbered estates inquiry commission: report of her majesty's commissioner's appointed to inquire into the Incumbered Estates Court …*, HC 1854‑55, [c.1938] vol. xix, 527, as well as numerous returns of sales under the encumbered estates commissioners. The *Return of number of properties in Land Court of Ireland*, HC 1890, vol. lx, 135 is one of a number of such reports that provides information on the names of landowners whose properties had been placed in the court, the names of petitioners (which gives a clear indication of where landlords had borrowed money), the date of when the petition was filed, the number of tenants concerned, the annual gross rental and the dates on which lots were put up for sale.[10]

SOURCES IN THE NATIONAL ARCHIVES OF IRELAND

The previous sections have offered details of what are the main sources available for the study of the landed estate in Ireland. There are other sources available to help

9 For the case of Lord Portarlington who almost bankrupted his estate as a result of his lavish expenditure on Emo Park, see Encumbered Estates Commission, *Report of the proceedings in the matter of the Portarlington estate* (Dublin, 1850). 10 The easiest way to access reference numbers for these papers is by typing 'incumbered estates' or 'land court' into the EPPI search facility.

one complete the overall picture; the importance of these depends on the focus of study. If that focus is agrarian crime which affected so many individual estates at different periods, the NAI houses a wealth of primary source material that reveals much about the nineteenth century and the first two decades of the twentieth century. These sources, as well as their provenance, strengths, weaknesses and so on, are discussed in much more detail in another work in this Maynooth Research Guides for Irish Local History series, Brian Griffin's highly informative *Sources for the study of crime in Ireland, 1801–1921* (Dublin, 2005). What follows here is therefore a basic introduction to these sources.

For pre-famine crime and outrage the State of the Country Papers, covering the period from 1796 to 1831, are a very important source. Of course, as has been pointed out by other historians, their provenance must be kept in mind: the documents were created in the main by magistrates, office-holders and informers. The first of these two groups were frequently alarmist regarding the state of the countryside and so distorted reality in order to draw the attention of the authorities to their perceived plight. The third group was frequently more concerned about receiving money or a pardon and so had few moral qualms about fabricating evidence.[11] The State of the Country Papers are catalogued in two calendars. The first calendar covers the period from 1796 to 1820 and the second the years from 1821 to 1831. These papers are richly suggestive of the areas of conflict which marred relationships between farmers and the cottier and labouring classes below them. They reveal the tensions that surrounded the price of conacre; the fears of conversion from tillage to pasture which would result in large-scale unemployment and limited access to land; the resentment of locals towards outside labourers; and, not least of all, the level of wages. They reveal that Irish rural society was certainly not simply divided between landlords and the rest; the 'rest' were as likely to be in conflict with each other as with the landowners.

The Outrage Papers which cover the years from 1832 to 1850 are similar in content to the State of the Country Papers. Their chief importance lies in the information they contain on the sustained and extended opposition to tithes that characterized much of rural Ireland during the 1830s and manifested itself in crime and outrage. Again, these sources were created mainly by the magistracy and the police who from the 1830s had assumed much more authority in the keeping of law and order in the countryside.

Marianne Cosgrave, Rena Lohan and Tom Quinlan's *Sources in the National Archives for researching the Great Famine* available in pdf form at http://nationalarchives.ie/topics/famine/famine.html and also published in *Journal of the Irish Society for Archives* (spring 1995),[12] highlights the importance of the archives of the chief secretary's office to a study of distress during the Great Famine.[13] The chief

---

11 N.J. Curtin, *The United Irishmen: popular politics in Ulster and Dublin, 1791–1798* (Oxford, 1994), p. 3; Griffin, *Primary sources for the study of crime*, pp 23–8.   12 For an excellent insight to the various sources available for the study of the Great Famine at local level, see the special editions of the *Clogher Record*, xvii, no. 1 (2000) and xvii, no. 2 (2001).   13 See also,

secretary's office was essentially the intermediary between the Irish administration in Dublin and the government in London. For the purposes of famine relief, it acted more or less as the intermediary between the various official relief agencies such as the Poor Law Commission, the Relief Commission and the Office of Public Works in Ireland and the British Treasury.[14] The office received reports, memoranda, letters and memorials concerning the distressed state of the country, many of these from local committees (usually dominated by local landowners), local clergymen or individual landlords. When the chief secretary's office became inundated with correspondence relating to the relief of distress from 1846 the decision was taken to file such correspondence separately. Usually referred to as the Distress Papers, these documents, therefore, form a sub-series to the registered papers of the chief secretary's office (commonly abbreviated as CSORP) and inform on various aspects of landed estate life during the crisis, illuminate on the role (and attitudes) of landlords at local level and tell of the plight of the wider estate community. The Distress Papers are indexed in four volumes in the NAI: CSO CR 70, index to Distress Papers, volume 1, 1846; CSO CR 71, index to Distress Papers, volume 2, 1846; CSO CR 77, index to Distress Papers, volume 1, 1846–47; CSO CR 78, index to Distress Papers, volume 2, 1846–47. Each volume is organized alphabetically under name of correspondent and further indexed in subsections under the name of the area to which they relate.

The Relief Commission Papers were generated by the Relief Commission established in November 1845 in response to the growing famine crisis. The remit of local commissions was to advise the government on the prevalence of distress and to oversee various projects aimed at the relief of the same through, for example, the distribution of Indian meal and to co-ordinate the activities of local relief committees. A high percentage of reports were compiled by lords lieutenant of the counties, resident magistrates, or poor law guardians, who, in the vast majority of cases, were local landlords. Following instructions issued by the commission in early 1846, local relief committees were established – there were over 650 in less than a year – which were again generally dominated by local landlords. Readers are directed to Marianne Cosgrave, 'Sources in the National Archives for researching the Great Famine: the Relief Commission papers' available at http://nationalarchives.ie/topics/famine/famine.html (and also published in *Journal of the Irish Society for Archives* (autumn 1995).

These papers are broken down into four series: RLFC1, comprised of administrative material; RLFC 2, distress reports received from individuals and various bodies at local level (memorials were very often signed and sent by local

Tom Quinlan, 'The registered papers of the chief secretary's office' at www.nationalarchives.ie/topics/Chief_secretary/CS.htm. A printed version of this article, with illustrative examples of documents, appears in *Journal of the Irish Society for Archives* (autumn, 1994), pp 5–21. **14** R.B. McDowell, *The Irish administration, 1801–1914* (London, 1964), pp 1–103; Kieran Flanagan, 'The chief secretary's office: a bureaucratic enigma' in *I.H.S.*, xxiv, no. 94 (1984), pp 197–225.

landlords); RLFC3, incoming letters (sorted according to barony for the period 1846–7); and RLFC4, returns from the constabulary, relief committees and others relative to the failure of the potato crop, activities of local relief committees and so on. A great deal of information can be accessed regarding absenteeism, landlord insolvency, landlord efforts to relieve distress on their estates, the reasons why some landlords refused to work with relief committees in their area, and even friction between neighbouring landlords whose attitudes towards relief schemes were often at variance. Given the dearth of pre-famine census material in Ireland, these records should be kept in mind: relief committees were instructed to compile lists of families in each townland with observations on their individual circumstances as a means to assessing the extent of relief measures necessary. Therefore, lists of distressed persons are available for a limited number of areas.

The CSORP for the post-famine period are most voluminous for periods of agrarian crisis such as the land war of 1879–82, the plan of campaign of 1885–91 and the period of United Irish League from its foundation in 1898 through the so-called ranch war of 1906–09 and, indeed, right up to the end of the Great War in 1918. To establish what records might be relevant to a local study, one has first to consult the large bound registers (or indexes) to incoming papers on open access on shelves in the NAI. Indexes are arranged by year and in alphabetical order under the initial letter of the name of the source from where they emanated or the subject matter to which they related. One can search, for example, under county name or lesser geographical denominations such as townland or parish. If the focus is agrarian crime, then the names of people involved including suspects and local magistrates are worth looking up. The index provides a reference number in the furthest left hand column. As papers related to the same incident were received over a period of time, they were amalgamated to form one file. This means that the original number given to a paper was often changed over and over again. Thus, numbers in the index were amended until the file was completed. Unfortunately, locating relevant records can be time consuming. It can also lead to a great deal of frustration for all too frequently one is informed that the requested file has not survived.[15] However, the registers themselves are of some value, given that there are brief descriptions of crimes, events, people involved and dates. In order to familiarize oneself with how to identify relevant files, one is advised to consult Tom Quinlan's guide on the registered papers.[16]

The Irish Crime Records covering the period from roughly 1848 to 1893 contain much relevant information as they deal with a period that witnessed a great deal of agrarian agitation associated with the post-famine Ribbonism of the 1850s, to a lesser extent Fenianism in the 1860s, the rise of the Land League from 1879 through the first phase of the land war (1879–82), the era of National League from the mid-1880s and the second phase of the land war (or Plan of Campaign.) The

---

15 Brian Griffin has noted how frustrating this can be for researchers in Griffin, *Primary sources for the study of crime*, p. 29, n.34, n.35.   **16** See footnote 13 above.

records contain, for example, four volumes of statistical returns of outrages, as well as abstracts of cases of persons arrested under the Protection of Persons and Property Act of 1881. This act gave the authorities the power to apprehend anyone suspected of violence, intimidation or the incitement of the same and to hold them in custody without trial. They are, therefore, as Brian Griffin points out 'an essential source for the study of the Land War in the early 1880s'.[17] From the Abstract of Prisoners' Cases, useful biographical details can be complied on activists at local level allowing, for example, for a detailed analysis of the social backgrounds of people arrested for suspected agrarian activity.

These records can be supplemented by the Crime Special Branch Reports generated by the Crime Special Branch of the RIC created on 1 October 1883 to deal with agrarian and other secret societies. These mainly consist of monthly reports compiled by divisional officers and county inspectors from February 1887 to January 1898 and thereafter until 1920 by county inspectors and the inspector general of the RIC. Indexes to these can be found behind the desk in the NAI.

There are also miscellaneous records such as those of the Chief Crown Solicitor's Office covering the period from around 1815 to 1921. The chief crown solicitors were the government's law agents in Ireland and their office was responsible for undertaking (or advising on) crown prosecutions. These are listed in three volumes which are again available behind the desk at the National Archives. There are, for example, scores of documents relating to the inquest on the so-called 'Mitchelstown massacre' of 9 September 1887 when three men were shot dead by the police during a National League demonstration in the town; hundreds of police reports on placards and posters used to summon Land League meetings; police reports on the meetings at Irishtown and Westport in County Mayo that were important to the progress of the Land League (reports are arranged alphabetically according to place names); as well as many crown briefs, indictments and reports of trials.

MEMOIRS, DIARIES, TRAVELLERS' GUIDES AND CONTEMPORARY WORKS

Although published memoirs, diaries, and contemporary works have their limitations as sources, which will be discussed presently, such personal accounts should not be dismissed as hopelessly biased or inaccurate.[18]

Unfortunately, there are all too few autobiographies and published memoirs of Irish landlords and those that survive are often fragmentary and digressive (and occasionally more than a little comical.) They tend to reveal more about the social

17 See Griffin, *Primary sources for the study of crime*, p. 42.   18 It should be noted that some estate collections, such as the Leslie papers in the NLI, contain memoirs and diaries that have not been published in full or published at all. In some respects such memoirs etc. may be more valuable as they are neither edited nor written according to the dictates of publishers or audience.

life of the landed class than the economics of landlordism or the management policy on estates.[19] Obviously this can be rather frustrating for the researcher who, having found an autobiography of the owner of the estate under study, finds nothing in it of value regarding estate life or estate management.

Some works were written during the turbulent years of the land war when a number of landlords or their agents attempted to correct the imbalance of the large number of books and pamphlets that attacked them and the system of landlordism. The autobiography of Sir William Gregory of Coole Park, County Galway, for example, reveals his apprehensions and fears during the Land League days of the early 1880s.[20] One needs to be discerning and critical in handling the information contained in this work or in works such as William Bence-Jones's *The life's work in Ireland of a landlord who tried to do his duty* (London, 1880) or William Steuart Trench's *Realities of Irish life* (London, 1868). Where doubts exist regarding any factual statement, the researcher needs to establish authenticity by cross-referencing with other primary sources where possible.

A number of other land agents have left their memoirs or collections of letters. William Robert Anketell's *Landlord and tenant: Ireland. Letters by a land agent …* (Belfast, 1869) records his comments on such subjects as leases, tenant improve-ments, tenant rights, capricious evictions, valuations and rents. S.M. Hussey, one of the partners of Hussey and Townsend, probably the largest land agency firm in Ireland in the nineteenth century, has left his *The reminiscences of an Irish land agent* (London, 1904). For an agent's opinions on estate management in pre-famine Ireland, see William Blacker, *Prize essay, address to the agricultural committee of the Royal Dublin Society, on the management of landed property in Ireland; the consolidation of small farms, employment of the poor etc. for which the gold medal was awarded* (Dublin, 1834). See also, G.F. Trench, *Are the landlords worth preserving? or, forty years management of an Irish estate* (London and Dublin, 1881) and 'One late an agent', *Landlordism in Ireland with its difficulties* (London, 1853). For opinions of landlords on the land question in pre-famine and post-famine periods the earl of Rosse's, *Letters on the state of Ireland by a landed proprietor* (London, 1847); the Knight of Kerry's *Irish landlords and tenants: recent letters to 'The Times' and further correspondence on the above subject* (Dublin, 1876); and John Hamilton, *Sixty years experience as an Irish landlord: Memoirs of John Hamilton, D.L., of St. Ernan's,* Donegal (London, 1894) are worth consulting. *The Irish Journals of Elizabeth Smith, 1840–50,* edited by D. Thomson and M. Mc Gusty (Oxford, 1980) is revealing regarding the Great Famine in County Wicklow and the reaction of a member of the landed class to the crisis.

Memoirs, published diaries and collections of letters such as these provide at least some useful factual information and they are one of the few historical sources that

---

19 This is true of works such as Lord Castletown, *Ego: random records of sport, service and travel in many lands* (London, 1923); Dunraven, *Past times and pastimes*; Lord Dunsany, *Patches of sunlight* (London, 1938); Elizabeth, Countess Fingall, *Seventy years young* (London, 1937); Lord Rossmore, *Things I can tell* (London, 1912); Duc de Stacpoole, *Irish and other memories* (London, 1922). **20** *Sir William Gregory, K.C.M.G., formerly member of parliament and*

record the particular concerns or interests of a landlord or an agent at a particular time. One can at least get an idea of how those of the landed class or those associated with it interpreted events such as the Great Famine, the land war, or the rise of the Land League as they unfolded.[21]

However, the weaknesses of such works must be kept in mind. Memoirs are after all collections of memories which are inevitably coloured by emotions. Memoirs are never all inclusive: because they are written retrospectively they are selective and the memories are remembered across a time gap through all the experiences the writer has had in the meantime. These memories are going to be affected by nostalgia or resentment. The time gap between the experience and the recording of it may in some cases be a lengthy one which means the writer's recollection of events may be vague or inaccurate. The objectivity of the writer must be questioned at all times. There is the danger that a landlord or agent may have falsified information in order to present himself in a more favourable light to his audience. Published collections of letters and diaries are more immediate than memoirs and are therefore probably more reliable as evidence but even they need to be approached with a certain amount of scepticism: were letters written with a particular agenda in mind? Was the writer careful in expressing personal anxieties? In the case of published diaries and journals, were entries written on the day or were they written with the benefit of hindsight? Are entries edited or watered down so as to please the readership (or, indeed, even the writer)? One must authenticate the historical content of the memoir by continuous reference to other primary sources in order to check the validity of the writer's memories.

The nineteenth century also saw the publication of a great number of travellers' accounts. These offer contemporary descriptions of places and people at particular times and some statistical information. Travellers tended to be attracted to Ireland during various crises and in a sense this tends to be one of their weaknesses as a source because they tend to be written by members of the upper or middle class whose observations are dictated by ideological convictions, their own bias and prejudice, the agendas of the social class to which they belonged, or, indeed, as in the case of Finlay Dun, the agenda of his employer, *The Times*.

sometimes governor of Ceylon. An autobiography, ed. Lady Gregory (London, 1894). **21** For an opposite viewpoint of the Land League, see Davitt, *The fall of feudalism in Ireland*. For a 'personal narrative' of the land war see W.S. Blunt, *The land war in Ireland, being a personal narrative of events* (London, 1912) and B.H. Becker, *Disturbed Ireland: being the letters written during the winter of 1880–81* (London, 1881). For an account of the operation of the plan of campaign on one estate see D. Keller, *The struggle for life on the Ponsonby estate* (Dublin, 1887). See also C. Russell, *'New views on Ireland'. Or, Irish land: grievances: remedies* (London, 1880). For contemporary account of the land acts, see R.C. Cherry & J. Wakely, *The Irish land law and Land Purchase Acts 1881, 1885, and 1887* (Dublin, 1888); A.G. Richey, *The Irish land laws* (London, 1880). On the Encumbered Estates Court see P.H. Fitzgerald, *The story of the Encumbered Estates Court in Ireland* (London, 1862); J.P. Prendergast, *Letters to the earl of Bantry, or a warning to English purchasers of the perils of the Irish Encumbered Estates Court, exemplified in the purchase by Lord Charles Pelham Clinton M.P., of two estates in the barony of Bere, County of Cork* (Dublin, 1854).

Dun came to Ireland in the early 1880s and wrote a series of newspaper articles on Irish landlords and landed estates which were later published in book form as *Landlords and tenants in Ireland* (London, 1881). Despite its weaknesses, the book is an important source as it offers a valuable, if brief, insight into the management of twelve individual estates in Ireland at the beginning of the land war as well as more general information on estates in counties Cork, Kerry, Down, Antrim, Derry, Tyrone, Donegal and Mayo.[22] In some cases, Dun gained access to family estate papers and reproduced some information from them. For example, he gives an estimate of the number of tenants on the 91,655-acre Fitzwilliam estate, the size of their holdings, and their rents. He shows the level of rent increase on the estate from 1800 to 1880. He points out that at the time of writing, rents had been well met 'testifying to the prosperity and solvency of the tenants'. Arrears stood at £5,000 or around 10 per cent of the rental. In 1846, arrears had stood at £10,000 but as a result of the famine they rose to £26,924 in 1853 of which £15,000 was written off. He claims that before and during the famine (1833–56), Fitzwilliam spent £23,586 on assisted emigration and £8,000 on other types of assistance for his tenants. He reclaimed an extensive home farm at a cost of £40,000 from which Fitzwilliam 'distributed annually to tenants and others several score of well-bred young shorthorn bulls, Border Leicester rams, and, latterly, Shropshires – a practice which tends greatly to the improvement of the farmer' rent paying stock.' In thirty-six years, Fitzwilliam expended £303,000 on estate improvements, or six years' gross rental of the estate.[23]

George Pellew's *In castles and cabins or talks in Ireland* (New York & London, 1888) and George Shaw Lefevre's *Incident of coercion: a journal of visits to Ireland 1882 and 1888* (London, 1889) offer accounts of landlord-tenant relations, observations on landlords, and evictions during the land war. Madame De Bovet's *Three month's tour in Ireland* (translated by Mrs Arthur Walter, London, 1891) contains a description of a monster meeting of the Irish National League in Waterford. For the Great Famine years see the marquis of Dufferin and Ava and G.F. Boyle, *Narrative of a journey from Oxford to Skibbereen during the years of the Irish famine* (Oxford, 1847) and [John Locke], *Ireland: Observations on the people, the land and the law in 1851; with especial reference to the policy, practice and results of the Encumbered Estates Court* (Dublin and London, 1852). For the pre-famine period, H.D. Inglis' *A journey through Ireland during the spring, summer and autumn of 1834* (2 vols, London, 1834) offers an assessment of the effects of absentee landlordism in Ireland and while Arthur Young's *A tour in Ireland, 1776–9* (A.W. Hutton ed., London, 1892) deals with the late eighteenth century, it is worth consulting.[24]

22 The twelve individual estates are the marquis of Downshire's Blessington estates in Wicklow and Kildare; the duke of Leinster's estates in Kildare and Meath; Earl Fitzwilliam's estate in Wicklow; the marquis of Waterford's estate at Curraghmore, Co. Waterford; Sir Henry Gore-Booth's Sligo estate; and the estates of the duke of Devonshire, Lord Bandon, Lord Kenmare, the knight of Kerry, Lord Dillon, Trinity College, and the London Companies. **23** F. Dun, *Landlords and tenants in Ireland* (London, 1881), pp 30–42. **24** Also of value may be F.B. Head, *A fortnight in Ireland* (London, 1852); M.A. Titmarsh, *The Irish sketch book* (London, 1842); and Alexis de Tocqueville, *Journeys to England and Ireland c.1835,*

While travellers' accounts may offer much valuable information, the researcher should be as discerning and critical with this information as with memoirs, diaries and autobiographies. Writing back in 1880, W.J. Sinclair warned: 'One must call for inquiry into the capacity of the tourist for extracting accurate information from the materials at his command, his impartiality in making use of them and the general correctness of the conclusions he has drawn from his facts.'[25] One must consider if the people being observed by the traveller allowed the latter to see only what they wanted him to see. Similarly, as in the case of Dun, for example, did landlords make available to him misleading information? Dun estimated that the duke of Leinster expended 20 per cent of his annual rental income on estate improvements between 1875 and 1881,[26] whereas estate accounts show that the figure was in fact significantly less. The point here is that a good deal of cross-referencing is again necessary, where possible, to authenticate information, particularly statistical information.

NEWSPAPERS

In his *Land and people of nineteenth-century Cork*, J.S. Donnelly jr. has shown the benefits to the local historian of making extensive use of newspapers as a source of information. Through a comprehensive study of local newspapers such as the *Cork Advertiser*, *Cork Constitution* and the *Cork Examiner*, Donnelly was able to gather much valuable information on landed estates in County Cork and how they were affected by the famine, agricultural depression, and the land war. Yet, although newspapers are one of the most accessible sources, they have remained largely underrated.[27]

The increase of literacy and prosperity in the post-famine period gave rise to an expanded readership so that by the late nineteenth century most counties had at least one newspaper. Local newspapers can indicate what landlord-tenant relations were like in an area; they can provide information on the social and economic conditions of tenants which is not often available in estate papers; they can very often provide graphic accounts of evictions and while landlords' reasons for evictions may be available in estate papers, newspapers are one of the few sources available that may offer some insight into tenants reactions to them. Local newspapers give accounts of rent strikes; they record levels of abatements granted by individual landlords; they may provide reports of landlord attempts at famine relief in the late 1840s; or report cases heard by the Land Commission courts from the early 1880s. They sometimes contain copies of memorials from tenants to landlords or communications received by tenants from their landlords, the originals of which may no longer exist. They also cover reports on local fairs and markets

ed. J.P. Mayer (London, 1958). **25** W.J. Sinclair, *Irish peasant proprietors: facts and misrepresentations* (Edinburgh & London, 1880), p. 3. **26** Dun, *Landlords and tenants*, p. 25. **27** Mary-Louise Legg, *Newspapers and nationalism: Irish provincial papers, 1850–92* (Dublin, 1998); see also Michael Murphy, *Newspapers and local history* (Chichester, 1991).

with useful details of cattle and agricultural prices down through the years. They may include advertisements of sales pertaining to estates or big houses and their contents.[28] Weekly reports on local tenant organizations such as the United Irish League compiled according to branch are often very illuminating.

Take, for example, a weekly edition of the *Leinster Leader* (22 January 1881). This edition was chosen at random to illustrate the wealth of information that can be accumulated regarding local estates during the land war. There are reports of Land League meetings and resolutions passed at them from about thirty different branches in Kildare, King's County and Queen's County; a very substantial article on a Land League meeting held at Castletown, Queen's County, listing those officers in attendance from that county and surrounding counties and giving an almost verbatim report of everything that was said; an article on the refusal of Lord Mayo's Kildare tenants to pay their rents; one on a deputation of tenants who approached Lord Fitzwilliam at Coolattin for an abatement of rents; a letter praising 'the usual and most liberal donation of clothing to the poor on the Drogheda estate' and the generosity of Lady Drogheda in supplying soup and food to '150 destitute persons'.

As Niamh O'Sullivan has shown, newspapers during the era of the land war were also important in providing powerful visual images of conditions in Ireland and she argues that the illustrations of Aloysius O'Kelly in the *Illustrated London News*, for example, were: 'subtly but significantly instrumental in elevating the Irish political situation from a British domestic irritant to an international cause'.[29] But, of course, illustrations, just the same as text, could be used to promote a particular political agenda, so one needs to be extremely discerning when approaching them for historical information.

To locate relevant local newspapers, one should consult James O'Toole's *Newsplan: report of the newsplan project in Ireland* (Dublin & London, 1992; revised edn, 1998 by Sara Smyth) which provides a list of all newspapers held in the main public libraries in Ireland and in the British library.[30] A full list of provincial newspapers for each county available in the NLI may be consulted at the desk. Sometimes issues which are not available in the main repositories may be found in local libraries or may even be consulted in the newspaper's office (providing the newspaper is still in existence).

As with other sources newspapers have their strengths and weaknesses. There is the likelihood that a certain editorial bias exists in most newspapers and, therefore, it is of some relevance to be aware of the identity of owners and editors of local

---

28 The value of newspapers to big house studies will be discussed separately in chapter four.
29 Niamh O'Sullivan, 'Imaging the Land War' in *Éire-Ireland*, xxxix (2004), p. 101.
30 Newspapers are listed according to title and they are cross-referenced according to county. Details regarding the life span of newspapers is given as are details on where they are to be found in hard copy or if they are available on microfilm. For other valuable works on newspapers in Ireland, see J.R.R. Adams, *Northern Ireland newspapers: checklist with locations* (Belfast, 1979); Rosemary ffoliott, 'Newspapers as a genealogical source' in Begley (ed.), *Irish genealogy: a record finder*, pp 117–38; N. Kissane, *The past from the press* (Dublin, 1985); H. Oram, *The newspaper book: a history of newspapers in Ireland, 1649–1983* (Dublin, 1983).

newspapers and their politics. For example, the *Northern Standard* in County Monaghan had a unionist bias while the *Dundalk Democrat*[31] served as its nationalist counterpart. However, the value of having two such newspapers circulated in one county means that the researcher can view events and reactions to them from opposing perspectives.

Newspapers of the early nineteenth century were selective in what they reported upon. If the researcher becomes aware of a significant event on an estate but finds no report of it in a local newspaper, this should not be seen as proof that the event did not actually take place. An editor may not have wished to offend members of his readership. Similarly, early newspaper editors often relied on local landlords or their agents or local schoolteachers for some of their news items. The interests of such 'reporters' must be kept in mind. It was not until the later nineteenth century that newspapers increased in size and shorthand reporters were employed to cover local events. Subsequently, reports became more detailed and their verbatim-type reporting allows the reader to be a little more discerning.

Unfortunately, few newspapers are indexed.[32] Therefore, researchers will need to spend a lot of time searching through weekly editions of local newspapers. They are perhaps best used for the study of an estate when one takes a particular topic over a relatively short period of time such as the Great Famine 1845–51, or the extended land war from the late 1870s. The patience that is required to search through weekly editions will be rewarded with a vast and variable range of information of significance that may not be extractable from other sources.

MISCELLANEOUS SOURCES

For those interested in the level of indebtedness of Irish landlords in the second half of the nineteenth century, L.P. Curtis jr.'s article on this topic shows how the mortgage records of Maynooth College[33] and the Representative Body of the Church of Ireland (R.C.B.)[34] can be used to good effect.[35] In 1869 the Church of Ireland received £8.5 million in compensation under the Disestablishing Act of that year, while Maynooth College received £369,000 under the Irish Church Act. Both the finance committee of the Church of Ireland and the trustees of Maynooth College invested a substantial proportion of their capital in mortgages to Irish landowners at interest rates of usually 4.25 per cent. Maynooth invested around £300,000 in mortgages to seven Irish landowners including two very

31 Although printed in Co. Louth, this newspaper was widely circulated in Co. Monaghan. 32 The *Leinster Leader* indexation project, set up in September 1988, was the first of its kind in the Republic of Ireland; see Mary Carroll, '*Leinster Leader* indexation project' in *Journal of the County Kildare Archaeological Society* (hereinafter *Kildare Arch. Soc. Jn.*), xviii, pt. ii (1994–5), pp 259–62. 33 These records are stored in the Russell Library, St Patrick's College, Maynooth, Co. Kildare. 34 Permission to consult these records should be sought through the Representative Church Body Library, Braemor Park, Rathgar, Dublin 14. 35 Curtis, 'Incumbered wealth'.

substantial loans to Lord Granard and Lord Cloncurry which between them
accounted for almost 50 per cent of the total invested. From 1871 to 1876 the RCB
approved 120 loans to Irish landowners and at its peak in 1877–8 had over £3.5
million tied up in Irish estates.

The mortgage ledgers of the RCB show the amount of the various loans
approved to landowners and one is able to see the effects of agricultural depression
and agitation from the early 1880s from the growth in interest arrears which are
also recorded. When these ledgers are used in conjunction with the annual reports
of the RCB[36] one gets a good indication of the pressures on both landlords to meet
financial obligations at this time and the pressures on institutions to safeguard their
investments. In 1886, for example, the annual report of the RCB shows that arrears
of interest stood at £35,000; by 1890 they had risen to £81,000; and by 1901 to
£135,000.[37] From 1885, in all cases in which a full year's interest was due, receivers
or agents under deed were appointed over estates by the RCB. The money invested
in mortgages to Irish landlords had now become a 'subject of anxiety' for the RCB
and its annual report of 1886 concluded: 'In the present state of uncertainty as to
the laws which may be enacted with reference to land tenure, it would be rash to
speak positively as to what may, or may not, be the loss on these investments. The
Representative Body can only repeat that they hope there will be no ultimate loss
of capital, though some loss of interest may be expected.'[38]

The importance of the Maynooth mortgage papers is that they contain a great
deal of correspondence between landlords and the college trustees from the early
1870s up to the early years of the twentieth century.[39] There are the initial loan
agreements which set out the loan amount agreed upon, the rate of interest, the
rate of penal interest in event of non-payment, the acreage and rental of the estate,
and the charges upon it. (However, one must be careful here as Lord Granard for
one did not bring the full extent of the charges upon his estate to the attention of
the trustees. It later transpired in court hearings that they were much greater than
he had initially claimed.) There are statements of interest accounts, private censuses
of tenants on some estates (most notably on the Granard estate), and details of the
break-up and sales of estates.[40]

Most revealing is the substantial volume of correspondence between landowners
or their representatives and the college trustees. This correspondence shows the
human side of the story which statistics and accounts cannot do. In December
1880, for example, Edward Murphy, agent to the Stewart estate in Dunfanaghy,
County Donegal, wrote to the bursar of the college: 'You will no doubt be aware
that even in the north of Ireland the tenants have combined against the payment

36 These may be consulted in the NLI.   **37** *RCB annual reports*, 1886, p. 11; 1890, p. 12;
1901, p. 14.   **38** Ibid., 1886, p. 44.   **39** The seven landlords were Lord Granard of Longford,
Lord Cloncurry of Kildare, R.J. Alexander of Antrim, B.R. Balfour of Louth, J.A. Stewart of
Donegal and Derry, Major Myles O'Reilly of Galway and Samuel Osborne of Meath.
40 The bulk of the documents pertaining to the Granard mortgage have been reproduced
in Terence Dooley, 'The mortgage papers of St Patrick's College, Maynooth' in *Archivium
Hibernicum*, lix (2005), pp 106–236.

of their rents ... I do not think it advisable in the present state of the country to resort to measures of coercion. Under these circumstances it occurs to me to ask you if you will permit the interest which will be due on 1st to stand over, without penal interest, until say the end of February.'[41]

For the late nineteenth century and up to independence in 1922, a useful source is the confidential monthly reports of the county inspectors of the RIC. These are part of The British in Ireland: Colonial Office CO 904, Dublin Castle records.[42] Reports are either handwritten or typed summaries of the main events in the county for each month of the year based on reports received by county inspectors from their district inspectors. The originals are available in the National Archives (Kew) but they are also available on microfilm in the NLI.[43] The county inspectors' reports vary, depending on the diligence of the individual officers and some can be quite illegible due to the quality of handwriting.[44] Most reports provide some information on estates on which agitation was taking place; details on significant land sales in the county during the month; and for the years from 1917 to 1922, the difficulties facing landowners in each county as lawlessness grew and land grabbing became a way of life during the revolutionary period. For example, the county inspector of Mayo reported in 1901 that negotiations for the sale of the Dillon estate had broken down because the tenants, 'at the instigation of local agitators', refused to complete the purchase of their holdings as the Congested Districts Board had insisted upon a clause reserving all sporting rights to the landlord. In the same month the Westmeath inspector reported the sale of the Nugent estate; the Wexford inspector reported the sale of the Keane estate; the Cavan inspector reported that that there was a no rent combination on the Fawcett estate because the landlord refused to accept the tenants offer of sixteen year's purchase on current rents; and the Galway inspector reported agitation on the Daly and Clanricarde estates. These records also contain important information on 'Anti-government organizations, 1882–1921', mainly secret police information on the United Irish League (quarterly returns relating to branches, lists of meetings, prosecutions of members, returns of outrages and so on), Sinn Fein, and a number of secret agrarian societies. Part one of the series, volumes 7–9, document secret service information about Ribbonism, Fenianism and agrarian disturbances from 1798 to 1867.

The revolutionary period proved, in many cases, to be the final catalyst in the decline of estates. The political revolution was accompanied by a social revolution

---

41 E. Murphy to Rev. Farrelly, 29 Dec. 1880 (Maynooth College Archives, 107/7). The mortgage papers should be used in conjunction with the *annual reports* of the president which are also available in the Maynooth archives. Again, these give more general information on the relationship between mortgagors and mortgagees in the late nineteenth and early twentieth centuries. Other primary sources which are useful in this respect include the *Irish Landowners' Convention annual reports, 1887–1919* available in the NLI. **42** For a valuable introduction to these records, see the bibliography of Fitzpatrick, *Politics and Irish life, 1913–21.* **43** There is an index of the colonial office (CO) papers available at the desk of the NLI CO904, parts ii–iv are composed of the county inspectors' monthly reports from 1892 to 1921. **44** These monthly reports were in turn summarized by the inspector general of the RIC for

in the form of a new land war. Chapter 1 has shown that many landowners had held on to extensive tracts of demesne and untenanted land (and, indeed, some retained much tenanted land) up to 1919. Because of their socio-political, economic and religious backgrounds landlords were to suffer outrage and intimidation particularly from 1920 to 1923 on a scale the like of which their class had not experienced in living memory. This included the burning of around 300 big houses.[45] Elements of this intimidation can be extracted from a study of local newspapers. However, much can also be gleaned from government files in the NAI. The Department of the Taoiseach, Department of Finance, and Department of Justice files contain reports on individual estates during this period and correspondence between landlords and these various departments. In June 1922, for example, Lord Powerscourt wrote to the Minister for Home Affairs drawing the latter's attention to the robbing, looting and intimidation that was rife around his estate at Enniskerry, County Wicklow.[46] The previous month Lord Castletown wrote to W.T. Cosgrave complaining that his tenants were refusing to pay their rents and that cattle drives were becoming all too common.[47]

Indexes to these files are to be found on the shelves in the NAI. The index to the Department of Justice files lists those which are related to 'land' (H77/–) giving a brief description of what is to be found in individual files such as 'demesne land at Newberry manor, Mallow'; 'estate of T. Wilson Walshe: lands of Killowen, Co. Wexford'; 'payment of rents by tenants: W.S. Hugo, Glenwood, Rathdrum, Co. Wicklow'. The Department of Finance files, also indexed, relate mainly to land purchase on individual estates in the 1920s; arrears of annuities; and compensation being sought by landowners for loss of property. The Department of the Taoiseach files mainly contain letters from landlords seeking protection from agitators during the revolutionary period. Here the index should be consulted under the headings of 'subjects', 'people' and 'places'. Even with the available indexes, much searching has to be done to see if the government files contain anything on a specific estate, so one should be prepared to spend some time going through them.

There is also a very substantial archive related to the land question post-independence to be found in the files of the various government departments, particularly the Department of the Taoiseach, the Department of Finance and the Department of Agriculture. Anybody interested in events at constituency level is directed to the University College Dublin Archives Department where the papers of post-independence politicians such as Frank Aiken, Ernest Blythe, Eamon de Valera, Sean MacEntee, Sean MacEoin and others are often quite revealing on local land division issues, as is the correspondence in the Fianna Fáil, Cumann na nGaedheal/Fine Gael archives.

the chief secretary.   **45** See chapter four.   **46** Lord Powerscourt to Minister for Home Affairs, 17 June 1922 (NAI, Dept. of Justice files, H5/389).   **47** Lord Castletown to W.T. Cosgrave, 1 May 1922 (ibid., H5/174).

CHAPTER 3

Irish big houses

INTRODUCTION TO THE HISTORIOGRAPHY
OF THE IRISH BIG HOUSE

Big houses have traditionally held a fascination for Irish writers of fiction, drama and poetry resulting in an outpouring of works since around the beginning of the nineteenth century. The relevance of these works as source material for the discerning historian will be discussed in the chapter which follows; suffice to say for now that the fact that many writers such as Maria Edgeworth, George Moore, Shane Leslie, Somerville and Ross and Elizabeth Bowen, came from big house backgrounds means that their works offer interesting sidelights to the historian on a variety of aspects of big house life, not least of all the attitudes of those inside looking out. Equally, the works of writers such as John McGahern and John Banville, whose cultural and class backgrounds are not the same as the aforementioned writers, afford an insight to the attitudes of those outside the big house looking in.

However, despite their centrality to Irish history (or possibly because of it!), it was not until the 1970s that Irish big houses and the family and servant communities who occupied them began to attract the level of attention from historians and specialists in art and architecture that they merit. As with the section on landed estates, any introduction to such secondary works here must be selective. As an important starting point the reader's attention is directed once again to www.irishhistoryonline.ie where searches under 'country house', 'big house', 'architecture', 'demesne' and related terms will turn up hundreds of publications, many scholarly and erudite and some antiquarian, but all important in varying degrees in the elucidation of some aspect of the history of individual houses or of some more general aspect of big house life.[1] Also of much value in this respect is

---

[1] Amongst the most valuable are, for example, M.D.C. Bolton, *Headfort House* (Kells, 1999); M.R. Carty, *History of Killeen Castle, County Meath* (Dunsany, 1991); Desmond Chaloner, 'Country house life in Meath 1810–17' in *Ríocht na Midhe*, 8 (1987), pp 16–31; N.E. French, *Bellinter House* (Trim, 1993); D.J. Griffin, 'A Richard Castle design for Headfort, Co. Meath' in Conleth Manning (ed.), *Dublin and beyond the Pale: studies in honour of Patrick Healy* (Bray, 1998); idem, 'Carton and Isaac Ware' in *Kildare Arch. Soc. Jn.*, xviii (1994–5), pp 163–75; John Kirwan, 'Mount Juliet' in *Journal of the Kilkenny Archaeological Society*, 50 (1998), pp 112–39; A.P.W. Malcomson, 'Bellisle and its owners' in *Clogher Rec.*, xvi, no. 2 (1998), pp 7–44; Frank Mitchell, 'The evolution of Townley Hall' in *Bulletin of the Irish Georgian Society*, 30 (1987), pp 3–61; Patricia O'Hare, *Muckross House, Killarney* (Dublin, 1998); Office of Public Works, *Castletown* (Dublin, 1995); Sean O'Reilly & Alistair Rowan, *Lucan House, Co. Dublin* (Dublin,

Edward McParland's, 'A bibliography of Irish architectural history', a catalogue of works relating to Irish architecture published before 1988,[2] while Toby Barnard's guide to sources for the study of material culture, also published in this series, is an obvious point of reference for those interested in the world of big house things.[3]

For anyone beginning a big house related study, there are a number of works which are essential reading: scholars such as Toby Barnard, Maurice Craig, Ann Crookshank, Desmond FitzGerald, Desmond Guinness, Mark Bence-Jones, Peter Somerville-Large, Edward McParland and William Ryan have made invaluable contributions to recording the architectural history of Irish big houses, describing their material culture, the lavishness of their interiors and contents, and overall recreating in print and picture their former splendour, contributions which, in turn, have awakened large sections of the public, public bodies and the Irish government to the importance of the future preservation of big houses in Ireland.[4] Others have produced learned works describing the historical evolution of the demesnes and parklands which surrounded so many big houses, as in Finola O'Kane's masterful study of eighteenth-century Irish landscapes where she explores: 'how and why the gardens were designed, who designed them, who used them, and for what purpose'.[5]

1988); Marquis of Sligo, *Westport House and the Brownes* (Ashbourne, 1982); also Dan Walsh, *100 Wexford country houses: an illustrated history* (Enniscorthy, 1996).   **2** Edward McParland, 'A bibliography of Irish architectural history' in *I.H.S.*, xxvi, no. 102 (1988), pp 161–212. **3** T.C. Barnard, *A guide to sources for the history of material culture in Ireland, 1500–2000* (Dublin, 2005).   **4** See, for example, T.C. Barnard, *Making the grand figure: lives and possessions in Ireland, 1641–1770* (New Haven & London, 2004); Maurice Craig, *Classic Irish houses of the middle size* (London & New York, 1976); idem, *The architecture of Ireland from the earliest times to 1880* (Dublin, 1989); Ann Crookshank, 'The visual arts, 1603–1740' in Moody & Vaughan (eds), *A new history of Ireland, iv, eighteenth-century Ireland*, pp 471–98; idem, 'The visual arts, 1740–1850' in ibid., pp 499–541; Brian de Breffny & Rosemary ffolliott, *The houses of Ireland: domestic architecture from the medieval castle to the Edwardian villa* (New York, 1984); Jane Fenlon, N.F. Figgis & Catherine Marshall (eds), *New perspectives: studies in art history in honour of Anne Crookshank* (Dublin, 1987); Desmond FitzGerald, David Griffin & Nicholas Robinson, *Vanishing country houses of Ireland* (Dublin, 1988); Desmond Guinness & William Ryan, *Irish houses and castles* (London, 1971); David Griffin, 'Country houses of County Laois' in P.G. Lane & William Nolan (eds), *Laois: history and society. Interdisciplinary essays on the history of an Irish county* (Dublin, 1999), pp 563–84; Mark Bence-Jones, *Twilight of the ascendancy* (London, 1987); idem, *Life in an Irish country house* (London, 1996); Michael McCarthy (ed.), *Lord Charlemont and his circle: essays in honour of Michael Wynne* (Dublin, 2001); Simon Marsden, *In ruins: the once great houses of Ireland* (Boston & London, 1997); Hugh Montgomery-Massingberd & C.S. Sykes, *Great houses of Ireland* (London, 1999); Sean O'Reilly, *Irish houses and gardens from the archives of Country Life* (London, 1998); Valerie Pakenham, *The big house in Ireland: an illustrated anthology* (London, 2000); Lindsay Proudfoot, 'Place and mentalite: the "big house" and its locality in County Tyrone' in Charles Dillon, H.A. Jefferies & William Nolan (eds), *Tyrone: history and society. Interdisciplinary essays on the history of an Irish county* (Dublin, 2000), pp 511–42; see also T.C. Barnard & Jane Fenlon (eds), *The dukes of Ormonde, 1610–1745* (Woodbridge, 2000); Agnes Bernelle (ed.), *Decantations: a tribute to Maurice Craig* (Dublin, 1992); Jacqueline Hill & Colm Lennon (eds), *Luxury and austerity* (Dublin, 1999). **5** Finola O'Kane, *Landscape design in eighteenth-century Ireland: mixing foreign trees with the natives* (Cork, 2004), p. 7.

Others have described the often forgotten ornate and architecturally important follies and garden buildings.[6]

Some of the above named writers have also contributed feature articles to *Country Life*, a magazine first founded in 1897 by Edward Hudson, a professional publisher, ostensibly to celebrate English country life.[7] Within a year or so, the magazine began to feature articles on Ireland (including an interesting early one on land issues and their potential repercussions for big houses).[8] Then followed articles on individual Irish houses and gardens, which were lavishly illustrated with photographs.[9] In 1899, for example, Farnham in County Cavan was featured with photographs showing off its new water supply.[10] By the early twentieth century, Irish houses began to feature more extensively because Edward McParland has claimed: 'Behind the Irish connexion with the journal is Edwin Lutyens. The Irish houses covered in the early days seem to have been selected because of their connexions with Lutyens.'[11] Thus there were articles on Lambay (1912 and 1929), Howth (1916 and 1930) and Heywood (1919).

Throughout the 1930s and 1940s articles continued to appear intermittently on Irish houses, gardens and furniture. The 1950s were bleak enough in terms of Irish coverage but then at the end of the decade Mark Girouard's first of a number of articles on Irish big houses appeared. Significantly, it was on Beaulieu, one of the most important surviving seventeenth-century houses, which to this day is still in the ownership of the original family, and is often considered the first unfortified house to be built in Ireland. Then followed contributions by such as the late John Cornforth, Maurice Craig (since as far back as the 1940s), Desmond FitzGerald (Knight of Glin), Christopher Hussey, Mark Bence-Jones, Alistair Rowan and Jeremy Masson. To date over twenty Irish houses have been featured in *Country Life*, the most recent being Hamwood in County Meath.[12] In the main these could be described as the great houses of Ireland, the majority of which, at least at the time of writing, were in the ownership of the original families, although Maurice

---

6 As well as O'Kane, *Landscape design* see Andrews, *Plantation acres*; Patrick Bowe, 'The Renaissance garden in Ireland' in *Irish Arts Review*, xi (1995), pp 74–81; James Howley, *The follies and garden buildings of Ireland* (New Haven, 1993); J.G.D. Lamb & Patrick Bowe, *A history of gardening in Ireland* (Dublin, 1995); Edward Malins & Patrick Bowe, *Irish gardens and demesnes from 1830* (London, 1980); Edward Malins & Desmond FitzGerald, *Lost demesnes. Irish landscape gardening, 1660–1845* (London, 1976); Terence Reeves-Smyth, 'Demesnes' in F.H.A. Aalen, Kevin Whelan & Matthew Stout (ed.), *Atlas of the Irish rural landscape* (Cork, 1997), pp 197–205; idem, 'The nature of demesnes' in J.W. Foster & H.C.G. Chesney (eds), *Nature in Ireland: a scientific and cultural history* (Dublin, 1997), pp 549–72; for studies of individual demesnes and gardens see Patricia Friel, *Frederick Trench (1746–1836) and Heywood, Queen's County and the creation of a Romantic demesne* (Dublin, 2000); Arnold Horner, 'Carton, Co. Kildare: a case study in the making of an Irish demesne' in *Quarterly Bulletin of the Irish Georgian Society*, xviii, nos 2–3 (Apr.-Sept. 1975), pp 45–101. **7** See O'Reilly, *Irish houses and gardens*, pp 6–25. **8** *Country Life*, 1 Dec. 1900. **9** For the importance of *Country Life's* photographic archive, see chapter four. **10** *Country Life*, 22 Apr. 1899. **11** Mc Parland, 'Bibliography of Irish architectural history', p. 162. **12** *Country Life*, 23 Feb. 2006; see also *Country Life Accumulative Index: vols i to cxciii to December 1999* (London, 2000).

Craig has written (briefly) on some smaller houses including Kilcarty, Mantua and Athgoe.[13]

A more recent generation of scholars has featured alongside the established experts in publications emanating from the Irish Georgian Society, an organisation founded in 1958 by Desmond Guinness and his late wife, Mariga 'for the protection of buildings of architectural merit in Ireland'.[14] The society began by publishing short bulletins aimed at drawing contemporary attention to important houses that were for sale or in danger of demolition. Shortly afterwards, the bulletin was expanded to include articles on houses and related aspects of their history, art and architecture, drawing upon the expertise of the likes of Desmond Guinness, Maurice Craig, Mark Bence-Jones and the prolific Desmond FitzGerald. In 1998, the bulletin was replaced by an annual journal, *Irish Architectural and Decorative Studies*, which continues to publish important and pioneering studies relating to many aspects of Irish big house life. A bibliography of articles in both the bulletins and journals can be consulted on the Irish Georgian Society website at www.igs.ie.[15]

But although much important work was published on the architecture of big houses and their material culture from the 1970s, considerably less was published concerning their history within the broader context of the changing social, political and economic developments of the nineteenth and twentieth centuries or descriptive of the lives of the people who built them, inhabited them, worked in them, gave life to them on a day-to-day basis and who, ultimately, witnessed their decline or fought for their survival. In this respect, the Irish big house lagged far behind its English counterpart.[16] It was this lacuna that inspired this author to undertake a systematic examination of the reasons for the decline of the big house in Ireland from the second half of the nineteenth century onwards in his *The decline of the big house in Ireland: a study of Irish landed families, 1860–1960* (Dublin, 2001).[17]

---

13 Maurice Craig, 'Some smaller Irish houses' in *Country Life*, cvi, no. 2738 (8 July 1949), pp 131–2; see also Rosemary ffolliott, 'Some lesser known country houses in Leinster and Munster' in *Irish Ancestor*, iii, no. 1 (1975), pp 49–51; Edward McParland, 'Sir Richard Morrison's country houses: the smaller villas' in *Country Life*, cliii, no. 3961 (24 May 1973), pp 1462–6. **14** For more details, go to www.igs.ie. **15** The Irish Georgian Society is also presently preparing a catalogue of theses and dissertations pertaining to architecture and the allied arts. When completed the new catalogue will be posted on the society's website. Other journals worth consulting include *Irish Tatler and Sketch*, *Irish Ancestor* and *Irish Arts Review*. In the 1960s (*c*.1963–8), the *Irish Times* ran a series of articles called 'People and Houses' which featured houses such as Ballinamona Park (25 Oct. 1968); Carriglass (21 Jan. 1964); Castle Blunden (27 Aug. 1966); Gurteen Le Poer (24 Dec. 1968) and so on; see 'Select bibliography' in Mark Bence-Jones, *A guide to Irish country houses* (revised ed., London, 1988), pp xxv–xxviii. **16** Cannadine's *The decline and fall of the British aristocracy* offers a great deal of information on the Irish situation; see also Mark Girouard, *Life in the English country house* (New Haven & London, 1978); idem, *The Victorian country house* (2nd ed., New Haven & London, 1981); David Littlejohn, *The fate of the English country house* (Oxford, 1997); Peter Mandler, *The fall and rise of the stately home* (New Haven & London, 1997). **17** See Bence-Jones, *Twilight of the ascendancy* and *Life in an Irish country house*; also Randal MacDonnell, *The lost houses of Ireland* (London, 2002).

This study attempted to bring a new dimension to the study of the big house in Ireland by examining the reasons for its decline within the context of historical economic, social and political developments.

THE BUILDING OF BIG HOUSES IN IRELAND: AN OVERVIEW

The earthen and timber fortresses built by the first wave of Normans to arrive in Ireland in the twelfth century were the precursors to their stone castles from the thirteenth century onwards which, in turn, were the precursors to the unfortified country houses which were to follow four centuries or so later. Very little of this medieval architecture now survives as part of an existing house, except for the round towers at Leixlip Castle or Kilkenny Castle or the medieval core of castles originally located within the precincts of the English Pale such as Dunsany and Fingall in Meath or Howth and Malahide in Dublin. Many more of the great castles such as Cahir in Tipperary, Blarney in Cork and Askeaton in Limerick now lie in ruins.[18]

Most Irish castles of the fifteenth to the seventeenth centuries were tower-houses. The majority of these were gradually deserted in favour of more modern, less defensive houses, although others were added to in a variety of different ways, sometimes with the addition of a plain lower Georgian construction as at Smarmore in Louth, or sometimes additions were built to the same height as the tower, as at Louth Hall, near Tallanstown, a house that is now abandoned and slowly falling into dereliction.

Because of the political upheavals of the sixteenth and seventeenth centuries and the uncertainties facing the new landed, mainly Protestant elite who arguably remained wary about their prospects in the Irish countryside, the semi-fortified house was slow to evolve. The earliest examples such as Portumna Castle in Galway (built by Richard Burke, earl of Clanricarde for an estimated £10,000[19]) or Burntcourt in Tipperary were designed along much the same lines as the Elizabethan and Jacobean houses of northern England. They were in some respects more practical as residences than the tower houses but they still retained defensive characteristics such as galleries and loops and a fortified outer wall. The English example followed through in their interior decoration with their great chimney-pieces and richly ornamented staircases. In Ulster there was a distinctively characteristic version of the semi-fortified house known as the 'Plantation castle', which looked more Scottish than English, with round towers and pointed roofs of the type at Ballygally in Antrim.[20]

---

18 See Brian de Breffny & Rosemary ffolliott, *Houses of Ireland* (London, 1975); H.G. Leask, *Irish castles and castellated houses* (revised edn., Dundalk, 1946); Niall McCullough & Valerie Mulvin, *A lost tradition: the nature of architecture in Ireland* (Dublin, 1987); Niall McCullough, *Palimpsest: change in the Irish building tradition* (Dublin, 1994); Tadhg O'Keefe, *Irish castles and castellated houses* (Cork, 1997). **19** Crookshank, 'The visual arts, 1603–1740', p. 476. **20** Bence-Jones, *A guide to Irish country houses*, p. xii.

But many of these early-sixteenth century semi-fortified houses were destroyed in the 1641 rebellion and later wars of the seventeenth century (Portumna survived only to be accidentally destroyed by fire in 1826.) Lismore in Waterford, for example, was successfully defended against rebel attacks in the early 1640s but eventually succumbed to Confederate forces in 1645 after it was badly damaged by fire and it was not until the 1810s that a major rebuilding project was undertaken to completely rebuild it. Similarly, Liscarrol Castle, the massive thirteenth-century home of the Barrys – described as 'the greatest surviving monument of the Anglo-Norman colony in South Munster'[21] – was captured by Confederates in 1645 and five years later destroyed by artillery under Sir Hardress Waller.

But if the seventeenth century was a century of destruction, this meant by extension that it was also a century of reconstruction. The Jephsons, for example, abandoned the war-damaged Mallow Castle in north Cork and converted the stables and service wing into a more modest, less defensive house.[22] Alterations to other houses in the second half of the century continued to reflect the settlers' insecurity. The Percevals had bawns (stoutly walled courtyards with corner towers) added to their fashionable Burton House in Cork around 1665. Ironically, these did not prevent the house from being destroyed by James II's retreating army in 1690.

It was only after the Williamite Wars had ended with the defeat of the Catholic King James in 1691 that settlers became confident enough to begin building defenceless houses. The most important of those built between then and 1720 tended to be very English in style, but they were also old-fashioned in that they lagged behind English architectural tastes. Thus when Stackallan House in County Meath was built in 1716, it was reminiscent of the type of English country house built some thirty to forty years before.[23] Many of the houses of this period were: 'usually modest in size and rectangular in ground plan, and had hipped roofs with overhanging eaves, dormer windows, and tall chimneystacks'.[24] They were in the main simple and functional and relatively few ostentatious architectural piles announcing the wealth of Irish landlords were built as yet, with some notable exceptions including Charleville Castle in Cork and Dunmore House in Kilkenny both of which have long since disappeared. Indeed, many Irish estates at this time had no sizeable house at all. As late as 1737, Lord Orrery exaggerated the point when he wrote to Tom Southerne: 'our nobility, like the old patriarchs, live in cottages with hogs, sheep and oxen', while a year later Samuel Madden claimed that 'in great estates of several thousand acres you will not meet with two houses of stone and lime fit (I will not say for a gentleman but even) for a farmer to live'.[25]

By the eighteenth century many landed families continued to reside in old houses: in Cork these included Castlelyons, Macroom, Blarney and Ballymaloe; in Meath, Dunsany and Killeen. But changes were afoot. The period from around 1720 to 1745 probably represented the apogee of big house building in Ireland,

---

21 Dickson, *Old world economy*, p. 36.   **22** Ibid.   **23** Bence-Jones, *A guide to Irish country houses*, p. xii.   **24** Crookshank, 'The visual arts, 1603–1740', p. 481.   **25** Orrery & Madden quoted in Crookshank, 'The visual arts, 1603–1740', p. 484.

when at least two-dozen sizeable houses, and probably scores of lesser ones, were built or at least begun.[26] Part of the reason for this spurt was that between around 1717 and 1730, many 21-year and 31-year leases fell in, allowing landlords to raise their rents possibly by as much as one third and, therefore, increase their prosperity.[27] Rents rose sharply once again between the 1740s and the 1760s (the beginning of a strong unpward trend which resulted in aggregated rents soaring to £12 million by 1815) and as L.M. Cullen has concluded: 'Landlords, whose incomes increased while incomes generally were stagnant, spent freely on sumptuary products, on wine, whose consumption rose sharply, and on house building.'[28] Economic prosperity, which manifested itself in high agricultural prices and greatly increased land value prices, was accompanied by a dramatic growth in banking and credit facilities and by the 1740s interest rates had fallen to their lowest levels for the entire eighteenth century.[29] All of this paved the way for big house construction.

The defensive nature of houses was now almost completely abandoned as prosperity also brought social and political stability. The Palladian, neo-Gothic or neo-Classical houses, which shot up throughout the country, replaced the embattled profile of the medieval tower houses. In place of the latter:

> there came a confident horizontality of bay and wing, in which not more than three storeys were thought necessary even for the grandest mansions. In the same more hospitable spirit, visual emphasis was now on doors and windows rather than on the protective elements of wall and roof; and the householder's power was asserted not by any show of impregnability but on the economic level, by designs whose studied irregularity was obviously the product of a single architectural shopping-spree.[30]

The construction of great mansions such as Castletown reflected peace and prosperity. It was in part designed by the Italian, Alessandro Galilei, and in part by Edward Lovett Pearce and it has been said that 'nothing quite so splendid was ever built again'; it represented the pinnacle of landed pretensions in Ireland.[31] It has been acknowledged that Pearce, probably the most noted Irish-born architect of the eighteenth century, brought about a revolution in the architectural taste of Irish aristocratic landlords.[32] His other best known works included the imposing Summerhill in County Meath and the extant Bellamont Forest in County Cavan, the latter, according to Maurice Craig: 'a very perfect and complete example of a Palladian villa',[33] which was undoubtedly inspired by Pearce's time spent in Italy and his admiration for Palladio's Villa Rotunda.

26 Craig, *The architecture of Ireland*, p. 180.   **27** L.M. Cullen, 'Economic development, 1750–1800' in Moody & Vaughan (eds), *A new history of Ireland, iv, eighteenth-century Ireland*, p. 177; Dickson, *Old world economy*, p. 195.   **28** Cullen, 'Economic development, 1750–1800', p. 177.   **29** Ibid., p. 195.   **30** J.H. Andrews, 'Land and people, *c.*1780' in Moody & Vaughan (eds), *A new history of Ireland, iv: eighteenth-century Ireland*, p. 237.   **31** Craig, *The architecture of Ireland*, p. 180.   **32** Bence-Jones, *A guide to Irish country houses*, p. xiii.   **33** Craig, *The architecture of Ireland*, p. 186.

Pearce's ascendancy in the 1720s coincided with the rise in popularity of the Palladian and Classical. When he died in 1733, the German-born Richard Castle (or Cassel) took up his mantle. Castle, who had arrived in Ireland via Holland and England, was probably brought to Ireland by Sir Gustavus Hume to build Castle Hume in County Fermanagh. He worked as an understudy to Pearce in the construction of Parliament House in College Green (now the Bank of Ireland.) Until his death in 1751, Castle was responsible for the design or redesign of many of Ireland's most famous and distinguished houses: Carton in Kildare, Hazlewood in County Sligo, Powerscourt and Russborough in Wicklow, Strokestown Park in Roscommon and Westport in Mayo to name but a few. Like Pearce, he favoured the Palladian plan of a central block joined to subordinate wings by straight or curving links, as at Carton, Powerscourt and Russborough. (As late as 1840, this plan was being used at Castleboro in Wexford, many years after it had gone out of fashion in England.) The wings served as outoffices or stables, whereas in England they were often used as additional reception rooms. Castle was also involved in the planning of more modest middling houses such as Ledwithstown in Longford.

But it would be foolish to consider that Irish big houses can be conveniently sorted into a few architectural categories. Many houses are in fact composites of a variety of styles fashionable at different periods: Lismore Castle, for example, is a composite of an early seventeenth-century and nineteenth-century castle incorporating towers of a much earlier medieval castle. Bantry House in Cork was originally built in 1720, modified between 1820 and 1830 and later extended between 1840 and 1850. Thus the existing architectural wholeness represents three distinct phases and points to the importance of understanding the changes in aesthetic taste and social fashion, sometimes influenced by such factors as the broadening of cultural horizons experienced by sons/heirs as they went on grand tours bringing home new ideas which determined the changing architectural form of houses.[34] Early in the eighteenth century, Sir James Jefferyes, owner of Blarney Castle in Cork, had extensive diplomatic and family connections on the continent in Holland, Poland and Sweden and according to David Dickson these continental influences 'were reflected in the castle's appearance: it was embellished with a part-Dutch, part-Gothic annexe early in the eighteenth century'.[35]

In other cases, the eighteenth century witnessed the demolition of old houses in favour of completely new structures. In 1715 the pre-plantation form of Castle Bernard in Cork was swept away in exchange for a brick and pilastered mansion. This was then enlarged in the next generation. Two generations later in 1789, it, in turn, was demolished and rebuilt in the Gothic manner.[36] However, in much of rural Ireland, fashions continued to lag far behind their English counterparts. In Munster in the 1760s–80s period, the Franco-Italian architect, Davis Ducart, was building Palladian mansions that were archaic by English standards.[37]

34 See *The diaries of Lord Limerick's grand tour 1716 to 1723*, ed. Earl of Roden (Dundalk, n.d.); Dickson, *Old world economy*, p. 96. 35 Dickson, *Old world economy*, p. 67. 36 Ibid., p. 97.
37 Ibid.

The lesser gentry continued to build small or middling but architecturally important eighteenth-century houses long after their more illustrious aristocratic neighbours had ceased. These tended to survive much more in their original totality and were typically two or three storeys over basement and five to nine bays wide. Mark Bence-Jones contends that

> good proportions and handsome joinery – shouldered doorcases, stairs with robust turned balusters – were generally all that the lesser gentry could afford to give dignity and elegance to the interiors of their houses. Plasterwork, apart from plain cornices and friezes, was generally beyond their means; though one sometimes finds simple stucco decoration in quite small houses, such as Summer Hill, Co Mayo.[38]

They served, as David Dickson puts it: 'their social purpose admirably: to impress social peers (and, perhaps more importantly, pretentious inferiors) as to a family's substance, standing and taste, and to provide for their genteel neighbours a venue for conspicuous hospitality, social intercourse and polite recreation.'[39]

Such houses, and probably even many of the great ones, were frequently designed by their owners or by local master builders. In the main, architects were still largely confined to public works or the most impressive big house projects supported by the grandest patrons. Shannongrove in Limerick was built between 1709 and 1723 to the design of a local mason called John O'Brien; Benjamin Crawley, a builder, probably designed Durrow Castle in Queen's County. Amongst the most famous of the amateur architects was Francis Bindon, who came to prominence following the death of Richard Castle in 1751. He had collaborated with Castle on Russborough,[40] and went on to design houses such as Coopershill in Sligo and Woodstock in Kilkenny but Mark Bence-Jones claims that 'despite his prominence as an architect and his large output, [Bindon] was only an amateur; a talented and well-connected member of the Co. Clare landed gentry who was also a successful portrait painter'.[41] The influential Nathaniel Clements was also an amateur. He designed Newberry Hall in Kildare and what is now Áras an Uachtaráin in the Phoenix Park and may have had a hand in the design of Beauparc in Meath. Clements favoured the wide-spreading Palladian layout, whereas most of Bindon's houses are tall blocks. These amateur architects or master builders probably found their inspiration or prototype in published plans including those to be found in works such as *Vitruvius Britannicus* (1715–25).[42]

In the houses of the rich commoners and nobility, one found the most elaborate and exquisite plasterwork. Amongst the best surviving examples are the ceilings of the gold saloon at Carton where the mid-Georgian, richly figurative baroque design exemplifies the once magnificent wealth and socio-political standing of the

38 Bence-Jones, *A guide to Irish country houses*, p. xv.   **39** Dickson, *Old world economy*, p. 95. **40** Craig, *The architecture of Ireland*, p. 188.   **41** Bence-Jones, *A guide to Irish country houses*, p. xiv.   **42** Crookshank, 'The visual arts, 1603–1740', p. 484.

FitzGerald family. Created in 1739, by the renowned Swiss-born stuccadores, Paolo and Filippo Lafranchini, the ceiling has been described as: 'the most sumptuous display of their skills in figurative stuccowork … [which] clearly illustrates their borrowings from Italian and French engraved sources.'[43] The design referred to as 'The courtship of the gods' is a typically allusive Classical arrangement containing a variety of mythological creations. The Franchini style soon influenced a whole generation of Irish stuccadores who flourished in the mid-eighteenth century.

Around the 1770s, the neo-Classical style of plasterwork, much more delicate and inspired by the recently discovered paintings at Pompeii and Herculaneum, came to Ireland. The Robert Adam rooms at Headfort are important enough to be now included on the World Monument List. James Wyatt designed rooms at Abbey Leix in Queen's County, Westport in Mayo and Curraghmore in Waterford (and possibly also at Farnham in Cavan, Ardbraccan in Meath and Avondale in Wicklow). His great masterpiece was Castle Coole in Fermanagh. But Irish craftsmen were also very much to the fore including Michael Stapleton known as the 'Dublin Adam' who worked on Lucan House in Dublin and Furness in Kildare. The fact that neo-Classical plasterwork could be created from moulds and so could be mass-produced meant that it came within the affordability of the lesser gentry.

Big house building in the second half of the eighteenth century was sustained by further economic growth from around 1785 to the end of the Napoleonic Wars in 1815. This period witnessed a correspondingly impressive rise in rent levels, possibly by up to 250 per cent in some cases. The 1780s and 1790s witnessed the construction of some of Ireland's most imposing houses such as the above mentioned Castle Coole with its giant porticoes and colonnades, and Emo Court in Queen's County described as: 'the domestic counterpart of Gandon's most famous public building, the Dublin Custom House.'[44] But such lavish spending projects were not without consequence: the construction of Emo Court almost broke the Portarlington family.

After the passing of the Act of Union in 1800 the politically active members of the landed class had less reason to spend time in Dublin and as the capital simultaneously lost its social appeal to London, more and more families retreated to the country, vacating the once fashionable squares of the city to spend more time in their big houses. Some received a great deal of financial compensation for the loss of their rotten boroughs, which they subsequently spent on embellishing their homes to the design of architects such as Francis Johnston, Richard Morrison and later his son, William Vitruvius. The Morrisons were essentially Classical architects although they could also dabble in Gothic. The latter, which first made its appearance in Ireland in the 1760s with the construction of houses such as Moore Abbey in Kildare, has been described as 'the architectural expression of the Romantic Movement'.[45] But it was really only after the Union that Gothic castles became extremely popular. A number of interesting theories have been put forward

43 See Joseph McDonnell, *Irish eighteenth-century stuccowork and its European sources* (Dublin, 1991).   44 Bence-Jones, *A guide to Irish country houses*, p. xvii.   45 Ibid., p. xviii.

as to why this became the case: some contend that as the architectural expression of the Romantic Movement, Gothic was considered more in keeping with the rugged Irish landscape; others that those who built Gothic castles from scratch or modified existing houses were giving an air of antiquity to their homes and their own family pedigree.[46] Owners taken by the style may even have been expressing their superiority over those around them. David Dickson writes of 'Big George' Kingston, son of the builder of Mitchelstown Castle, and one of the wealthiest landlords in Munster, that he was:

> A man of passionate extremes and deep insecurities, he was at home in the aristocratic world of Regency London and sought to transplant that world to Mitchelstown. In 1823, he set about rebuilding the castle on the scale of a royal palace and saw himself in almost feudal terms, heir of an ancient Geraldine lordship ensconced in his neo-Gothic extravaganza.[47]

But as Maurice Craig points out, whatever merit these theories have, the fact was: 'the romantic fashion for irregularity was now just hitting European architecture (having affected gardening a few generations earlier), so that, once again, if only for a moment, Ireland was bang up to date'.[48] The Gothic Charleville Forest in King's County was built from scratch; Markree in County Sligo was converted from a plain Georgian house as was Killua and Tullynally, both in County Westmeath; Duckett's Grove in County Carlow became a Gothic extravaganza. But in the decades in the lead up to the Famine, universal architectural uniformity remained hard to find: the period saw the construction of the Elizabethan-Revival Kilruddery in Wicklow, the Tudor-Gothic Camlin in Donegal, the Italianate Edermine in Wexford, while in Ulster, the more restrained Classical style, as in the Argory in Armagh, continued to dominate big house architecture, as in the rest of Ireland where the smaller houses 'continued to be unselfconsciously Classical.'[49]

The Great Famine marked something of a watershed in big house building. Construction, at least by families dependent almost exclusively on rental incomes, came more or less to an end. Some of the great houses built in its aftermath were owned by families that had made their fortunes outside agricultural rents – in brewing, linen manufacture, distilling and trade – and who wished to buy into the landed way of life in order to achieve social respectability and perhaps even political status. Thus, Arthur Guinness, Lord Ardilaun, built St Anne's and Farmleigh in Dublin and Ashford Castle along the Galway–Mayo border (as well as purchasing English homes); Andrew Mulholland, the linen magnate and father of the first Lord Dunleath, built Ballywalter Park in Down; while Mitchell Henry, a wealthy English merchant, built the magnificently situated Kylemore Abbey in Connemara.[50]

46 Ibid., p. xviii.   **47** Dickson, *Old world economy*, p. 493.   **48** Craig, *The architecture of Ireland*, p. 248   **49** Ibid.; for a study of the Argory see Olwen Purdue, *The MacGeough Bonds of The Argory: an Ulster gentry family, 1880–1950* (Dublin, 2005).   **50** John Ussher Sharkey, *St Anne's: the story of a Guinness estate* (Dublin, 2002); Kathleen Villiers-Tuthill, *History of Kylemore Castle*

The effects of the Great Famine on Irish big houses have yet to be researched in great detail but scores of houses belonging to bankrupted landlords appeared in the Encumbered Estates Rentals along with their estates.[51] What happened to most of these remains to be seen but their future was undoubtedly varied: Ballynahinch Castle in Galway, for example, built in the eighteenth century by Richard 'Humanity Dick' Martin, found new wealthy owners and continues to survive in the present day as a four star hotel; on the other hand, Palace Anne in Cork, a very distinguished early eighteenth-century red brick house, was abandoned in the mid-1850s and had become a ruin twenty years later.[52]

The mid to late Victorian period did witness the building of Ruskinian-Gothic houses such as the second Portumna Castle in Galway, the High-Victorian Gothic Knocktopher Abbey in Kilkenny, the severely Baronial Ashford Castle, the Tudor-Revival Killarney House in Kerry, and the enormous Elizabethan-Revival Dartrey Castle in Monaghan. Palmerston in Kildare was one of the very few examples of Queen Anne Revival style. Some of the architects who dominated this period included James Franklin Fuller and Charles Lanyon who practised out of Belfast along with his young partner, William Henry Lynn. English architects continued to work in Ireland: William White designed the imposing Victorian-Gothic Humewood in County Wicklow and Edwin William Godwin designed Dromore Castle in Limerick for the earl of Limerick. The latter is interesting, not only because it was 'the most archaeologically correct C19 Irish castle, rising from a wooded ridge above a lough' but perhaps more so because it was begun in 1867, the year of the Fenian Rising, and is said to have been deliberately designed with fortification in mind. Thus the *Building News* of the time reported: 'in the event of the country being disturbed, the inmates of Dromore Castle might not only feel secure themselves but be able to give real shelter to others'.[53] The castle was eventually dismantled in the 1950s when a new owner could not be found and rates were unaffordable. In 1988 Mark Bence-Jones wrote of it: 'The ruin remains; as solid as any of the old ruined castles of the Irish countryside, but larger and more spectacular than most of them.'[54]

Hardly surprisingly, given the nature of the socio-economic and political developments from the late 1870s,[55] the building of big houses in Ireland became a mere trickle. There are extremely few Edwardian country houses: Hollybrook in County Cork was built in 1903–4 and around the same time, Sir Edwin Lutyens remodeled Lambay Castle in Dublin and designed its surrounding landscape.

But while the building boom slowed down considerably in the post-famine period, it did not mean the end of big house embellishment. By the mid-nineteenth century big house building in Ireland had arguably come to its natural conclusion or perhaps the fact that so few houses were built from scratch by landlords is a strong indicator of the need for retrenchment learned from the famine. In general, landlords did not have the massive fortunes of their eighteenth-century ancestors to begin building projects from the foundation up but when they

and Abbey (Connemara, 2002).   **51** See chapter four.   **52** Bence-Jones, *A guide to Irish country houses*, pp xix, 230.   **53** Ibid., pp 110–11.   **54** Ibid., p. 112.   **55** See chapter one.

began to reap the rewards of an improved economy from the mid-1850s to the late-1870s they returned to embellishing their homes and remodeling them to suit changing tastes and fashions and, in some cases, to meet social expectations. Their magpie-like owners continued to scour the Continent during their grand tours, as their forefathers had done, seeking bargains from the palaces and great houses of the more impoverished continental aristocracy that would provide symbolic expressions of the lifestyle that they deemed appropriate to their class.[56] From 1851 to 1858 the duke of Devonshire spent an estimated £48,000 on the renovations at Lismore Castle.[57] In 1854 the earlier *porte cochere* at Kilkenny Castle was extended to become the front hall linking the two wings of the castle and a Moorish staircase was built adjoining the picture gallery that housed over 180 paintings. A year later, a single-storey two bay bow-ended wing was added to Clonbrock and the interior of the house redecorated. In 1861 Lord Clanricarde spent at least £12,000 on the rebuilding of Portumna after the old house had been gutted by fire.[58] In 1874 the building of a porch at Burnham in Kerry for Lord Ventry cost £1,200 while in 1880 additions to Tullyra in Galway cost £6,700.[59]

LANDSCAPE EMBELLISHMENT

By the second half of the eighteenth century, tastes in location were changing as rapidly as tastes in design. There was a preference for locating houses within demesnes characterized by 'hilly sites, distant vistas and rolling lawns; a view of water was now particularly esteemed'.[60] Demesnes are defined historically as 'the lands held by the manor for its own use and occupation'.[61] Their origin can be traced to the early medieval tenurial system when, as Terence Reeves-Smyth has pointed out: 'a proportion of the manorial lands were set aside "in demesne" to produce both goods and profits for the estate.'[62] Therefore, they assumed at an early stage importance as 'home farms' producing for the market and the big house. The first Ordnance Survey maps show that by the early nineteenth century, demesnes probably covered around 6 per cent of the country.[63] They ranged in size from a little over a hundred acres to upwards of around 1,500 acres. They usually included a home farm used to keep the big house self sufficient, a kitchen garden to service the family's needs, gardens and lawns for ornamentation and leisure purposes, woodland for the rearing of game, parkland for the grazing of cattle, and a wide variety of outoffices for the housing of animals and utilisation by demesne

56 The many auction catalogues which began to appear from the 1920s are excellent indicators of the extent and richness of Irish house contents; see, for example, Christies, *Powerscourt, Enniskerry, Co. Wicklow: catalogue of Old Masters pictures, French, English and Irish furniture, silver and a collection of arms and armour to be sold 24–5 September 1984.* **57** Proudfoot, 'Estate management in Waterford', p. 533. **58** Estimate of building costs of works carried out by B.T. Patterson, Builders, 1860–1933 (Irish Architectural Archive (IAA), B/09). **59** Dooley, *The decline of the big house*, pp 34–5. **60** Dickson, *Old world economy*, p. 97. **61** Reeves-Smyth, 'Demesnes', p. 197. **62** Ibid. **63** Ibid.

employees such as gardeners, masons and carpenters. The great demesnes were surrounded by high stone walls which ran for miles.

Occasionally landlords and architects had difficulty in compromising on the choice of location. Thus in 1824 Henry Westenra wrote of his disagreement with William Vitruvius Morrison regarding the proposed location of Rossmore Park in Monaghan:

> I have received Morrision's answer to my observations. He adheres rigidly to his own idea on the subject. I certainly cannot actually disapprove of his plans, but I do think he might have made them upon a better arrangement, to suit the situation and the aspect. He writes in a rage, I think at being found fault with, and huffily declares he finds it impossible for him to alter or amend his plan, and that it gives him more complete satisfaction than any he ever produced … [The location preferred by Westenra] is a very uncommon and a very beautiful place unlike every other. The house should therefore be constructed in an uncommon, but picturesque manner, unlike every other and in accordance with the place.[64]

There were many houses like Powerscourt and Westport which were exceptional in their locations, taking maximum advantage of dramatic natural scenery to become part of an integrated aesthetic experience. A further important element of this wholeness was the creation of gardens, and the ornamentation of demesnes and landscapes.[65] In the first three decades of the seventeenth century formal gardens had been extended and laid out to surround big houses with alleyways and hedges. More and more exotic plants were introduced. Fountains and statuary became almost obligatory, as did ponds and sometimes terracing. In 1639 the earl of Cork instructed his agent, Walley, to make the gardens at Lismore 'a paradise'.[66] By the latter part of the century, grandees, in particular, had the wealth to redesign the landscape around their homes into formal landscapes and gardens and so the late seventeenth century saw the laying out of many fine Baroque formal gardens at a time when as Edward Malins and the Knight of Glin have argued: 'landscaping became a social and economic necessity'.[67] Nearly contemporary with these were the formal gardens laid out in the Dutch manner, with clipped hedges and straight canals, such as those at Stillorgan in Dublin in 1695:

64 H.R. Westenra to Lord Rossmore, 26 Dec. 1824 (copy) (IAA, RPD 54.5).   **65** Malins & Bowe, *Irish gardens and demesnes from 1830*; also Mary Davies, 'Kilruddery Co. Wicklow: a timeless garden with a sense of peace' in *Irish Garden*, 1 (1) (1992), pp 8–10; idem, 'Belvedere House, Co. Westmeath' in *Irish Garden*, 1 (3) (1992), pp 8–10; Ann Golden, Belinda Jupp & Thomas McErlean, 'Recreating Kylemore – an exercise in garden archaeology' in *Irish Garden*, 9 (1) (2000), pp 40–43; Nigel Everett, 'The gardens of Bantry House, Co. Cork' in *Irish Garden*, 9 (2) (2000), pp 62–64; Horner, 'Carton, Co. Kildare: a case study of the making of an Irish demesne'.   **66** Crookshank, 'The visual arts, 1603–1740', p. 483; see Bowe, 'The Renaissance garden in Ireland'; Terence Reeves-Smyth, *Irish gardens and gardening before Cromwell* (Cork, 1999).   **67** Malins & Glin, *Lost demesnes*, p. 1.

The gardens abounded in straight avenues and alleys with curious edgings of box, carefully clipped yew trees, knots of flowers, topiary work and grassy slopes, and possibly there might have been, as there was in Bullein's nursery, the representation of a boar hunt or hare chase cut out in box. Three artificial fish ponds, laid out, like everything else, on strictly rectangular lines, lay to the south of the house.[68]

One of the best paintings of a late seventeenth-century garden in the French Baroque style is that of Carton *c.*1738 by Van der Hagen (plate 13). This oft produced work depicts a fairly typical grand, late seventeenth-century formal demesne with 'its Baroque geometry embraced *bosquets*, orchards, kitchen gardens, a bowling green and a canal, with plain grass *plats* bordered by topiary beneath the Palladian house windows. The front court was pierced with iron ballustrading to allow views down the crows-foot avenues of lime.'[69] Avenues had become ubiquitous by the 1730s. Almost all houses had at least one tree-lined approach (often lime but sometimes elm and chestnut) and, as at Carton, the grander houses frequently had an intricate web of avenues stretching for miles from the demesne wall and gate lodge to the house. (The most complete late seventeenth-, early eighteenth-century garden to have remained intact is the earl of Meath's gardens at Kilruddery in Bray, County Wicklow.)

By the mid-eighteenth century, there was something of a rebellion in taste against the rigidity of the formal garden and a move towards the concept of a more natural landscape.[70] As Anne Crookshank put it:

… ordered informality superseded the rigidity of the enclosed formal garden. The vistas of pleached alleyways gave way to panoramic views of great areas of park which merged gently into the countryside and which incorporated such natural or created features as waterfalls, curling streams or lakes. The ha-ha [a sunken ditch] with its ability to preserve the immediate surroundings of the house from being sullied by farm animals without any obvious fencing to create a visible break, became a common device. The use of statuary continued, as the park usually included architectural features such as temples, obelisks, or hermitages, created partly as necessary accents in the planned wildness and partly as romantic reminders of antiquity. Flowers were banished to the walled gardens, set at some distance from the house.[71]

Finola O'Kane's study of the Carton landscape illustrates how it was opened up in this way to give it a more natural look. James FitzGerald, first duke of Leinster and his wife, Emily, were largely instrumental in planning the redesign of the parkland, ably assisted by gardening experts such as Philip Collinson and Charles

68 F.E. Ball, *The history of the county of Dublin* (6 vols, Dublin, 1902), i, 122; quoted in Malins & Glin, *Lost demesnes*, p. 8. **69** Reeves-Smyth, 'Demesnes', p. 199. **70** Malins & Glin, *Lost demesnes*, p. 31; see also Reeves-Smyth, 'Demesnes', p. 201. **71** Crookshank, 'The visual arts, 1740–1850', pp 509–10.

Hamilton. Their initial ambition to design a landscape comparable to some they had admired in England and elsewhere soon gave way to their own designs.[72] The formal gardens and avenues evident in the Van der Hagen painting were swept away, the flower gardens were banished to walled gardens at a distance from the house and replaced with an idealized conception of natural landscapes. By 1747 Emily was delighted that the avenue trees had been cut down and 'a very fine lawn' laid out before the house which she thought was: 'the greatest beauty a place can have'. More land was acquired so that the demesne was expanded to five times its original size. This expansion took in the required undulating ground, water and valleys to be found south of Carton. Land was acquired to the south-east so that the demesne could be connected to the developing town of Maynooth. A connecting avenue of lime trees terminated at the old Geraldine 'council house', originally part of the FitzGerald's medieval castle complex and stone piers and gates were erected at the entrance to the town and at the opposite end of the lime avenue guarding the demesne. The Dublin entrance to the demesne was the one used by the family, aristocratic friends, relatives and other important guests. Its meandering route offered vistas, carefully framed by clusters of trees, of the Ryewater, Waterstone Cottage, the Prospect (or Tyrconnell) Tower, the south-western lawns and the house itself. The Ryewater was widened and a lake feature was constructed. In December 1762 Emily wrote to her husband: 'New river is beautiful. One turn of it is a masterpiece in the art of laying out, and I defy Kent, Brown or Mr Hamilton to excel it: this without flattery'. And to emphasize the role she and her husband had played in this design, she continued:

> And now that you may not be too vain, the shape of the island in its present state is not pretty: whether its rising so much above the water be the cause of it or not I can't tell, but it wants that grace and easy pretty turn. The end is extremely well hid at present, and when the banks are dressed and green it will be altogether a lovely thing.[73]

These were just some of the changes undertaken on one demesne to ensure that the vista from the big house was now of wide, open expanses of parkland and copses of trees. Patricia Friel's *Frederick Trench (1746–1836) and Heywood, Queen's County: the creation of a Romantic demesne* (Dublin, 2000) provides an illuminating insight to how the creation of the Heywood landscape was determined by the life experiences of Frederick Trench. His education and exposure to the cultural and intellectual fashions of the day led him to move hills, dam rivers and create the lakes necessary to mould his romantic landscape.[74]

---

72 These changes are described in O'Kane, *Landscape design*, pp 89–130.   73 Lady Emily FitzGerald to Marquis of Kildare, 10 Dec. 1762 in *The correspondence of Emily, duchess of Leinster (1731–1814)*, ed. Brian Fitzgerald (3 vols, Dublin, 1949–57), i, 150.   74 See also J.A. Ryan, 'The garden at Heywood, Ballinakill, Co. Laois' in *Irish Arts Review Yearbook* (1991–92), pp 95–8.

As with most other aspects of big house life, the Great Famine had a negative impact on gardening and landscape design. Depreciated incomes meant less to invest. In the years after the famine, it was really only the better-off landlords who developed landscapes. But some changes did take place: formal parterres were reintroduced around many houses, sometimes with balustraded terracing and rose-gardens and rock gardens were developed.[75] From the 1880s, further economic cutbacks affected gardens as well as houses. It was at this stage that the famous Irish horticulturist, William Robinson, advocated the concept of the 'wild' garden, that is the planting of 'perfectly hardy exotics under conditions where they will grow without further care', which subsequently became very popular in Ireland leading, for example, to the creation of rhododendron gardens.[76] The passing of the 1923 Land Act, which empowered the Irish Land Commission to acquire compulsorily untenanted estates and demesnes, was hugely detrimental to the eighteenth- and nineteenth-century gardens and landscapes. However, there are a few which have survived intact, some in private ownership such as Abbey Leix in County Laois and others, including Heywood in the same county, under the care of the Office of Public Works.

THE DECLINE AND FALL OF THE BIG HOUSE IN IRELAND[77]

The eighteenth and early nineteenth centuries had witnessed the heyday of the Irish big house. Great houses such as Carton, Kilkenny Castle, Castletown and Powerscourt were in many ways purposely built to meet the requirements of housing great collections of paintings and portraits by artists such as Carravagio, Van der Hayden, Breughel, Gainsborough, Holbein, Van Dyck, Rubens Gainsborough and so on, books and curios bought on the Continent during the grand tour, or Irish furniture and silver.[78] Collections of family portraits to which landed families attached great importance and displayed openly to their social equals symbolized the importance attached to preserving the family lineage. Huge libraries were created by house owners as an expression of what they held important and essential to maintaining a certain standard of life, and to project an image that their owners were aware of what was fashionable reading at the time of purchase or essential reading at any time.[79] Opulent reception rooms such as the gold saloon at Carton and grand dining-rooms formed the showpieces of grandeur aimed at impressing guests. In the same way that land was entailed to keep estates intact, heirlooms were settled to prevent them being sold off and so as J.P. Neale wrote in 1820: 'The mansions of our nobility and gentry, completed at a vast expense, and manifesting

75 Reeves-Smyth, 'Demesnes', p. 203. **76** Ibid., p. 205. **77** Much of what follows in this section is drawn from Dooley, *The decline of the big house*. **78** For the example of Sir John Leslie, see Seymour Leslie, *Of Glaslough in the kingdom of Oriel and of the noted men who have dwelt there* (privately published, 1913). **79** Shane Leslie, *The Irish tangle for English readers* (London, 1946), p. 138.

a corresponding magnificence of appearance, are many of them the depositories of the choicest specimens of art in the collections of pictures or galleries of sculpture.'

Servants, perhaps more than anything else, were the outward symbols of the luxurious and leisured lifestyles led by Irish landlords, their families and, of course, their guests. They were an integral part of the values and style of living that characterized big house life. In the same way that landlords were acutely conscious of standards in the way that they built up art collections and libraries during the nineteenth century, they were conscious of the standards of servants. The guests they invited to their homes were used to moving in high social milieus, where the quality and number of servants indicated the status level of a home. For that reason professionally trained servants and particularly ones born in England were widely employed in Irish houses.[80]

Large-scale investment in big house building, their subsequent running on an annual basis, later improvements and embellishments and the creation of gardens and demesne landscapes were more often than not underpinned by heavy borrowing. L.M. Cullen has made the important point that the study of the problem of landlord indebtedness in the eighteenth century 'may not be to attempt to delineate a progressive process of indebtedness over time but to discern the contrasting fortunes and reasons for them to families at any one point in time'.[81] David Large was one of the very few historians to look at landlord wealth in the eighteenth century and although his contribution throws up as many questions as it provides answers, one of his main contentions that indebtedness was a serious matter for many landowning families by 1815 seems very valid.[82] There were houses such as the once magnificent Castlelyons in Cork which did not even survive the eighteenth century. Having been accidentally burned in 1771, the family's declining financial position meant it was never rebuilt.[83]

Debts accumulated over successive generations could break even the most powerful families. In the eighteenth century the FitzGerald estate centred on Carton was around 70,000 acres in size. An impressive and rising rent roll in the eighteenth century sustained the building, running and renovations that took place at Carton and on the demesne from the late 1730s until around the Great Famine. But while the gross rental was impressive, so obviously was the expenditure which went hand in hand with running a great house, maintaining two Dublin houses (Kildare House, later Leinster House, now the seat of Dáil Éireann, and Frascati in Blackrock) and a London house and generally living the extravagant lifestyle of Ireland's premier peer. In the eighteenth century the most damaging expenses were the exorbitant family charges faced by successive dukes. James FitzGerald, first duke of Leinster and his wife, had nineteen children (ten of whom survived to majority) and so in 1766 the duke confessed to his wife that expenditure on Carton was 'a folly considering the number of children we have'.[84] When William FitzGerald

---

80 Dooley, *The decline of the big house*, pp 146–70.   **81** Cullen, 'Economic development, 1750–1800', pp 179–80.   **82** Large, 'The wealth of the greater Irish landowners', p. 44. **83** Dickson, *Old world economy*, p. 79.   **84** A.P.W. Malcomson, *The pursuit of an heiress:*

succeeded his father as second duke of Leinster, he also inherited massive debts of almost £150,000. Mortgages used for the redevelopment of Carton were just one element compounded by the extremely onerous family charges resultant from the number of his own siblings and the jointure payable to his mother who was to outlive him by ten years and so continue to be a financial burden on the next generation as well. The duke had to provide portions of £10,000 to each of his three sisters who married. His brothers, including Lord Edward FitzGerald, were endowed with outlying portions of the estate and possibly also with cash. These financial arrangements would probably have bankrupted the Leinster estate at this time were it not for the second duke's astute marriage to the only child of Lord St George of Headford Castle in Galway in 1774. The sale of her inheritances raised £60,000 which went some way to reducing his capital debt but the long-term damage had been done and the Leinster estate was to be the first of the great estates to be broken up under the 1903 Wyndham Land Act.

Having somewhat recovered from the effects of the Great Famine, the agricultural depression and agitation of the late 1870s and 1880s[85] were to have grave consequences not only for the social and, indeed, political power of Irish landlords, but, of course, also for their economic power and ultimately for their big houses. The consequences of rental decline resultant from rent strikes, the enforced or voluntary granting of abatements and the fair rent fixing terms of the 1881 Land Act had a dramatic effect on big house expenditure. Big houses were ruinously expensive to maintain and the amounts spent on their annual upkeep could often mean the difference between profit and loss on an estate from the 1880s. When this became the case, cutbacks became the order of the day: servants were released, town property was sold, in some cases the big house was temporarily closed down or rented out to wealthy Americans, as in the case of the earl of Fingall's Killeen Castle in Meath in the late 1880s and early 1890s.[86] Similarly, Fingall's county neighbours, the Taylours, closed Headfort between 1904 and 1908 and retrenched to rented accommodation in Hampshire.[87]

As of yet, houses were not sold. For landlords they still symbolized their social standing in a local community and they would have been reluctant to diminish this perception. At any rate, buyers were not readily available. Instead there began the sale of big house contents. Of great importance in this respect was the introduction of the Settled Land Act in 1882 which for the first time allowed owners or trustees to break the entail in order to sell house contents (or outlying landed property.) There was a lively market, particularly in America, for paintings, rare books, Irish silver and furniture, assets that had been unaffected by agricultural depression. Few Irish houses of note did not have a Reynolds, Romney, Van Dyck, Rembrandt or Rubens any of which could fetch significant five-figure sums, particularly from eager American plutocrats.[88] The sale of a few paintings here and there or a library

aristocrtatic marriage in Ireland, 1750–1820 (Belfast, 1982), p. 4. **85** See chapter one. **86** Fingall, *Seventy years young*, pp 116–17, 186; Dooley, *The decline of the big house*, pp 79–111. **87** Dooley, *The decline of the big house*, p. 108. **88** Littlejohn, *The fate of the English country*

of books was not as noticeable as a country house.[89] While most sold to pay their debts, there were cases of landlords such as Lord Powerscourt who sold paintings in the 1880s in order to fund the building of west-wing bedrooms at his home.[90] But the likes of Powerscourt was an exception. Above all else, and with very few exceptions, most owners sold to survive and the remodeling or modification of houses that had taken place at various stages during the previous two centuries or more all but came to an end by the early1880s.

Arguably the economic windfall of the Wyndham Land Act in 1903 offered a chance of respite and most landlords who sold in the early years enjoyed at least a temporary affluence. Big house social life retained much of its former grandeur up to the war years [91] Servants remained plentiful (as is exemplified in the household schedule returns of the 1911 census), an outward expression of the desire of landlords to cling on to certain aspects of the old way of life. While big houses, stripped of their landed estates, may have become something of an anachronism, they were still affordable as long as investments paid regular dividends and farming remained viable for those who retained extensive demesne farms.[92] Professional financial advisors such as Sir Ernest Cassels created investment portfolios made up of 'the most fanciful stocks and shares'.[93] As a result many families (temporarily) turned a new economic corner as worldwide investments in stocks and shares proved initially lucrative.[94]

The case of the Clonbrock estate is again instructive.[95] Having sold his estates by 1915 for £250,000, Luke Gerald Dillon had most of this capital to invest. His share portfolio was very much a global one with investments in South America, the USA, Canada, Australia, New Zealand and so on but he invested only around £2,000 in Ireland in Great Northern Railway preference stock.[96] No longer having expenses such as quit rents, head rents, estate improvements and a variety of other charges to meet, Clonbrock found himself at least as well off as when he had been dependent upon rental income, in fact probably considerably better off if the increased expenditure on the maintenance of the big house after 1915 is anything to go by.[97] However, from the late 1920s everything changed dramatically because the crash in stocks and shares (allied to the massive death duties incurred at Clonbrock's death and the agricultural depression in Ireland which decimated farming income) wiped out almost the entire family fortune. In 1930, the year after the Wall Street Crash, house expenditure dropped from almost £700 the previous

house.   **89** Valuation of diamonds and jewellery for His Grace, the Duke of Leinster, 1883 (PRONI, Leinster papers, D3078/2/10/2); *Catalogue of pictures, plate, antiquities etc. at Carton, Kilkea Castle, 13 Dominick St. Dublin and 6 Carlton House Terrace, London* (Dublin, n.d.). **90** M. Wingfield, *A description and history of Powerscourt* (London, 1903), p. 74.   **91** For changes in social life post-World War I see Shane Leslie, *The film of memory* (London, 1938), pp 110–19; Seymour Leslie, *The Jerome connexion* (London, 1964), pp 34–6, 58.   **92** Dooley, *The decline of the big house*, pp 112–45.   **93** For the case of the Leslie family of Glaslough see Leslie, *The Jerome connexion*, p. 36.   **94** Dunraven, *Crisis in Ireland*, p. 21.   **95** See also chapter one.   **96** Dooley, *The decline of the big house*, p. 117.   **97** Ibid., pp 120–1.

year to £270, estate expenditure dropped from £6,000 to £4,900 and while over £300 was paid in house salaries in 1929, nothing was paid in 1930. From that year onwards, house and estate went into irreversible decline.

It was a situation that became all too familiar in many big house communities in Ireland after 1918. Economically many landlords floundered on the rocks of agricultural depression in the post-war decades and the simultaneous attempts by an independent Irish government to acquire compulsorily their remaining estates.[98] The Taylours, for example, who had vacated Headfort in the 1890s managed to return in 1908 and lived there quite comfortably until ravaged by the great depression of the 1930s. While they spent an average of around £2,000 per annum on the upkeep of the house throughout the 1920s, the depreciation of investments meant this expenditure was cut to under £300 by the late 1930s. The running of the house simply became unaffordable and so it was leased to a preparatory school.[99] In the end it seems that nothing was as necessary for the upkeep of big houses in Ireland as the regular rental income that had sustained them for generations.

The revolutionary period realized the fears of Irish landlords which had been growing since the land war began some forty years previously. During these years, but particularly from 1920 to 1923, landlords, largely because of their socio-political, economic, cultural and religious backgrounds, were to suffer outrage and intimidation on a scale the like of which their class had not experienced in living memory, not even at the height of the land war of the 1880s.[1] A major feature of this intimidation was the burning of big houses.

During the War of Independence from January 1920 to the calling of the Anglo-Irish Truce in July 1921, an estimated seventy-six big houses were burned in the twenty-six county area of the present Irish Republic, predominantly in counties most affected by violence, especially Cork where twenty-six were burned. In the Civil War which followed, an estimated 199 houses were burned between January 1922 and April 1923, again predominantly in the Munster region. The complexity of reasons behind these burnings has been elucidated by this author elsewhere.[2] Suffice to say here that during both wars, the breakdown of law and order, the abandonment by the RIC of outlying rural barracks during the War of Independence, and the absence of an effective law enforcement body for much of the Civil War created the conditions to allow the IRA or local agrarian agitators

---

98 See chapter one.   **99** Dooley, *The decline of the big house*, p. 144.   **1** See R.B. McDowell, *Crisis and decline: the fate of southern Unionists* (Dublin, 1997); also Patrick Buckland, *Irish Unionism I: the Anglo-Irish and the new Ireland, 1885–1922* (Dublin, 1972); idem, *Irish unionism, 1885–1923: a documentary history*; Terence Dooley, 'Monaghan Protestants in a time of crisis, 1919–22' in Comerford et al. (eds), *Religion, conflict and coexistence in Ireland*, pp 235–51; Peter Hart, 'The Protestant experience of revolution in modern Ireland' in Richard English & Graham Walker (eds), *Unionism in modern Ireland: new perspectives on politics and culture* (Dublin, 1996), pp 81–98; Alvin Jackson, *Col. Edward Saunderson: land and loyalty in Victorian Ireland* (Oxford, 1995).   **2** For the burning of big houses in Ireland see Dooley, *The decline of the big house*, pp 171–207; also Peter Martin, 'Unionism: the Irish nobility and revolution, 1919–23' in Augusteijn (ed.), *The Irish revolution, 1913–1923*, pp 151–67.

(often one and the same) to attack houses for a variety of reasons: because they were to be used by the British military forces as substitute barracks (or by either side of the IRA during the Civil War); as a reprisal for the burning of homes of IRA or Sinn Féin supporters in a locality; for agrarian purposes of forcing a landlord to leave an area and therefore free his untenanted lands for redistribution amongst the local people; or simply as a diversion for groups of idle young men.

To replace big houses, their contents or often both required large-scale funding. In the vast majority of cases, big house owners were unable to claim on their insurance policies as they did not cover riot and civil commotion. They were, therefore, dependent on what compensation became available to them from the British and/or Irish Free State governments under the terms of the 1898 Local Government (Ireland) Act, the Criminal Injuries (Ireland) Acts of 1919 and 1920 or the Damage to Property (Compensation) Act of 1923.[3] In almost all cases, the compensation paid to owners was not enough to allow them to rebuild their houses in their former splendour. Some houses such as Kilboy in Tipperary and Springfield Castle in Limerick were rebuilt on a much smaller scale, the latter using only the nineteenth-century Gothic wing.[4] Others built smaller houses elsewhere in Ireland, particularly in south County Dublin or north Wicklow, away from their original estates where they felt they would be safer. Other owners did not rebuild at all either because their awards were too small to allow them to do so, or because they were reluctant to come back to live in Ireland. Instead, they took whatever compensation they could negotiate and moved permanently to England and thus once great houses such as Summerhill in Meath were left to disappear completely from the landscape.

After the so-called Troubles of the early 1920s, the old landed class became psychologically more insular than ever before. Their political connections to Britain were severed and the British army officer class had departed Ireland by 1922. Most found it difficult to sever their old emotional ties and they therefore found themselves in a state of limbo, floating between Britain and Ireland but belonging to neither. For the big houses that remained with their original owners, much had changed by the 1930s. Lavish dinners, balls and hunting parties had become a thing of the past. Servant numbers declined rapidly in the years after 1918: wage rates rose beyond most owners' affordability; middle-class employers required more workers and were prepared to pay them more and provide them with more leisure time; better education eventually became the nemesis of deference. The legal and professional classes had by now begun to regenerate themselves, severing the social links between that stratum and the old landed class that had existed in the past.

On an economic front, rising income tax levels hit big house owners disproportionately and reflected the Free State government's desire to capitalize on the wealth of the landed class (the situation was very much the same in Britain.) Death duties rose dramatically and the consistently high levels of property taxes (rates) all

3 Dooley, *The decline of the big house*, pp 197–207.   **4** Lord Dunalley, *Khaki and green* (London, 1940), p. 248.

contributed to the sale, dismantling (a roofless house was rates free) and abandonment of Irish big houses from the 1920s. Before 1935, Battersby and Sons alone had sold at least sixty big houses in Ireland including Bishopscourt and Killashee in Kildare, Kylemore Abbey in Galway and Ravensdale in Louth.[5] The sale of houses continued relentlessly up to the 1980s so that today only a small percentage of the big houses that survive, probably in the region of 10–15 per cent, do so in the ownership of the original families. In the main, they were sold because people could no longer afford to live in them. While some purchased houses remained in private ownership others were put to a variety of new uses as hotels, hospitals, schools, agricultural research centers, government offices, factories and more recently country clubs. Others were demolished after unsympathetic government departments purchased them along with their lands. These included Burton Hall in Carlow, sold to the Land Commission in 1927, and Coole Park in Galway, sold to the Department of Lands in the same year. In the 1950s it became fashionable to demolish houses such as Dunsandle in Galway, Courtown in Wexford, and Mote Park and Frenchpark in Roscommon because of the shortage of materials in postwar Ireland. And many more such as Dalyston in Galway, Derrycarne in Leitrim and Hollymount in Mayo were not sold at all but simply abandoned by their owners.[6] Concurrently, the sale of big house contents grew at an unprecedented rate from around 1918. Heirlooms and works of art were no longer sold to provide extra finances to maintain a leisured lifestyle, they were sold in order to help their owners survive. Huge quantities of Irish silver and furniture, important art collections and the contents of libraries were dispersed throughout the world.

The more modest houses of the lesser gentry had a better chance of survival, becoming in many cases the homes of large farmers. They also had the distinct advantage of remaining fashionable, being small enough to allow the family owners to maintain them in a servantless world, and being much more economically friendly when it came to such practical developments as the installation of electricity or central heating.

After independence, Free State/Irish Republic governments were slow to show any type of sympathy or concern for the plight of big houses. There was little appreciation in government circles for their cultural heritage value. When, in February 1944, Sean Flanagan TD asked Sean Moylan, Minister for Lands, if he would hand over the country houses situated on Land Commission-divided estate lands, instead of allowing them to fall into decay or be demolished, the minister replied:

> Residences on lands acquired by the Land Commission for division which are not suitable for disposal to allottees may be demolished in order to provide material for building smaller houses for allottees or may be sold by public auction, at which it is open for such bodies as the deputy mentions to bid for them.[7]

---

5 Dooley, *The decline of the big house*, p. 141. **6** See Simon Marsden, *In ruins: the once great houses of Ireland* (Boston & London, 1997). **7** *Dáil debates*, vol. 92, 23 Feb. 1944, 1518.

Around the same time in the 1940s, abandoned and disused mansions were considered only in terms of how they might be used as hospitals in a bid to eradicate the tuberculosis health crisis in Ireland and at another stage how they might be used for the advantage of such organizations as An Óige, the Irish Tourist Board or the Youth Training Body.[8] Towards the end of October 1943, the cabinet decided that the Department of Local Government and Public Health should carry out a survey of 'disused country mansions' and 'examine the question of their utilisation in consultation with any other Dep[artment]s concerned'.[9] County managers were circularized to provide a list of disused mansions in each county prior to their survey by housing inspectors.[10] Copies of these reports were forwarded to the Department of Defence, Department of Industry and Commerce, the Irish Land Commission and the Office of Public Works. By then, the Irish army had been in occupation of a number of derelict big houses such as Carton, using them as temporary barracks, during the Emergency. In 1944 the Department of Defence responded to the government survey reporting that 'the experience gained by the use of such buildings for the accommodation of troops during the Emergency indicates that they are quite unsuitable for military purposes, and accordingly the Dep[artmen]t is not interested in their future use'.[11] The OPW stated that it was 'very unlikely that any of the premises could be economically used for services for which accommodation is normally provided by that Dep[artmen]t.' The Irish Tourist Board felt that 'many of the houses are only suitable for demolition and salvage' and they expressed interest only in whether the 'salvaged materials might render it possible for them to proceed with the construction of holiday camps'. Interestingly, only a few months before, in July 1944, when the *Irish Press* ran a leading article on the possibilities of converting derelict country houses into youth hostels,[12] the leaders of An Óige and the Irish Tourist Association 'warmly commended' the article. Shortly before, An Óige, founded in 1931, had purchased Aughavannagh House in Wicklow, a former residence of both Charles Stewart Parnell and John Redmond, for just £350.[13] The secretary of An Óige thought more houses might also be used for adult holiday homes (providing they were located in 'holiday districts') as there were 'more than half a million factory workers here [in Ireland] for whom cheap holiday accommodation was needed'.[14]

Finally, the Minister for Local Government and Public Health concluded that

> the result of the survey to provide buildings suitable for conversion into hospitals for sanitoria has been very disappointing. The no. of houses found

8 My thanks to Irene Furlong for bringing this information to my attention.   **9** P. Ó Cinneide to secretary of Minister for Local Government and Public Health, 30 Oct. 1943 (NAI, Dept. of the Taoiseach files, S13344A).   **10** Secretary of Minister for Local Government and Public Health to P. Ó Cinneide, 25 May 1944 (NAI, Dept. of the Taoiseach files, S13344A).   **11** Letter from Minister for Local Government and Public Health to secretary of Department of the Taoiseach, 30 Nov. 1944 (NAI, Dept. of the Taoiseach files, S13344A).   **12** *Irish Press*, 15 July 1944.   **13** Ibid., 19 July 1944.   **14** Ibid.

suitable is very small. Most of the houses were built when requirements in regard to sanitation and hygiene were not what are required now. Many of them are without a water supply and a great no. of them without even proper sanitation.[15]

Other commentators, a very small minority, it should be added, were less convinced. In September 1944 Gertrude Gaffney wrote in the *Irish Independent* that big houses should be considered as convalescent homes. Referring to two mansions about to be demolished, she pointed out: 'One of them seems to be in perfect order and the other boasts splendid dance floors. Surely a dance floor is just what is needed to accommodate a row of hospital beds'. She contended that 'such mansions present so many possibilities for the recreation and the welfare of the people that their destruction should be stopped without delay'.[16] Letters appeared from others in the *Irish Times* to the same effect.[17]

It seems, therefore, that government bodies were extremely wary of taking over big houses, probably as much for economic reasons as political ones. The Department of Local Government and Public Health effectively ended the speculation by concluding that the survey showed only: '5 (provisional no.) suitable for tourist accommodation; 325 unsuitable for any public purpose'.[18] In the end only a handful of big houses passed into government hands at this time to be used as agricultural training centres (such as Johnstown Castle in County Wexford and Ballyhaise in County Cavan) or, like Muckross in County Kerry, to lie vacant for many years before its tourism potential was exploited.[19]

As Irene Furlong's work has shown, the integration of tourism and culture in independent Ireland demonstrated little signs that the future preservation of big houses would be a priority. The contrasting fate of a number of houses in the post-independence decades illustrated the narrow definition of Irish heritage that prevailed. In 1932 Arthur Vincent, a wealthy American, gifted Muckross House in County Kerry and 10,000 acres of Ireland's most scenic parkland to the state. Vincent's self-proclaimed vision was: 'to see not only the youth of Ireland, but young people from all parts of the world, come to Muckross. I want it to be a playground for youth.'[20] It lay vacant for almost a decade when in 1940, during the Emergency, it was one of the houses occupied by the Irish army. Only the locals seemed concerned. Killarney Urban District Council passed a resolution on 15 October 1940:

15 Letter from Minister for Local Government and Public Health to secretary of Department of the Taoiseach, 30 Nov. 1944 (NAI, Dept. of the Taoiseach files, S13344A). **16** *Irish Independent*, 1 Sept. 1944. **17** Ibid. **18** Report by Department of Local Government and Public Health, 'Utilization of disused country mansions', 17 May 1945 (NAI, Dept. of the Taoiseach files, S13344A). **19** Dooley, *The decline of the big house*, p. 253. **20** Quoted in *Irish Times*, 29 June 1954.

It seems to us incredible, and certainly a slight to the donor, that the government would consent to allow this beautiful national park and residence to be converted to any such use ... their preservation and maintenance is of very special and vital importance to the people of Killarney and the tourist industry.[21]

After the Emergency it continued to lie idle and then in 1950 the secretary of the Killarney Tourist Association, acting upon a resolution passed by the town's urban district council wrote to the government suggesting that the house should be used as a summer retreat for the president of Ireland.[22] Nothing came of this either. Four years later, it was reported that the Kerry County Committee of Agriculture were to have talks with the Minister for Agriculture about the prospects of using Muckross as an agricultural training college. The *Irish Times* was despondent about the house's future: 'Muckross House remains a silent and lonely sentinel on the shore of the Middle lake. As successive governments have failed to find a use for it, it seems it will eventually fall into decay.'[23] It was not until the 1960s that the government finally decided to open the house to the public.

In the summer of 1942, Coole Park, the ancestral home of Augusta Lady Gregory, one of the founding members of the Abbey Theatre, was razed to the ground, fifteen years after it had been sold to the Forestry Section of the Department of Agriculture and eleven years after her death in 1931. There was no debate on the issue in the Dáil. In December 1947 reports appeared that Edgeworthstown in County Longford was to be demolished because of its decaying state. A writer in the *Irish Press* wrote:

A day or two ago I passed the house where Maria Edgeworth lived most of her long life ... We are told that it is to be pulled down, which seems a great pity. There were good Edgeworths and bad Edgeworths, but for the sake of the little lady who was Ireland's first great novelist and who loved the Irish people, that house of many memories should be preserved.[24]

In between, around the beginning of the Emergency, Avondale, the County Wicklow home of Irish nationalist leader, Charles Stewart Parnell (a Protestant landlord) was turned into a museum. It was approaching the fiftieth anniversary of his death in 1891. Irene Furlong has concluded:

The moral climate obtaining in Ireland in the 1930s and 1940s was such that literary works and their authors were fair game, and the physical legacy of an ascendancy figure such as Gregory was not regarded as a desirable part of the

21 Quoted in Irene Furlong, 'State promotion of tourism in independent Ireland 1925–55' (unpublished Ph.D. thesis, NUIM 2002), p. 332. **22** Secretary of Killarney Tourist Association to the Taoiseach, 17 May 1950 (NAI, Dept. of the Taoiseach files, S6355). **23** *Irish Times*, 29 June 1954. **24** *Irish Press*, 4 Jan. 1948; quoted in Furlong, 'Tourism', p. 333.

cultural heritage of the nation. On the other hand, the political fervour of the 'soldiers of destiny' easily enabled the establishment of a museum to honour the 'Great Chief' at a time when Ireland's neutral stance required the bolstering of its isolated psyche by nationalist memorials.[25]

It was not until the 1950s that the efforts of a small lobby group of aesthetes (most notably Desmond Guinness and his late first wife, Mariga, and later Desmond FitzGerald, Knight of Glin and Professor Kevin B. Nowlan) brought the plight of big houses to the public attention. Through the work of the Irish Georgian Society, these individuals and others sought to preserve big houses as part of the Irish national heritage. They continued to face a number of major obstacles. For example, the repercussions of the harsh tax regimes of successive Irish governments was epitomized in the forced sale of Malahide Castle in the mid-1970s. The house and its contents were offered to the state in lieu of the Talbot de Malahide family's tax liability but the government of the time was not farsighted enough to accept one of the most distinguished of all Irish castles. It and its contents were sold and most of the latter was dispersed throughout the world (with the exception of the portrait collection which remains in the National Gallery of Ireland), representing, from the perspective of the built heritage, perhaps the most deplorable consequence of the tax legislation of the pre-1980s period. Moreover, there remained a marked dichotomy in Irish society between the minority who viewed historic houses as the creations of master architects and craftsmen, cultural artefacts worth preserving for future generations, and the majority who would quite gladly have seen them razed to the ground either because they were completely apathetic to big houses or else they perceived them to be symbols of hundreds of years of colonial oppression at the hands of usurping landlords who shared none of the cultural, religious or political beliefs of the native population. Given these difficulties, the praiseworthy efforts of these individuals, the Irish Georgian Society, An Taisce (The National Trust for Ireland founded in 1948) and public bodies such as the Office of Public Works and Dublin and Fingal County Councils to preserve houses such as Kilkenny Castle, Emo Court, Malahide, Newbridge and Ardgillan are all the more commendable.

CONCLUSION

In 1941, in an essay entitled 'The big house', Elizabeth Bowen wrote the following:

> The big house has much to learn – and it must learn if it is to survive at all. But it also has much to give. The young people who are taking on these big houses, who accept the burden and continue the struggle are not content,

---

25 Furlong, 'Tourism', p. 329.

now, to live for themselves only; they will not be content, either, to live 'just for the house'. The young cannot afford to be stupid – they expect the houses they keep alive to inherit, in a changed world and under changed conditions, the good life for which they were first built. The good in the new can add to, not destroy, the good in the old. From inside many big houses (and these will be the survivors) barriers are being impatiently attacked. But it must be seen that a barrier has two sides.[26]

Arguably, it was not until the mid-1980s that barriers began to come tumbling down (as, indeed, they did throughout Europe) and since then there has been a noticeable change in government and public attitudes towards big houses. In 2002, one owner summarized the gradual change as follows:

> I've lived through public desire to pull the place down, through indifference, through reluctant acceptance that it should stand, to a desire to preserve it, and now at last we are seeing an acceptance that it really is important Irish workmanship.[27]

In September 2004 An Taoiseach, Mr Bertie Ahern TD, speaking at the opening of the Third Annual Historic Houses of Ireland Conference at the National University of Ireland, Maynooth, told the audience:

> For too long the historic house was not seen by many as part of a shared Irish heritage – nor indeed was it viewed as a heritage worth preserving. Fortunately, times and opinions have changed radically since then. The Irish big house is increasingly valued today for its architectural significance; for the wealth of design created for the most part by Irish craftspeople; and for the valuable insight it offers us into an era that has had such an influence on shaping our history.[28]

In this relatively recent public adoption of historic houses as an important part of the Irish inheritance, changing political and cultural attitudes have undoubtedly gone hand in hand with advances in education and scholarship. The latter are epitomized, for example, by the establishment in September 2004 of the Centre for the Study of Historic Irish Houses and Estates at the History Department at the National University of Ireland, Maynooth, with public and private funding.[29] The primary objectives of the CSHIHE are to secure and enhance public appreciation of historic properties in the coming years by education, research, and scholarly

26 Bowen, 'The big house' in Lee (ed.), *The mulberry tree*, p. 30.   **27** Andrew Kavanagh, owner of Borris House, Co. Carlow, in conversation with this author, 27 May 2002.   **28** For the full text of the Taoiseach's address, see www.taoiseach.gov.ie/index.asp?docID=2145. **29** See www.historicirishhouses.ie; for inadequacies in the education system that remain to be addressed see Alan Kirwan, 'The Republic of Ireland' in Giles Waterfield (ed.), *Opening doors: learning in the historic environment* (Hampton, Middlesex, 2004), p. 139.

publication.[30] The purpose of this research guide is not just to contribute to that process of education by providing information on sources that are available (chapter four) but perhaps more importantly to stimulate others to explore new areas of big house studies (chapter five) that may further encourage the dismantling of the barriers in people's minds.

Positive initiatives have also been influenced by wider European and world developments; for example, the UNESCO Convention concerning the protection of the World Cultural and Natural Heritage, drawn up in 1972 and ratified by Ireland in 1991, recognized that it was/is the duty of the state to preserve, conserve and transmit this heritage to future generations. In 1985, the Convention for the Protection of the Architectural Heritage of Europe (known as the Granada Convention) was drawn up by the Council of Europe, although not ratified by Ireland until 1997. Significantly, the Convention viewed the protection of heritage in a wider European context setting out that the aim of the Council of Europe was 'to achieve a greater unity between its members for the purpose, *inter alia*, of safeguarding and retaining the ideal and principles which are their common heritage'. The Granada Convention was important in that it made it incumbent upon each party to the agreement to take statutory measures to protect its architectural heritage. In Ireland the Local Government (Planning and Development) Act 1999, since consolidated in part iv of the Planning and Development Act, 2000, addressed the Convention's directives to implement appropriate supervision and authorization procedures to protect listed buildings by force of law. In Ireland the importance of historic houses, their parks and gardens to Irish and European cultural heritage consequently became more generally accepted as did the fact that houses, their contents and their surrounding curtileges provided the only architectural evidence of the intermediate historical period between the most prosperous era of the landed class in eighteenth-century Ireland and their gradual decline from the late nineteenth century.

The contribution of the Irish government through the introduction of fiscal changes, most notably the development of a support structure of grants and tax relief for existing owners under section 482 of the Irish tax acts, as well as legislative provisions to protect the built heritage through the planning code, the provision of an architectural heritage advisory service, the appointment of conservation officers to many local authorities and the establishment of the National Inventory of Architectural Heritage on a statutory basis have all been equally important.

At a regional level, community councils (such as Crossmolina with regard to Enniscoe) and local government authorities (such as Fingal County Council, Roscommon County Council and Westmeath County Council in regard to Ardgillan, Newbridge, Malahide, King House and Belvedere) began to build on the premise that local big houses could be promoted as significant local tourist attractions. Moreover, the increased prosperity of Ireland since the late twentieth century has produced a large number of wealthy entrepreneurs and entertainers

30 See www.historicirishhouses.ie.

who, along with certain foreign business persons, have purchased and restored (or are restoring) houses such as Abbey Leix in Laois, Ardbraccan in Meath, Carton in Kildare, Castlehyde in Cork, Charleville in Wicklow, Killua in Westmeath, Lyons in Kildare, Stackallen in Meath, and Tudenham in Westmeath to name but a few.

But despite all these positive initiatives, the lack of adequate financial resources to maintain many of the big houses, particularly those in the ownership of the original families, has remained a problem. In 2001, in a bid to establish the current state of Irish houses, this author was commissioned by the Department of the Environment, Heritage and Local Government and the Irish Georgian Society to identify, through interview with fifty owners or managers, the threats to the future of a sample of fifty houses (including four town houses) and to make recommendations regarding the steps necessary to safeguard all historic houses into the future as part of the country's national heritage. In September 2003 the report, *A future for Irish historic houses? A study of fifty houses* was published.[31] Its central recommendation called for the establishment of a viable national trust-type organisation for Ireland to safeguard the future of the remaining historic houses, while at the same time acknowledging that very often the most cost effective way of safeguarding historic properties is to provide assistance to dedicated private owners, trustees or managers of state and institutionally owned properties to allow them help themselves in maintaining and running these houses.

A year after the publication of the report, in September 2004, An Taoiseach, Mr Bertie Ahern TD, announced the establishment of an independent Irish Heritage Trust at the Third Annual Historic Houses of Ireland Conference.[32] It has a mandate to acquire properties of significant heritage value where there is a risk to their heritage value, so as to provide for their proper conservation, maintenance and presentation and their future public enjoyment and appreciation. The Trust will operate as a charity and will have a remit to maximize non-Exchequer resources in support of its activities. It will also operate under a strong commercial ethos to build up income from individual membership, corporate support, commercial ventures and to encourage the involvement of volunteers. The government has pledged to meet the Trust's establishment and initial running costs from the vote of the Minister for the Environment, Heritage and Local Government. It will also contribute 75 per cent of the first endowment fund, to a maximum of €5.5 million, needed to meet conservation, maintenance and presentation costs. (The proportion of the State's contribution to future endowment funds will diminish as the Trust establishes itself sufficiently to maximize its own fund-raising capabilities.) It is not the government's financial contribution that is significant, which obviously it is not, but rather the intimation that the worst days for the big houses in Ireland are over, at least in terms of recognition of their importance to Irish and European cultural heritage.

---

31 Terence Dooley, *A future for Irish historic houses? A study of fifty houses* (Dublin, 2003).
32 www.taoiseach.gov.ie/index.asp? docID=2145.

CHAPTER 4

Sources for the study of Irish big houses

The aim of this chapter is to introduce the reader to the most important primary sources available for the study of an Irish big house and its demesne and landscape surroundings. As in chapter two, what is described is the ideal and the sources of most relevance to the researcher will depend on the actual focus of the study. Two points need to be emphasized at the outset: firstly, as in chapter two, the sources are not arranged in any hierarchical order of importance. Secondly, the reader must bear in mind that most of the sources already described in chapter two may be of some relevance to the study of big houses. While specific points may be made about repeat sources in this chapter, the reader is directed back to chapter two for information on locations, strengths and weaknesses and so on. Finally, as with the National Archives in chapter two, sources accumulated in the Irish Architectural Archives (IAA) will be discussed as a unit simply because this repository represents the most appropriate starting point for research into individual Irish big houses.

IRISH ARCHITECTURAL ARCHIVE

The Irish Architectural Archive was established in 1976: 'to collect and preserve material of every kind relating to the architecture of the entire island of Ireland, and make it available to the public'.[1] It has recently been relocated to impressive offices at 45 Merrion Square, Dublin and is open to the public Tuesdays to Fridays, 10 a.m. to 5 p.m. No appointment is necessary and there are no research fees. For an introduction to the IAA, see its website at www.iaa.ie.

The collections housed in the IAA, as the website points out: 'comprise the largest body of historic architectural records in Ireland and as such constitute a vital national cultural resource'. These records include 250,000 Irish architectural drawings ranging in date from the late seventeenth to the late twentieth centuries, a large proportion of which pertain to Irish big houses. If architectural plans for various phases of construction and remodeling of an individual house exist, they are illuminating, for example, on changing architectural tastes and fashions that were determined by such factors as changes in ownership, British or continental influences, increased prosperity, and even the acquisition of titles (in Sir John Leslie's case, for example, it was said that one of the reasons he rebuilt Glaslough in County Monaghan in the early 1870s was to celebrate his elevation to the baronetcy)[2].

---

1 www.iarc.ie.   2 Shane Leslie's unpublished autobiographical sketch (NLI, Shane Leslie papers, MS 22,884).

The IAA has also over 400,000 photographs constituting a very significant visual history of Irish historic buildings. Again big houses feature prominently. These photographs along with other important collections such as the Clonbrock and Lawrence collections in the National Photographic Archive or less well-known collections such as the Magan collection on deposit in the Offaly Historical and Archaeological Society Office in Tullamore are critical in providing a freeze-frame image of houses at certain stages of their existence. The importance of these photographic collections is that they provide images of many houses that have long since vanished from the rural landscape.[3]

During the period of its existence, the IAA has also accumulated files on hundreds of individual houses, comprising, for example, newspaper cuttings, copies of journal articles, miscellaneous correspondence, auction catalogues and so on. Its comprehensive library has more than 15,000 publications including a full collection of *Country Life*.

One of the most important projects undertaken by the IAA in recent times has been the creation of The Irish Architectural Archive's Biographical Index of Irish Architects under the direction of Ann Martha Rowan.[4] This index, as the title suggests, contains biographical information on Irish architects or architects who worked in Ireland from 1720 to 1940. The cut-off dates were chosen because 1720 is the date at which Rolf Loeber's *A biographical dictionary of architects in Ireland, 1600–1720* (London, 1981) ends, while 1940: 'marks the natural break in architectural and building activity in Ireland caused by the Second World War'.[5] The complete index may be consulted in the IAA's reading room and it is hoped that in the future it will become available online.

In Northern Ireland, the Department of the Environment offices in Waterman House, Hill Street, Belfast, houses records of the same nature as the IAA. Between 1969 and 1993, all of the buildings in Northern Ireland were assessed for their architectural and historic interest. Two per cent of these met the criteria necessary to be included in the Statutory Listing of Historic Buildings (ranging 'from the grand mansion to the humble cottage'[6]) in accordance with article 42 of the Planning (Northern Ireland) Order 1991. A second survey is currently under way to re-assess the original listings and to identify additional buildings worthy of protection. The Northern Ireland Buildings Database holds information on 9,000 buildings in total, including a good many country houses, with details on dates of construction, exterior descriptions, architect(s), and criteria for listing.[7]

In the creation of the database and for other administrative and recording purposes, paper files were created, very similar in type to those available in the IAA.

3 For more on photographs, see below.   4 Howard Colvin's *A biographical dictionary of British architects, 1600–1840* (3rd edn., New Haven and London, 1985) remains an invaluable work of reference in relation to architects who were resident in Ireland such as James Gandon and Edward Lovett Pearce and, indeed, many others who were responsible for the design of Irish houses but who were non-resident.   5 See www.iarc.ie.   6 See www.ehsni.gov.uk/built/buildings/building.shtml.   7 www.eshni.gov.uk/built/mbr/buildings_database/build.asp.

These files are predominantly for houses and landscapes in Northern Ireland but some houses in the other three Ulster counties of Monaghan, Donegal and Cavan are also included.[8]

MAPPING IRISH COUNTRY HOUSES: DATABASES, PUBLISHED GUIDES AND OTHER WORKS

To date, the most comprehensive published guide available is Mark Bence-Jones's *A guide to Irish country houses* (revised ed., London, 1988). This guide, arranged alphabetically according to the most recognized name of the house, provides brief introductions to houses and in many cases illustrations. While very important, it should be emphasized that this guide is also extremely limited. It provides information on only around 2,000 houses (not all of which are strictly speaking big houses but in some cases hunting lodges) which is probably only between a third and a quarter of all those originally in existence. As Bence-Jones himself admitted, this was by no means an exhaustive listing; it was: 'a single-handed effort produced in a very limited time'.[9] And he pointed to the possible obstacles that would face those who might attempt a more ambitious project in the future, namely that knowledge of a demolished house is often limited to a single photograph (if even that) and relevant records pertaining to the history of surviving individual houses are often scarce, most notably documentation relating to their architectural history. For this reason, some of the individual house details in his guide are extremely short. For example: 'Aghada House, Aghada, Co. Cork. A late Georgian house by the elder Abraham Hargrave, built for John Roche between 1791 and *ca* 1808.'[10]

At present, the most ambitious attempt to locate and describe all the big houses in existence in Ireland by the nineteenth century is being undertaken at the Centre for the Study of Historic Irish Houses and Estates at the National University of Ireland, Maynooth. The CSHIHE's database of Irish country houses has been created in co-operation with Dr John Keating of the Department of Computer Science at NUIM and is capable of infinite expansion over time. When completed

---

8 See also the Ulster Architectural Heritage Society website at www.uahs.org.uk for information on its activities 'to promote the appreciation and enjoyment of architecture from the prehistoric to the present in the nine counties of Ulster, and to encourage its preservation and conservation', not least of which has been the publication of a number of excellent works including Earl of Roden, *Tollymore: the story of an Irish demesne* (Belfast, 2005); C.E.B. Brett, *Buildings of north Co. Down* (Belfast, 2002); idem, *Buildings of Co. Armagh* (Belfast, 1999); Robert McKinstry et al., *The buildings of Armagh* (Belfast, 1992) and many more which can be accessed at www.uahs.org.uk/publics.html.   **9** Bence-Jones's *A guide to Irish country houses*, p. vii.   **10** Ibid., p. 2; other similar more regional works include Valerie Bray, *Houses of Kerry* (Whitegate, 1994); Anna-Maria Hajba, *Houses of Cork, vol. 1, north* (Whitegate, 2002); Dan Walsh, *100 Wexford country houses: an illustrated history* (Enniscorthy, 1996); H.W.L. Weir, *Houses of Clare* (Whitegate, 1986); see also Terence Reeves-Smyth, *Irish country houses* (Belfast, 1993).

it is hoped that the database will have information on all the country houses in existence in Ireland, the date of construction, the families who were associated with them, the architect(s) who designed them (where identifiable), as well as a brief description of each house and how it evolved architecturally over time (where possible). Attempts will also be made to identify and locate the primary sources relating to each house and to compile a comprehensive bibliography of secondary works in which each house is mentioned. Illustrations will be provided where appropriate.

Other relevant databases are currently in existence or in the process of construction. The 'Connacht Landed Estates Project', located at the Centre for the Study of Human Settlement & Historical Change at NUI Galway, under the direction of Professor Gearóid Ó Tuathaigh with research by Marie Boran and Brigid Clesham, began in the autumn of 2005. Its objective is:

> To conduct a survey of the landed estates which existed in the five counties of Connacht between *c.*1700 and *c.*1920 and to create a database of information relating to each estate. The database will include details of surviving archival and printed resources relating to the estate as well as information relating to its location and the families who owned it.[11]

The National Inventory of Architectural Heritage is a section of the Department of the Environment, Heritage and Local Government charged with identifying and recording the architectural heritage of Ireland from 1700 to the present day. The website www.buildingsofireland.ie is the online representation of the survey work carried out to date. The site is updated on a continuous basis. The recorded information for country houses includes the name and address of each house; a registration number (a unique number assigned to each individual building surveyed); the date of the house's construction (or approximate period where not otherwise known); a description outlining the main architectural and distinguishing features of the house and finally an appraisal: 'a qualitative account of why the building is an important part of Irish architectural heritage'.

Since about 2003, the Department of Environment Heritage and Local Government has also been developing a national inventory of heritage gardens and designed landscapes. Information on around 5,500 heritage gardens and designed landscapes has been accumulated into a very substantial and important archive. The information gathered in paper files has been added to a digital database that will be published on the World Wide Web in the near future.

In the compilation of such databases a wide variety of primary sources are important in the identification, location and description of houses. One of the main starting points for the nineteenth century are the early Ordnance Survey maps. Such maps accurately locate houses and demesnes and when used in conjunction

---

11 Information kindly provided to this author by Professor Gearóid Ó Tuathaigh, Marie Boran and Brigid Clesham.

with surveyors' notebooks, they can offer further enlightenment on demesne buildings, avenues leading to the house, gatehouses or lodges, gardens, orchards and so on. Other earlier maps such as the road maps of Taylor and Skinner (1778) roughly locate many (though by no means all) houses.[12]

To identify houses in existence in the eighteenth and nineteenth centuries, a variety of other sources may be consulted. For example, Francis Grose's *Antiquities of Ireland* (1791) and *The post chaise companion through Ireland* (1786) provide some detail, if only locative. The statistical surveys of the early-nineteenth century mentioned in chapter two can sometimes be useful in piecing together relevant information including the approximate date of construction of a house where no more reliable information is to be found (even though in his *Statistical observations relative to the county of Kilkenny 1800, 1801* (1802), William Tighe made the remark: 'It is not the object of this work to describe the seats of proprietors, though many deserve notice'.)[13] For example, in Coote's *Statistical survey of Monaghan* (1801) Blayney Castle is described as a new house built recently near the ruins of the old castle, so the present structure probably dates to the 1790s. (Other genealogical sources tell us that the eleventh Lord Blayney married in 1796, which possibly also points to the late 1790s as the date of construction.)[14]

Lewis's *Topographical dictionary* provides a narrative image of a large number of houses in pre-famine Ireland, many of which have long since disappeared. However, Lewis, very much dependent upon the patronage of the landed class, was slow to criticize and, therefore, wrote continuous complimentary descriptions of houses and demesnes. For example, Lewis described Currah, the Limerick home of Sir Aubrey de Vere as an 'elegant residence' situated 'in the centre of a wide, fertile, undulating demesne, enriched with luxuriant woods and plantations and embellished with a picturesque lake; the mansion is of hewn limestone with a front of beautiful design commanding the lake; there are three entrances to the park, of which the lodge at that from Adare is the most handsome'.[15] He was generally fulsome in praise of the houses around Monaghan town:

> The principal seats are Rossmore, the residence of the Right Hon. Lord Rossmore, a handsome mansion in the Elizabethan style, situated in an extensive and beautifully diversified demesne, abounding with wild and romantic scenery and commanding some fine distant views; Castle Shane, of E[dward] Lucas, Esq., an ancient mansion in a highly enriched and tastefully embellished demesne ... with a handsome entrance lodge in the later English style of architecture...; Cornacassa, of Dacre Hamilton, Esq., pleasantly

12 George Taylor & Andrew Skinner, *Maps of the roads of Ireland, 1778* (Dublin, 1969 ed.). 13 Tighe, *Statistical observations relative to the county of Kilkenny 1800, 1801*, p. 588; I would like to thank Geralyn White for bringing this reference to my notice. 14 Unpublished statistical surveys for parishes in Co. Louth can be found at www.jbhall.freeservers.com (an excellent starting point for anybody interested in the local history of Co. Louth). 15 Lewis, *Topog. dict. Irel.*, i, 9.

situated in a highly cultivated and well-planted demesne; and Camla Vale, of
Lieut. Col. Westenra, brother of Lord Rossmore, a spacious and handsome
residence, situated in grounds tastefully laid out and adjoining the demesne
of Rossmore Park.[16]

Lewis is, therefore, more important as an indicator of the existence of houses in
Ireland than as a reliable source for their appearance and design and it should be
noted that his *Topographical dictionary* is less useful when searching for descriptions
of houses belonging to the lesser gentry.

In 1818–20 J.P. Neale (1780–1847), an architectural draughtsman, now best
remembered for his sketches of great houses, began publication of his eleven
volume *Views of the seats of noblemen in England, Wales, and Scotland and Ireland* (first
series, 6 vols, 1824; second series, 5 vols, 1824–9) which in total comprised 732
plates. It contains some of the best images of pre-famine Irish country houses
(predominantly of the larger classification such as Carton, CastleFreke and so on).

The Ordnance Survey memoirs, now published as a series under the editorship
of Angélique Day and others, provides similar information to Lewis. In 1824 the
British prime minister, the duke of Wellington, authorized a townland survey of
Ireland with maps at the scale of 6", to facilitate a uniform valuation for local
taxation. The memoirs were written descriptions recording all the relevant
information that could not be included on the maps themselves (memoir being a
term used in the eighteenth century to describe topographical descriptions
accompanying maps).[17] As Angélique Day et al. point out: 'The Memoirs are a
uniquely detailed source for the history of the northern half of Ireland before the
Great Famine'.[18] (Unfortunately between 1839 and 1840 the memoir scheme
collapsed as no further financing of the project was forthcoming from Westminster,
so the southern half of the country was never covered.) Like Lewis, the memoirs
offer varying degrees of information on country houses (usually under the heading
'Gentlemen's Seats'). We are told merely that Drummoey Glebe at Essexford,
Killanny, County Monaghan was: 'a substantial and commodious house but has
nothing striking in appearance'. On the other hand:

> Dawson Grove, the residence of Lord Cremorne, containing 494 acres of land
> and 103 of water, ranks amongst the most handsome noblemen's seats within
> the province. The 'magnum dorsum' of Drummore runs through his
> lordship's demesne, forming in combination with Fairfield, lately purchased
> from T. C. Stewart Corry Esquire, amounting to 585 acres of land and 165 of
> water, a beautiful chain of undulation, interspersed with lakes and islands, and
> adorned with plantations and ornamental grounds of great extent and beauty.
> The house, quadrangular, large and commodious, but heavy in appearance,

---

16 Ibid., pp 383–4.   17 *Ordnance Survey memoirs of Ireland, xl: counties of South Ulster, 1834–8,*
ed. Angélique Day and Patrick McWilliams (Belfast, 1998), p. viii.   18 Ibid., p. ix.

stands upon a highly eligible site commanding a very beautiful, though not extensive, prospect.[19]

It should not be any surprise that given the dramatic effect which the Great Famine had on many estates, forcing their owners to put lands and in many cases houses on the market, the Encumbered Estates Rentals[20] are a valuable source of information to the social and architectural historian. As Desmond Guinness has pointed out, these were: 'the mid-nineteenth century equivalent of auctioneers' photographs issued with the bills of sale published by the Encumbered Estates' Commission and its successor bodies, the Landed Estates' Court and the Land Judges' Court.'[21] The rentals contain scores of lithographs (and later photographs) of houses of estates which became insolvent during and after the Great Famine 1845–51. M.C. Lyons' *Illustrated incumbered estates Ireland, 1850–1905* (Clare, 1993) provides a good introduction to the illustrations and type of detail which accompanied them. One of the most significant houses to feature in the rentals was Castlehyde, Fermoy, County Cork, said to have been designed by Davis Ducart and subsequently enlarged by Abraham Hargreave sr. In December 1851, it was sold by its owner John Hyde to Arthur Guinness for just under £4,000, at a time when the brewing dynasty was consolidating its social position amongst the Irish landed class. The rental description reads partly as follows:

> The mansion houses stands on the north side of the River Blackwater, within about one mile of the garrison town of Fermoy, and 12 of the Mallow station on the Great Southern and Western Railway ... The river, which runs through the demesne ... for upwards of a mile, affords angling for both salmon and trout, and has a fine long reach for boating. The demesne is ornamented with several acres of very fine old oak timber. The gardens, with the pleasure grounds attached to them, are laid out in terrace walks in the old style, with handsome old-clipped hedges of yew and box; and comprise with the orchards – which are productive of the best kind of cider apples – about 22 acres.[22]

The subsequent ownership of all houses and their rateable valuation (not just those in the Encumbered Estates' rentals) can be traced by using the cancelled or field books in the archives of the Valuation Office.[23] If attempting to trace an individual house, one simply needs to know the name of the townland and electoral division in which it was located. These books are also an invaluable guide to changing rateable valuation which is noted in the margins. Accompanying comments offer reasons for the change or point to the date of destruction or demolition of houses, in many cases occasioned by the rise in rates.[24]

---

19 Ibid., 131, 114. **20** See chapter two. **21** Desmond Guinness, 'Foreword' in Lyons, *Illustrated incumbered estates Ireland*, p. vii. **22** Quoted in ibid., p. 20. **23** See chapter two. **24** See chapter three.

Griffith's printed valuation provides a comprehensive listing of country houses for the post-famine period. The printed valuation should also be used in conjunction with the cancelled books discussed above.[25] The aforementioned *Return of untenanted lands in rural districts, distinguishing demesnes on which there is a mansion* ... is, as the title suggests, obviously useful.[26] Genealogical sources and other works of reference provide details of residences as well as family histories (births, marriages, deaths, sometimes place of education, army or other careers, club membership) and estate acreage. There are a variety of the same, the most informative being the aforementioned John Bateman, *The great landowners of Great Britain and Ireland,* reprinted with introduction by David Spring (Leicester, 1971); U.H. Hussey de Burgh, *The landowners of Ireland* (1881); *Burke's landed gentry of Ireland* (various editions); *Burke's peerage and baronetage* (various editions); *Burke's Irish family records* (various editions); G.E. Cockayne, *Complete peerage of England, Scotland, Ireland etc., extant, extinct, or dormant* (8 vols, Exeter, 1887–98, revised edn. by Vicary Gibbs and others, 13 vols, London, 1910–49); and *Thom's Almanac and Official Directory* (1845–) which provides details on the resident magistracy.

The *Georgian Society Records* of 1913 feature a select list of Irish country houses with historical sketches. In 1914, Sir Albert Richardson published his *Monumental classic architecture in Great Britain and Ireland* which was even more select. In 1915, T.U. Sadleir and P.L. Dickinson's *Georgian mansions in Ireland* appeared with similar information, though on a greater number of houses (including some smaller ones).

A detailed survey of the 1901 and 1911 census household schedule returns would provide much detail on big houses inhabited by townland at the beginning of the twentieth century, as well as a general idea of the community in which the house or estate was located.[27] (Some household returns survive for the 1891 census, but very few exist for an earlier census.)[28] Household schedule returns (or census enumerators' books) were compiled by the census enumerators. They are the census forms which were completed by each individual householder. For the 1901 and 1911 censuses there are two forms available. Form A, completed by those present, constitutes: 'a return of the members of the family and their visitors, boarders,

25 See chapter two.   **26** HC 1906, c.177.   **27** E. Margaret Crawford, *Counting the people: a survey of the Irish censuses, 1813–1911* (Dublin, 2003); see also Vaughan & Fitzpatrick (eds), *Irish historical statistics.* Also very useful in this respect are B. Collins, 'The analysis of census returns: the 1901 census of Ireland' in *Ulster Local Studies,* 15 (1) (1993), pp 38–46; Rosemary ffolliott, 'Irish census returns and census substitutes' in Begley (ed.), *Irish genealogy: a record finder;* S.A. Boyle, 'Irish manuscript census records: a neglected source of information' in *Ir. Geography,* ii (1978), pp 110–25.   **28** The household schedule returns for 1861, 1871, 1881 and 1891 were destroyed by government order. Those for 1821, 1831, 1841, 1851 were almost entirely destroyed in the fire at the Four Courts in 1922. Those that survived may be found in J.G. Ryan, *Irish records: sources for family and local history* (Salt Lake City, 1988); see also Declan Cooney, '1821 census of the parish of Munsterconnaught' in *Breifne,* viii, no. 34 (1998), pp 877–83; Theo McMahon, 'Some county Monaghan abstracts from the 1821 census' in *Clogher Rec.,* xiv, no. 1 (1991), pp 89–114; D. Sheridan, '1841 census – Killeshandra parish' in *Irish Family History,* ix (1993), pp 62–86.

servants, etc. who slept or abode in this house on the night of ...' It provides such information as the relationship of those present to the head of the family, their religion, their education (essentially their ability to read and write), their age, rank, profession or occupation, marital status, where they were born and their ability to speak and/or write Irish. Form B is another tabulated form, though completed by the enumerators, and attached to the household enumeration forms for their district. It records details on houses specifying the number of rooms in use, the number of windows and whether the house had a slated or other type of roof.

The household schedule returns for the twenty-six counties are available in the NAI, while those for the six-counties are in PRONI. To locate the household schedule return of a big house, one simply needs to know the townland in which it was located. Often, this townland is specified as the demesne, for example Charleville demesne, Castlesaunderson demesne and so on. One then goes to the *Townland index* to find the DED number in which the townland was located. Indexes for each county are divided by DED with a reference number for the townland within the DED. These two numbers and the name of the county are required to order the household schedule returns.

One can use both forms A and B to gather information on such things as the approximate size of the big house on an estate, at least as far as can be gauged from the number of rooms 'in use' specified by owners on their returns. However, while most owners probably provided an accurate estimate of the total number of rooms in the house, there were undoubtedly others who interpreted their instructions literally and gave merely the number of rooms 'in use' on a daily basis. One can also find information on the number and type of outoffices attached to a big house. Similarly, data can be gathered on servants – the number employed, their religion and place of birth. Again, one needs to be careful here for census returns show that many landlords were absent on the night on which the 1901 and 1911 forms were completed and therefore it is probable that some of their servants were with them and that what remained in many houses was merely a skeleton staff.

ESTATE PAPERS

Estate papers are as important to the study of big houses as they are to the estates on which those houses are located and arguably there is a vast amount of material yet to be fully mined that will shed light on just how landed families lived their lives within (and without) their houses and demesnes.

All aspects of the economic life of the big house, from its building to its everyday maintenance, was tied to a large extent, if not totally, to that of the estate. Estate accounts have already been discussed in some detail in chapter two. Now we need to look at them specifically in light of what they tell us about the running of the big house.

Unfortunately, sources such as specifications, estimates and bills relating to the original building of houses are rather rare. Where they do exist, they provide the obvious starting point. In chapter two, the richness of the Clonbrock estate collection was referred to in relation to the management of the estate. The same is equally true of the house. There are bills, receipts, correspondence and estimates for building works on Clonbrock between 1782 and 1824; the same for the building of outoffices, demesne walls and a coach house for the period 1828–30; specifications for the addition of servants' apartments in 1832; and for additions to the main block of the house in the same year; specifications for the building of a mill and other buildings on the estate in 1842; correspondence, estimates and bills of costs for improvements carried out on the house 1856–67, including a bill for the painting and redecorating of the house in February 1862; contractors' bills for the installation of a sewerage system in 1879; the same for various improvements carried out to the servants' quarters 1892–1901, including the installation of a hot water system. There are also housekeeping accounts and household and general expenses books for considerable periods that detail every item purchased and sold from the house on a daily basis. There are hundreds of bills and receipts for household goods supplied to the Dillons from the mid-eighteenth century up to the late 1920s by local retailers in Ahascragh and Ballinasloe and from merchants in Dublin, Paris and Vienna. Besides, the obvious information on goods purchased and expenditure incurred, these accounts illuminate on how the house was furnished, the lifestyle of the family and significantly their attitudes to 'fashionable buying'. Moreover, there is a wealth of local social history to be gleaned from such sources – information on local booksellers, clothiers and tailors, dressmakers, wig makers, medical suppliers, sports goods suppliers, furniture, fine art, gold and silver dealers and a myriad of others. All of these written records are enhanced by a collection of architectural drawings – plans and designs for a variety of buildings and related works on the house and estate – as well as the wonderful Clonbrock photographic collection.

An examination of the dating of the Clonbrock records pertaining to building and embellishment reflects various highs and lows in big house life in Ireland. There were, for example, high levels of building in the late eighteenth and early nineteenth centuries which in the main were periods of prosperity for many landlords such as Clonbrock. Building works declined, but were not completely abandoned, in the 1820s and 1830s as the economy slowed down. There is little evidence of work during the famine years. As the economy began to recover from the effects of that crisis, building improvements recommenced and major alterations were carried out between 1856 and 1867 (including during the bad years of renewed depression in the early 1860s which hardly affected the estate because of Clonbrock's astute management policy). However, as a result of the decrease of rental income following the fair rent fixing terms of the 1881 Land Act and the further (if rather minimal effects) of the Plan of Campaign, the house was the first part of the estate to suffer. In April 1887 Clonbrock's agent wrote: 'His lordship has reduced his establishment considerably but unless times change he cannot uphold his present one'.[29]

29 J.R. Mahon to G.C. Mahon, 25 Apr. 1887 (NLI, Mahon papers, MS 22,231).

Retrenchment became a part of late-nineteenth century and early-twentieth century life for many like Clonbrock.

Arguably big houses also had a political function. At the most basic level, they were gathering places and nurseries of the political elite until well into the nineteenth century. In this respect, personal and political papers of individual family members are of great importance. The political papers of Luke Gerald Dillon (1834–1917) of Clonbrock are a veritable treasure trove waiting to be mined. By the 1860s, Dillon was immersed in local and national politics. He had served in the diplomatic service in the 1850s, being appointed second secretary at Vienna in 1862. The following year he returned to Clonbrock. He became high sheriff of Galway in 1865 and served two terms as private secretary to the viceroy of Ireland in 1866–68 and again in 1874–76. In the 1880s, he was a member of the Irish Land Committee (formed in response to the Land League), the Property Defence Association (established in 1880 to protect landlord interests in the face of Land League agitation), and the Land Corporation of Ireland (founded by Carlow landlord Arthur MacMurrough Kavanagh in 1883 to utilize farm land from which tenants had been evicted and for which no new tenants could be secured because of the fear of boycotting and intimidation). He was also a member of the executive committee of the Irish Landlowners' Convention (founded in 1887 to protect landlord interests against the National League), and of the lesser known Galway Grazing Landowners' Protection Association. In addition, Dillon was an active Unionist and a leading member of the Irish Unionist Alliance.[30] His correspondents include most of the leading landlords of his time in Britain and Ireland over a very lengthy and important period in Irish history, particularly in terms of the economic and political decline of Irish landlords.

The Clonbrock estate investment books are important in detailing where he invested the capital received from the sale of his estate under the 1903 Land Act. Such records are unfortunately all too rare. Clonbrock's investment portfolio was truly global and until the end of the Great War, profitable. However, the great depression that followed and culminated in the Wall Street Crash of 1929, allied to high levels of death duties which affected the estate in the 1920s, decimated the Clonbrock share portfolio. When the investment account books are scrutinized in conjunction with the estate and house accounts, one gets a very clear picture as to how the economic depression impacted upon the house which went into irreversible decline from 1930.[31]

Obviously, the social history of a house is inextricably linked to the social lives of the family (or families) who inhabited it. At local level, social life, particularly for the lesser gentry, was often centred on the big house or its surrounding gardens, woodland, walks, in some cases lakes (manmade as at Carton or natural as at Dartrey), tennis courts, croquet lawns and so on.[32] Big house visiting was a national

---

30 Ball, 'Clonbrock papers', p. 78.   **31** See Dooley, *The decline of the big house*, pp 116–20, 119–21.   **32** Ibid., pp 44–78.

pastime for the Irish landed class and so some estate collections contain lists of guests to be invited to dinners, balls and other functions and/or signed visitor books, the comments on which are in themselves worthy of a scholarly analysis. The diaries of Lady Alice Howard of Shelton Abbey in County Wicklow described her social life in some detail as she travelled from house to house.[33] Gentlemen's diaries record their participation in shooting and hunting parties at home and abroad.

As already mentioned, servants were an integral part of big house life. Servants' wage books usually provide information only on names, job descriptions and wages. Account books show that servants were sometimes given tea and sugar as part of their wages.[34] This was particularly true of servants who worked outside the house such as laundry maids who usually received provisions once a week from the house. For a time, beer money or even the luxury of having a bath were perceived bonuses.[35] Wage books and accounts are important in comparing the numbers of servants employed in great, middling and lesser houses and contrasting wage structures from one house to another. However, they are of very little use in trying to ascertain where servants came from, what was their own social background and so on. The household schedule returns of the 1901 and 1911 censuses allow for an examination of servants' religion, place of birth, literacy and age. It is to be lamented that such returns do not exist for the previous century when servants were much more plentiful in Irish country houses.

It is also to be lamented that very few servants working in Irish country houses left any form of record of their lives (though it is possible that interviews carried out with former big house servants may be available in places such as the archives of the Folklore Department at UCD or the archives of RTÉ, for instance).[36] Servants occasionally appear in the published memoirs of country house family members but these were the favoured few, presented as loyal retainers who never questioned their status or role in big house life.[37] Some estate collections do contain letters of application from servants which, if nothing more, can be important in revealing their perceptions of what they deemed important in the eyes of prospective employers. For example, one twenty-one year old girl who applied for a position at Farnham in Cavan in the early 1890s was quick to point out in her letter that she was 'a Prodestant [*sic*]'.[38] Some indication of employment policy can also be gleaned from the advertisement columns of the national newspapers,

33 See, for example, Diaries of Lady Alice Howard (NLI, Howard papers, MS 3,600); A directory of people to be invited to balls at Kilkenny Castle, 1880–1912 (NLI, Ormonde papers, MS 23,552); Diary of visitors to Headfort Castle, 1887–92 (NLI, Headfort papers, MS 25,369).   34 Of some value in respect of wage levels is *Report by Miss Collet on the money wages of indoor domestic servants in Great Britain* [Cd 9346], HC 1899, xcii, 22.   35 See Dooley, *The decline of the big house*, pp 146–70; Mona Hearn, *Below stairs: domestic service remembered in Dublin and beyond, 1880–1922* (Dublin, 1993), pp 60–82; Pamela Horn, *The rise and fall of the Victorian servant* (Dublin & New York, 1975).   36 See N.S. Smith, *George: memoirs of a gentleman's footman* (London, 1984).   37 See, for example, Elizabeth Bowen, 'The most unforgettable character I've met' in Lee (ed.), *The mulberry tree*, pp 254–65.   38 M. Crawford to Lady Farnham, n.d. [1893] (NLI, Farnham papers, MS 18,616).

particularly the *Irish Times*, which specified the requirements of employers (usually in such terms as 'Protestant', 'sober', 'honest', 'equal to duties', 'early riser' and so on) or the qualities of those seeking a position (in much the same terms.)[39] Similarly, estate collections occasionally contain written agreements between employers and staff that detail duties expected of the servants.[40] The wonderfully diverse (if at times frustratingly fragmented) nature of estate records means that occasionally one finds a particular type of record in one collection, not to be found in many others. For example, the Gore Booths kept 'Rat account books' at Lissadell where one penny was paid for each rat caught. From 20 June to 6 July 1846, 531 rats were caught in the kitchen and outoffices. In his reminiscences of life at Lissadell in the 1860s, S.A.W. Waters wrote of a rather gruesome nightly pastime enjoyed in the kitchen:

> Late at night rats used to continually pop in and out of this hole [near the kitchen range]. The smokers used to make a pool by putting in a coin apiece. Then each in turn took a large knife and stood beside the hole, holding the knife just over it. As a rat put its head out, down came the knife, and, with luck, the rat lost its head. The game was that each subscriber got five minutes with the knife and the one who killed the most rats took the pool.[41]

A much more conventional and extremely important source in regard to household management in the eighteenth century is the 'Rules for the government of the Marquis of Kildare's [later duke of Leinster's] household, 1763–1773'[42], which, for a time, was in this author's possession having kindly been loaned to him by the family of the present duke of Leinster. This is a rather remarkable (and probably unique) 113-page document which seems to have been circulated and possibly copied by other great house owners (aristocrats and archbishops alike) elsewhere in the United Kingdom and may very well have been the rulebook that formed the template for others to follow.[43] It sets out the tasks of individual servants, the remuneration they were to receive, what they were to eat and when, how and where they were to live and the disciplinary measures to be taken in the event of a breach of any condition of employment. The document represents a very good example of how Ireland's premier aristocrat attempted to order his household

39 For some indication of servants' desired conditions of employment, see Mary MacMahon, 'Servants' in *The Celt*, xvi (Nov. 1857). **40** See for example, Book of labourers' agreements on Ballyglunin estate, 1879–90 (NLI, Blake of Ballyglunin papers, MS 27,000); 'Rules to be observed by the lodge-keeper at Kilkenny Castle' (NLI, Ormonde papers, MS 24,951). **41** S.A.W. Waters's reminiscences (PRONI, D/4131/D/2/1); I am very grateful to Mr Dick Hunter for bringing this source to my attention. **42** A copy of the same in the archives of Alnwick Castle was used by Patricia McCarthy in 'Vails and travails: how Lord Kildare kept his household in order' in *Irish Architectural and Decorative Studies*, vi (2003), pp 120–39. **43** On the copy used by Ms McCarthy, there is a note: 'For his Grace the Duke of Northumberland with the Archbishop of Cashel's compliments. 24 January 1795, Stephen's Green, Dublin'; ibid., p. 121.

at the same time as he was bringing order to his house and physical setting and, indeed, the lives of the wider tenant community which inhabited the estate. It also hints at the difficulties not only in retaining servants in a large household over a period of time (an incentive of one year's wages as a bonus was provide to any lower servant who stayed for five years) but also the difficulties there must have been in maintaining the discipline of a large staff on a day-to-day basis.

In tracing the architectural history of a house, its decoration, the planning of its landscape and, indeed, family life, personal correspondence and diaries (published and unpublished) can be of immense value. For example, the diaries of the earl of Cork for the early seventeenth-century are an extremely rich source for the reconstruction of the grandeur of early-seventeenth century interiors.[44] By far the richest man in Ireland of his time, he was involved in the building or reconstruction of at least eight great houses in Ireland (as well as the town of Bandon.) His diaries record the furnishing he was constantly buying, silver plate he imported in great bulk from England or brought from Dublin, tapestries, glass, china and so on. On 28 June 1624, he recorded in his diary:

> bought of Mr Arthur of Dublin, merchant, two suites of tapestry hangings …
> [one] for my dining chamber at Lismore, … the other … for the long
> chamber in Youghal …, also ten yards of crimson velvet … to make chairs,
> stools, and a window cushion … I also bought of Mr Smyth the upholsterer,
> in Dublin, a gilt bedstead, and an Indian gilt table …, and for them … tassels
> and fringes of crimson silk and silver to finish the chairs, stools and cushion.[45]

Similarly, the correspondence of Lady Emily FitzGerald is important for what it reveals regarding her rôle and that of her husband in the embellishment of Carton house and demesne.[46] In December 1762, she wrote to her husband about their success in transforming the Carton landscape, praising the layout of the new river but complaining about the unattractive appearance of the island in the river.[47]

Household inventories also yield a great deal of valuable information about material culture.[48] These inventories were sometimes compiled for legal purposes of probate, sometimes on the change of ownership and sometimes (particularly after the 1882 Settled Land Act) to identify those contents which might be sold and least missed. It is probably fair to conclude that the vast majority of inventories belong to the larger houses. Such inventories are of particular value where they list contents according to room and outbuildings. To have inventories from different generations would obviously reveal much about changing trends and tastes, picture

---

44 These form part of the Lismore papers available in the duke of Devonshire's home at Chatsworth in England. **45** Quoted in Crookshank, 'The visual arts, 1603–1740', p. 477.
46 *Correspondence of Emily, duchess of Leinster (1731–1814)*, ed. Fitzgerald, i, 150; see also Brian Fitzgerald, *Emily, duchess of Leinster, 1731–1814: a study of her life and times* (London, 1949).
47 See *Correspondence of Emily, duchess of Leinster*, ed. Fitzgerald, i, 150. **48** See Jane Fenlon, *Goods & chattels: a survey of early household inventories in Ireland* (Kilkenny, 2003).

collections, altering fashions in room usage, if not also about the changing economic circumstances of the house owners. Some inventories are more restricted,
confining themselves to valuables such as plate, silver, and paintings. The Esmonde
Papers on deposit in the National Archives contain many useful photographs,
particularly of the interior of Ballynastragh in Wexford which seem to have been
taken to coincide with the drawing up of an inventory of the house's contents for
insurance purposes in the early nineteenth century.

Some of the major collections contain library inventories which provide
invaluable evidence of the reading tastes of the Irish landed class.[49] The Acheson
Library at Gosford in Armagh, the Percy Library at Caledon in Tyrone, the Shirley
Library at Lough Fea in Monaghan were all noted by Sir Shane Leslie as notable
among 'the great libraries which were collected in the specious days'.[50] Many of
these great libraries were dispersed from the 1920s and in some cases long before
as landlords sought to supplement declining income. The National Library of
Ireland and the Irish Architectural Archive house some published catalogues relating
to these auctions.[51]

Even the inscription on some of the family silverware can provide important
leads to a fuller examination of a family's history. For example, a Victorian shaped
oblong tea tray, engraved with armorials and an inscription, was presented to
Charles Powell Leslie of Glaslough, MP for County Monaghan from 1852 to 1871,
by his tenantry in 1844. This was on the eve of the Great Famine and the rather
lengthy inscription suggests that distress already prevailed, that the tenantry had
asked for a reduction in rents and that this had been granted. Part of the inscription
reads as follows:

> Sir, we your tenants present ourselves before you on this auspicious occasion,
> assuring you of our sincere prayers for your long enjoyment of health and
> happiness, and to thank you for your generous and extensive reduction of our
> rents, you will therefore accept of the warm expression of our gratitude, and
> believe it to be genuine and voluntary, and that it pervades and gladdens
> every circle downwards to the most humble cottage on your property.[52]

An inscription on a large pair of Victorian presentation six-light candelabra
presented to the second marquis of Sligo (1788–1845) and later sold at auction is
interesting and points to Sligo's rôle in the administration of the colonies. It also
demands investigation of his gross income derived not only from his extensive

49 See Pat Donlon, 'Property of a gentleman: the library at Annaghmakerig' in *Linen Hall Review*, iv (1987), pp 9–11; Bernadette Cunningham & Máire Kennedy (eds), *The experience of reading: Irish historical perspectives* (Dublin, 1999). **50** Leslie, *The Irish tangle for English readers*, p. 138. **51** For example, *Catalogue of library of J.R. Garstin of Irish literature to be sold by private auction, 1918; Catalogue of the entire library from Doneraile Court … to be sold by auction … on 17 and 18 December 1969.* **52** *Important silver and gold … which will be sold by auction by Sotheby Parke Bernet & Co., 3rd May 1984* (in author's possession).

estates around Westport in Mayo but also his 20,000-acre plantation in Jamaica. In 1837 one of the candelabra presented to him was inscribed as follows:

> Presented to the Most Noble Howe Peter Marquis of Sligo by the Negroes of Jamaica in testimony of the grateful remembrance they entertain for his unremitting efforts to alleviate their sufferings and to redress their wrongs during his just and enlightened administration of the government of the island and of the respect and gratitude they feel towards his excellent lady and family for the kindness and sympathy displayed towards them. 1837.

The other was inscribed with the names of 114 signatories and read: 'Presented to the Most Noble Howe Peter Marquis of Sligo, the emancipator of the slaves by the inhabitants of the town and neighbourhood of Westport. 1838'.

Auction catalogues, another important source of information on houses, are sometimes found in estate collections, although the Irish Architectural Archives and the National Library are the best places to search for the same, as well as the archives of auction houses such as Sotheby's and Christie's which contain many catalogues of sales of Irish house contents (with the added bonus that the Christie's catalogues, for example, have informative introductions written by country house experts such as Hon. Desmond FitzGerald to houses such as Malahide (1976), Newtown Park (1976), Luttrellstown (1983), Powerscourt (1984) and Cabinteely (1984).)

In April 1937 over 5,000 books were sold from the Dartrey library in Rockcorry, County Monaghan as part of a massive auction of house contents which took place over four days. The unwitting testimony contained in the auction catalogue informs of the travel arrangements put in place by Millar and Beatty auctioneers to take people to and from Dublin, Belfast, Cork, Galway, Waterford, London and Northern Ireland. The attention of prospective buyers was 'called to the fact that furniture over 100 years old can be imported duty free into the United Kingdom'.[53] The catalogue suggests the richness of the house contents listed according to the room from which they were sold and special attention was drawn to the works attributed to El Greco, Guido Reni, Zoffany, Hugh Hamilton, Allan Ramsay, Coates, Guercino, Linglebach and others of the early English, Flemish and Italian schools. The catalogue in this author's possession notes the prices paid for some of the contents including thirteen guineas for the Zoffany attributed landscape of Dawson Grove, the family seat.

NEWSPAPERS

As with estate life, the value of newspapers to the study of big houses and their families is largely determined by the focus of the study and they are probably of most use when a study is limited to a relatively short time span. They can inform

---

53 Catalogue is in this author's possession.

for example on how big houses became important social venues for the gathering of landed families at particular events such as race meets or coming of age celebrations. For the Punchestown meeting of April 1880, the *Leinster Express* listed sixteen big houses from which approximately 400 family members and guests left on one day to attend the races. Local newspapers can be useful in tracing births, marriages and death of members of the aristocracy and gentry. They contain descriptions of landed family weddings (the receptions were usually held in the big house) along with lists of wedding guests and the gifts they gave the bride and groom. They similarly reported on funerals, often providing lists of those in attendance (at least the local dignitaries) as well as lengthy memorials to the deceased.

In the early twentieth century other events took on a new social significance. During the third Home Rule crisis, Sir John Leslie of Glaslough voluntarily opened his demesne to allow the Ulster Volunteer Force to drill there and such drills became spectator events akin to the early days of the American Civil War (1861–65) when southern families picnicked on hilltops overlooking battlefields. Thus, on 16 April 1914 the *Belfast Newsletter* reported:

> A fairly large crowd of spectators witnessed the operations, amongst those present being Mrs Leslie, Mrs Guthrie, Lord and Lady Kerry (sic), Lady Caledon, Mrs Crowsley, the Venerable Archdeacon Abbott … The place chosen for the operations was ideal as timber cutting had been in progress and the fallen trees and hilly ground provided splendid cover for the attacking force. At the conclusion tea was supplied to the men by Col. and Mrs. Leslie who along with the members of the house party present were indefatigable in attending to their wants.

Newspapers, local and national, are invaluable for a study of the effects of the revolutionary period 1916–23 on Irish country houses, particularly the burning of around 300 of them during the War of Independence (1919–21) and the Civil War (1922–3). In the wake of their destruction, papers frequently reported on the compensation cases which followed. From the 1920s, national (and local) newspapers, particularly the *Irish Times*, advertised hundreds of country houses for sale in Ireland and are, therefore, one of the best indicators of the cumulative effect of the political, economic and social factors which brought about their decline. Moreover, auction notices feature a good deal of detail on the contents of houses and outbuildings and so can be very informative regarding the material culture of a household.[54]

---

54 Sources for the study of material culture are described in Barnard, *A guide to sources for the history of material culture in Ireland*.

THE *DUBLIN* [LATER *IRISH*] BUILDER

The first volume of the *Dublin Builder* appeared in 1859. It was a monthly journal
devoted to 'architecture, engineering, sanitary improvement, the sciences and arts'
and was the brainchild of its proprietor and editor J.J. Lyons, himself an architect
and Fellow of the Royal Institute of Architects in Ireland. In his first editorial, Lyons
pointed out that the function of the new journal was to fill a vacuum:

> Justly may the numerous classes identified with the building and constructive
> arts in Ireland writhe under the stigma that they alone of their craft in the
> three sister kingdoms pursue their career un-represented by that powerful
> advocate 'the Press', and are unable to point to any national and professional
> periodical devoted to their enlightenment, to the maintenance intact of their
> rights and privileges and forwarding of their general interests.[55]

In December 1866, the journal was renamed the *Irish Builder and Engineering
Record* because: 'the word "Dublin" gave to it rather a *local* significance'.[56] Its
renaming at this time is significant as it coincided with the post-famine upturn in
the economy which, in turn, led to the last significant phase of big house
redevelopment (as opposed to building.) Various editions of the journal contain
important information on a variety of Irish houses, particularly those under
modification (or construction) from the 1860s. On 15 November 1869, for
example, the journal contains a sketch of the recently rebuilt Oaklands in County
Tyrone, home of Viscount Stuart. The architect is named as William Hastings of
Belfast, the builder as John Murphy, his site representative as Robert Flanagan and
the plumber as John McGee, all from Belfast. The chief new features of the house
are described in some detail and the cost of the reconstruction of the house
estimated at £10,000. The edition of 1 March 1870 points out that reconstruction
work on Summerhill in County Meath, the home of Lord Langford, not restored
since its partial destruction by rebels in 1798, had just been commenced. Again,
architects and others involved in the project are named.

Other significant articles over the years include the reminiscences of prominent
architects such as J.F. Fuller who, in the jubilee edition in 1909, described his
architectural ventures in Ireland since 1861, mentioning the work he carried out
on a variety of houses such as Annamore in Sligo (then home of Charles O'Hara),
Mount Falcon in Mayo (home of Utred Knox), Ashford Castle in Mayo (the home
of Lord Ardilaun) and Kylemore Castle (now Abbey) in Galway: 'every stone for
which (Dalkey Granite) was sent from Dublin by ship to Letterfrack.' In the
December of 1872 edition, we learn that the Architectural Association of Ireland
was discussing the possibilities of concrete, less than a decade before Clonalis House
in Roscommon became the first mass concrete country house to be built in
Ireland.

55 *Dublin Builder,* Jan. 1859.   **56** *Irish Builder,* 15 Dec. 1866.

CONTEMPORARY PUBLISHED WORKS,
MEMOIRS AND AUTOBIOGRAPHIES

Traveller's guides of the eighteenth and nineteenth century, written by the likes of William Makepeace Thackeray, the Halls (husband and wife) and Henry Inglis, often provide freeze frame introductions to country houses at particular stages in their life, a description perhaps of their architectural style, occasionally a glimpse at their interiors, and frequently the nature of demesne and wider estate developments.[57] Even the most innocuous remark can inform on a house maybe no longer in existence.[58] In his journey through County Louth (where his cousin the Revd Alias Thackeray was Church of Ireland rector in Dundalk), William Thackeray made the following interesting point about English attitudes to Irish demesnes:

[The demesne at Annsbrook] is as pretty and neatly ordered as any in England. It is hard to use this comparison so often, and must make Irish hearers angry. Can't one see a neat house and grounds without instantly thinking that they are worthy of the sister country; and implying, in our cool way, its superiority to everywhere else? Walking in this gentleman's grounds, I told him, in the simplicity of my heart, that the neighbouring country was like Warwickshire, and, the grounds as good as any English park. Is it the fact that English grounds *are* superior, or only that Englishmen are disposed to consider them so?[59]

In the 1920s and 1930s there was a flush of memoirs written by members of the Irish landed class. This was not unique to Ireland; in England members of landed families were doing likewise.[60] Some wrote because they had genuine literary flair; others wrote for the money and some who did not need the money: 'merely wrote to record the world that others had lost, but to which they still very largely hung on'.[61] Terence de Vere White once commented that these were by and large

books of reminiscences by Irishmen who went out to govern New South Wales, or otherwise achieved eminence, [that] begin with a short chapter containing a joke; the next deals with a school in England; then Oxford or Cambridge. The bulk of the book is composed of chapters on London and life abroad ... Ireland is left like the shell of the egg out of which the chicken emerged.[62]

57 See C.J. Woods, 'Irish travel writing as source material' in *I.H.S.*, xxviii (1992), pp 171–83.   **58** See, for example, S.C. & A.M. Hall, *Ireland: its scenery, character &c.* (3 vols, London, 1841–3); Henry Inglis, *A journey throughout Ireland* (London, 1834); R.C. Hoare, *Journal of a tour in Ireland, A.D. 1805* (London & Dublin, 1807); H. Worcester-Smith, *A sporting tour through Ireland, England, Wales and France* (2 vols, Columbia, SC, 1925).   **59** W.M. Thackeray, *The Irish sketch book of 1842* (London, 1879 ed.), p. 265.   **60** Cannadine, *The decline and fall of the British aristocracy*, pp 399–402.   **61** Ibid., p. 400.   **62** Terence de Vere White, *The Anglo-Irish* (London, 1972), p. 168; quoted in Elizabeth Grubgeld, *Anglo-Irish autobiography: class, gender and the forms of narrative* (New York, 2004), p. 2.

This is true of many published memoirs such as Lord Castletown's *Ego* (London, 1923) which has as its subtitle *Random records of sport, service, and travel in many lands* and contains chapters entitled, for example, 'A trip abroad', 'College life', 'The Franco-Prussian war', 'Rocky mountain adventures', 'More of the Wild West' and so on. But there are a great deal of similar works that are much more revealing about life in an Irish country house. Memoirs by the likes of the earl of Dunraven, the earl of Midleton, Lady Fingall, the Duc De Stacpoole, and Elizabeth Bowen very much lament the demise of their class and a way of life.[63] The Leslies of Glaslough (now Castle Leslie) were well served by three literary members of the family, Sir Shane, his daughter, Anita and Shane's brother, Seymour.[64] Elizabeth Bowen's *Bowen's Court* (London, 1942) evocatively captures the decline of a house in the late nineteenth and early twentieth centuries. It not only offers important detail on the physical plant but also provides a strong sense of what the house, its contents and its surroundings meant to the owner, an impression than cannot be readily gleaned from any source other than a memoir of this nature. The same is equally true of Mervyn Wingfield, seventh Viscount Powerscourt's *A description and history of Powerscourt* (London, 1903). This work provides a detailed record of the acquisition of contents for one of the most famous of all Irish big houses built between 1731 and 1740 to the design of Richard Castle.[65] For the earlier period the correspondence of Emily, duchess of Leinster (1731–1814) is instructive regarding the interior and exterior embellishment of Carton House and its landscape, while the published letters of Mary Delany covering the span 1731–68 are a much quoted source for historians of Georgian Ireland.[66]

It is perhaps in helping to recreate the social and cultural worlds of the landed class that such memoirs or published diaries, correspondence and so on are of most

63 The following is but a short selection of autobiographies, published memoirs and autobiographies: Castletown, *Ego*; Lady Clodagh Anson, *Book: discreet memoirs* (London, 1931); idem, *Another book* (London, 1937); Earl of Desart and Lady Sybil Lubbock, *A page from the past* (London, 1936); Duc de Stacpoole, *Irish and other memories* (London, 1922); Nicolette Devas, *Two flamboyant fathers* (London, 1966); Joan de Vere, *In ruin reconciled: a memoir of Anglo-Ireland, 1913–1959* (London, 1990); Dunraven, *Past times and pastimes*; Richard Edgeworth, *Memoirs of Richard Lovel Edgeworth: begun by himself and concluded by his daughter, Maria Edgeworth* (2 vols, London, 1820); Fingall, *Seventy years young*; *Sir William Gregory …: an autobiography*, ed. Lady Gregory; M.E.L. Lenox-Conyngham, *An old Ulster house and the people who lived in it* (Dundalk, 1946); Earl of Midleton, *Records & reactions, 1856–1939* (London, 1939); George Moore, *Hail and farewell* (London, 1911); Frank Pakenham, *Born to believe: an autobiography* (London, 1953). 64 Shane Leslie, *The end of a chapter* (London, 1916); idem, *The film of memory*; idem, *The Irish tangle*; idem, *The landlords of Ireland at the crossroads* (Dublin, 1908); idem, *Long shadows* (London, 1966); idem, *The passing chapter* (London, 1934); see also his semi-autobiographical novel, *Doomsland* (London, n.d.); Seymour Leslie, *Of Glaslough*; idem, *The Jerome connexion*; Anita Leslie, *the Marlborough House set* (New York, 1975); idem, *The gilt and the gingerbread: an autobiography* (London, 1981). 65 See Dooley, *The decline of the big house*, pp 19–24. 66 *Correspondence of Emily, duchess of Leinster (1731–1814)*, ed. Fitzgerald; *Letters from Georgian Dublin: the correspondence of Mary Delany, 1731–68*, ed. Angélique Day (Belfast, 1991); see also Patricia Pelly & Andrew Tod (eds), *The highland lady in Dublin, 1851–1856: Elizabeth Grant of Rothiemurchus* (Edinburgh, 2005).

value but it remains important to ask all the relevant standard questions of them that one would ask of any legitimate historical source: when describing historical events how close to the event is the retelling of it? Was the narrator is a position to see first hand what happened or is he or she relying on somebody's else account? Why were the memoirs written in the first place – as a sincere effort to record one's life or as a means of making money (which, as noted above, became something of a phenomenon in 1930s Britain)? Moreover the same weaknesses sometimes exist in travellers' descriptions of houses that are inherent in their judgements of management policy on individual estates: too often the writer is much too deferential to the house owner to be critical of his architectural taste (or his lifestyle).

PAINTINGS, TOPOGRAPHICAL DRAWINGS AND OTHER IMAGES

Patrick Duffy has rightly pointed out that 'paintings, drawings, and the work of landscape artists have been much underused as a source of evidence for historians' and that they hold a great deal of relatively untapped research potential.[67] William Laffan has similarly concluded that 'topographical drawings can be of direct use in determining the conservation of buildings they depict'.[68] Irish landscape painting became popular from the seventeenth century. By the eighteenth century, the enthusiasm of country house owners for landscape paintings resulted in the publication of illustrated books of scenery. Probably the most famous of these books was Thomas Milton's *Collection of select views from the different seats of the nobility and gentry in the kingdom of Ireland* (1783–93) for which he employed eminent landscape artists such as Thomas Roberts (1748–78) and William Ashford (*c.*1746–1824). Reference has already been made to the value of the lithographs in the Encumbered Estates rentals and the drawings contained in works such as J.P. Neale's *Views of the seats of noblemen*.

The publication of William Laffan (ed.), *Painting Ireland: topographical views from Glin Castle* (Tralee, 2006) bears testimony to the wealth and diversity of topographical sketches of country houses, their demesnes, parklands and other accoutrements. After all, the collection on which this work is based is drawn from one house only, granted that of one of Ireland's foremost collectors, Desmond FitzGerald, Knight of Glin.[69] However, due to the financial pressures faced by Irish country house owners in the past, the vast majority of houses have at various stages been stripped of many of their paintings which have subsequently been dispersed throughout the world. This began back in 1882 when the Settled Land Act of that

---

67 P.J. Duffy, 'The changing rural landscape 1750–1850: pictorial evidence' in Raymond Gillespie & B.P. Kennedy (eds), *Ireland: art into history* (Dublin & Niwot, CO, 1994), p. 26. **68** William Laffan (ed.), *Painting Ireland: topographical views from Glin Castle* (Tralee, 2006), p. 14.   **69** See also Anne Crookshank & Knight of Glin, *Ireland's painters, 1600–1940* (New Haven CT & London, 2002); idem, *Irish portraits, 1660–1860* (London, 1969); Anne Crookshank, 'A life devoted to landscape painting: William Ashford (*c.*1746–1824)' in *Irish Arts Review Yearbook*, xi (1995), pp 119–30.

year, referred to in the previous chapter, acted as a catalyst in the break up of house collections.

Ann Crookshank and the Knight of Glin have been responsible for the creation of the most important and largest visual archive of Irish painting in Ireland, and possibly in the world, which since 2002 has been administered by the Irish Art Research Centre at Trinity College, Dublin (Triarc).[70] The archive contains around 38,000 photographic images as well as some exhibition catalogues, research notes, correspondence and so on. A great many of the photographic images are of paintings that cannot be easily accessed as they are in private collections closed to the public or located overseas. As the website for Triarc points out:

> The material in the archive is a valuable resource not only for history of Irish art, but also for other historical disciplines. The large number of landscape paintings, depicting scenes from across the country, provide an invaluable source for local historians, architectural historians etc.; the portraits and genre scenes are an equally important point of reference for researchers in social history.[71]

Triarc's ambition is to digitise these images and, therefore, provide web-based access to the archive.

Paintings and drawings can allow for an examination of the architectural evolution of houses and landscapes. In the Glin collection, for example, we see evidence of the architectural structure of Curraghmore in County Waterford before its Victorian remodelling. The two views of Carton (see plates 13 and 14) separated by under forty years show the great changes that took place over that period as formal gardens gave way to a more natural landscape. The first by William van der Hagen was painted in 1739, shortly before the old house was demolished. The second by Arthur Devis was painted in 1776 and shows that the alleyways and parterres of the van der Hagen have been replaced by newly-planted trees and shrubs and the newly-created lake is a focal point of the backdrop.

Despite their obvious value, paintings (possibly more so than topographical sketches) should not be regarded as an exact factual record of a place's appearance at a particular time. As Duffy points out: 'From the point of view of the historian … the canvas as a document must be cross-checked against the often dry and tedious written word.'[72] A patron's wishes to omit some unimpressive physical feature may have influenced a painter's final creation or a landscape may have been enhanced in order to embellish a big house setting. A painter may have been influenced by prevailing stylistic conventions. It is, therefore, important to consult other sources in tandem with extracting information from sketches and paintings.

---

70 Open to researchers, Monday to Friday from 9 a.m. to 5 p.m. by appointment only; see www.tcd.ie/History_of_Art/IARC; see also www.nationalgallery.ie/html/paintings.html; www.huntmuseum.com. **71** www.tcd.ie/History_of_Art/IARC, 11 Apr. 2006. **72** Duffy, 'The changing rural landscape 1750–1850', p. 27.

It is now also accepted that photographs can provide a unique insight to aspects of life in Ireland from the nineteenth century onwards not always provided by the written or printed source. As Noel Kissane wrote in his introduction to *Ex Camera*: 'Photographs evoke a sense of the past more potent than actual reportage. Their impact is immediate and crosses the barriers of language, age and educational abilities.' They can be rich in the information they provide to the local historian.[73]

The existence of a huge body of photographs in the Irish Architectural Archives and lesser collections in local repositories has been referred to above. Also of great importance are the photographic collections of the National Library of Ireland housed in the National Photographic Archive, Meeting House Square, Temple Bar in Dublin.[74] These collections comprise approximately 600,000 photographs. The huge Lawrence collection of 40,000 glass plate negatives dating from 1870 to 1914, to which an index will soon be available as a searchable on-line database, is of particular significance to those seeking images of Irish country houses during this period.

Likewise, the magnificent Clonbrock collection containing 2,000 glass plates spanning the years 1860–1930. The National Library acquired this collection in 1977 for the princely sum of £25 and the cost of transportation. It provides the perfect visual companion to the very comprehensive manuscript collection of Clonbrock estate papers acquired by the library the previous year. The photographs were mainly taken by Luke Gerald Dillon, fourth Baron Clonbrock (1834–1917), and his wife, Augusta (1839–1928), daughter of Lord Crofton of Mote Park in Roscommon. When they first took up their hobby, probably around 1860, amateur photography was becoming fashionable amongst members of the landed class in Ireland, presumably many other houses other than Clonbrock had their own studios and darkrooms (then usually referred to as photograph rooms.) The Clonbrock photographs provide what is probably the most authentic, varied and substantial record of life on a large Irish landed estate available. It contains portraits of three generations of the Dillon family and many of their friends, photographs of the house and its demesne, its servants, estate workers and tenants, as well as photographs of local community events and activities involving the family. A database of the index to the collection has recently been web-enabled (although images are not attached).[75]

The *Country Life* Picture Library's photographic collection dates back to the foundation of the magazine in 1897.[76] Among the 400,000 or so photographs are many specially commissioned photographs relating to the Irish houses featured in the magazine showing architectural features, as well as magnificent interior views of furniture, paintings, antiquities and so on. In some cases such as Lambay Castle, they record a visual history of houses and their contents over a period of time, but

73 See, for example, Liam Kelly, *Kiltubrid, County Leitrim: snapshots of a rural parish in the 1890s* (Dublin, 2005).   74 Open to the public Monday – Friday, 10 a.m. – 5 p.m. and Saturdays, 10 a.m. – 5 p.m.   75 See www.nli.ie/a_coll.htm.   76 See www.countrylife.co.uk/picturelibrary/about.html.

equally important they record much of what has subsequently been lost or dispersed. The library located at Stamford Street in London may be visited by appointment and prints of any negatives it holds can be supplied by post.[77]

IRISH TOURIST ASSOCIATION TOPOGRAPHICAL
AND GENERAL SURVEY

In the 1940s, as a means towards the promotion of cultural tourism in Ireland, the Irish Tourist Association commissioned a topographical and general survey in the twenty-six counties. The survey was carried out at parish level and covered the following: topography (a brief description of outstanding scenic views in the district, natural attractions or unusual topographical features); geology (caves, eskers and so on); sports and games played in the area; amenities and general information on parks, public services, entertainment venues, industries, public monuments and so on); accommodation and catering; and, most pertinently from the point of view of this study, the survey asked for information on 'mansions, castles and estates of imposing character'.

In Daingean in County Offaly, the surveyor noted: 'Mount Lucas, on the main Dublin Road, three miles to the east of Daingean, is the only mansion of note remaining. It was formerly the residence of the Lucas family, but within recent years has been taken over by the Land Commission and divided into smaller holdings.'[78] The survey for Kinlough in County Leitrim carried out in 1943 provides the following snapshot of Lareen House:

> The estate is small, 152 acres... The land is let out in tillage and pasture. There are no gardens. An avenue almost a half-mile long, leads to the house which is now in a ruined condition. Due to its destruction by fire some years ago [c.1933] only the walls now remain together with the porch and entrance door. It was a two-storey building with plain windows and a plain porch. It had a frontage of about 65 [feet], width of about 35 [feet]. There were eight apartments on the ground floor.[79]

This type of information is very important in dating the disappearance of individual houses from the rural landscape.

On completion of the survey, the files, including extensive photographic collections, were, it seems, inherited by Bord Fáilte. They remained in the Bord's possession until 1983 when Dr Peter Harbinson, archaeologist to Bord Fáilte, enquired if *An Chomhairle Leabharlanna* (the Library Council of Ireland) would be

77 See O'Reilly, *Irish houses and gardens*.   78 Irish Tourist Association topographical and general survey of parish of Philipstown, Co. Offaly (Tullamore Library).   79 Irish Tourist Association topographical and general survey of parish of Kinlough, Co. Leitrim, 1943 (Leitrim County Library).

prepared to take over the files generated by the survey and distribute them to the various county libraries.[80] The Library Council did so. However, not all seem to have survived. This author has gained access to files pertaining to counties Wicklow, Donegal, Offaly and Leitrim. The only way to ascertain if they have survived for a county is by enquiry through county libraries.

READING THE RUINS[81]

The drive for the conservation and restoration of historic buildings has generated much valuable research material for the future. Conservation reports, commissioned by individuals, organisations, committees, government departments and so on can be hugely informative. Such reports usually begin with a historical introduction to the house, which is interesting in its own right, before proceeding to the main purpose of the report, for example, to enquire into the work necessary to be carried out on the roof of a house. In a report of this nature, the reasons for and the extent of the damage to the roof is described and much historical detail given. For instance a report on the state of the roof at Burton Park in County Cork in 2005 stated:

> The wall plates all around were completely rotten and the whole roof structure had been changed, possibly at the restoration in the 1890s ... In the reconstruction in the late-19th century, the dormer windows appear to have been put in and the balustraded parapet erected round the front and 2 side elevations. At this time, the purlins at the front were cut in order to form the large dormer windows and no support was given to the cut ends of the purlin which subsequently began to sag.[82]

Structures can be read as historical evidence in the same way as written records. In the reconstruction of Killua, County Westmeath, the architect, Mattie Shinnors, has produced a sequence of maps partly from the archaeological examination of the ruins and partly from a range of primary sources that are very informative regarding the evolution of the house from a late eighteenth-century, neo-Classical box into a medieval pile by the 1830s to the design of James Shiel (see plate 27). As a report on Killua pointed out: 'The results of the metamorphosis (at Killua) was evident at the outset of the job and as the research on-site progressed, the effects of such

---

80 Thomas Armitage [director *Chomhairle Leabharlanna*] to 'Dear Librarian', 21 Feb. 1983 (Ballywaltrim library, Bray).   **81** In compiling this section I have benefited greatly from the advice of Mattie Shinnors, architect in charge of the reconstruction of both Killua and Tudenham in Co. Westmeath, houses which up to a few years ago were in great danger of disappearing from the Irish landscape.   **82** This information is drawn from 'Report on the completion of the work to the roof at Burton Park ... in October 2005' by O'Carroll Associates, Convent Road, Roscommon.

cataclysmic change to the structure became apparent'.[83] The dating of these changes is also informative. In 1814, possibly just before the economic downturn impacted, a new dining room was added. This represented the Chapman family's rise in local social circles; a grand dining room became a prerequisite to rising social expectations. In 1821, the house was given a round tower presenting a Gothic appearance and the whole of the following decade witnessed a rather dramatic period of Gothicisation on the Killua demesne with Clonmellon Lodge, a triple-towered Gothic folly, and Killua Lodge both constructed. This was part of a much wider trend. Around the same time, Shiel was also working in County Westmeath on the Gothic transformation of Tullynally and the building of Knockdrin Castle from scratch.[84] Then, in the 1830s, a library and museum were added at Killua. There was no further development in the 1840s which reflected the disastrous effects of the Great Famine. As soon as the economy showed signs of recovery in the post-famine period, the Chapmans once again indulged in a new phase of building. 1854 saw the addition of a south-east tower to compliment the 1821 tower. Would it have been built earlier had the economy not floundered? The final phase of development was in 1858 when an existing corridor was removed and three new bedrooms added. There was no further development. Until about three years ago Killua lay in ruins, but its ruins offered enough evidence to Mattie Shinnors and his dedicated team of experts to begin one of the most ambitious schemes of big house reconstruction undertaken in Ireland on behalf of its owners Allen and Lorena Sanginés-Krause, a development which is due to be completed by around 2010.

WORKS OF FICTION

Oliver MacDonagh concluded that 'literature is its own end' but he believed that it can also help to serve the historian, not as an historical source as the term is ordinarily understood, but in the case of the novel it 'can yield insights and possibilities of recovering special portions of the past, for which we shall search in vain in any other matter'.[85] The big houses of Ireland (and, indeed, various aspects of the land question)[86] has exuded a certain mystique which has attracted numerous

83 Mattie Shinnors to this author, 19 June 2006. 84 See chapter three. 85 Oliver MacDonagh, *The nineteenth-century novel and Irish social history: some aspects* (O'Donnell lecture, UCC, 21 April 1970), p. 3. 86 See, for example, William Carleton, *Traits and stories of the Irish peasantry* (Dublin, 1833); Canon P.A. Sheehan, *The graves of Kilmorna: a story of '67* (New York, 1915); Anthony Trollope, *The landleaguers* (New York, 1979 ed.); C.J. Kickham, *Knocknagow or the homes of Tipperary* (Dublin, 1873); Padraic Colum, *The land* in Colum, *Three plays* (Dublin, 1963 ed.); Walter Macken, *The bogman* (London, 1952); Tom McIntyre, *The Charolais* (London, 1969); Michael McLaverty, *Lost fields* (New York, 1941); Patrick Kavanagh, *Tarry Flynn* (London, 1972 ed.); John B. Keane, *The field* (Dublin, 1993 ed.); Rutherford Mayne, *Bridge Head: a play in three acts* in Curtis Canfield (ed.), *Plays of changing Ireland* (New York, 1936), pp 405–71; John McGahern, *That they may face the rising sun*

writers from the beginning of the nineteenth century and which has resulted in an outpouring of works of fiction – novels, short stories, drama and poetry, all too numerous to name in this guide. In this respect the reader's attention is drawn to the bibliography of Otto Rauchbauer's *Diskurse und builder zum anglo-irischen landsitz im zwanzigsten jahrhundert* (2002). These works of literature are supplemented by a variety of literary studies of the big house novel genre, many of which are insightful including Jacqueline Genet (ed.), *The big house in Ireland: reality and representation* (Dingle, Co. Kerry, 1991) and Vera Kreilkamp, *The Anglo-Irish novel and the big house* (Syracuse, NY, 1998).[87]

As noted at the beginning of this chapter, very many of the nineteenth and twentieth-century writers who used the big house as a backdrop to their novels and plays were themselves born into the Irish landed class including Maria Edgeworth, George Moore, Lady Morgan, George A. Birmingham [Rev. Hannay], Edith Somerville and Martin Ross, Lennox Robinson, Shane Leslie and Elizabeth Bowen.[88] For the historian, the descriptions of the architectural characteristics or the interior layout and furnishings of Irish big houses by these writers are of some value. For example, Lady Morgan, in her early-nineteenth century novel, *The wild Irish girl*, describes a boudoir in an Irish castle as follows:

> The walls were rudely wainscoted with oak, black with age; yet the floor was covered with a Turkey carpet, rich, new and beautiful – better adapted to a London dressing-room than the closet of a ruined tower. The casements were high and narrow, but partly veiled with a rich drapery of scarlet cloth: a few old chairs, heavy and cumbrous, were interspersed with tabourets of an

(London, 2002). See also Peter Costello, 'Land and Liam O'Flaherty' in King (ed.), *Famine, land and culture in Ireland*, pp 169–79. **87** See also Adrian Frazier, *George Moore, 1852–1933* (New Haven & London, 2000); Victoria Glendinning, *Elizabeth Bowen, Portrait of a writer* (London, 1977); W.J. McCormack, *Ascendancy and tradition in Anglo-Irish literary history from 1789 to 1939* (Oxford, 1985); Grubgeld, *Anglo-Irish autobiography*; Dorothy Kennedy, 'The big house in Irish literature: a study of Somerville and Ross, W.B. Yeats and Sean O'Casey' in *Bulletin of Irish Georgian Society*, xxxii (1989), pp 6–30; Colin Smythe (ed.), *Lady Gregory: fifty years after* (Gerrards Cross, 1987). **88** See, for instance, Elizabeth Bowen, *A world of love* (London, 1967 edn.); idem, *The last September* (London, 1987 edn.); George A. Birmingham, *The country gentleman* (London, 1913); idem, *An Irishman looks at his world* (London & New York, 1919); Joyce Carey, *Castle Corner* (London, 1950); Maria Edgeworth, *Castle Rackrent* (London, 1800); T.J. Farrell, *Troubles* (London, 1975); Aidan Higgins, *Langrishe, go down* (London, 1966); Molly Keane, *Mad Puppetstown* (London, 1985 edn.); idem, *Two days in Aragon* (London, 1985 edn.); idem, *Fuel House* (London, 1986); George Moore, *A drama in muslin* (London, 1886); Lennox Robinson, *The big house: four scenes in its life* (London, 1928); Edith Somerville & Martin Ross, *The big house of Inver* (London, 1925); idem, *The real Charlotte* (London, 1894); see also John Banville, *Birchwood* (London, 1978 edn.); idem, *The Newton letter* (London, 1982); Brian Friel, *Aristocrats* (Dublin, 1980); John McGahern, 'Eddie Mac' and 'The conversion of William Kirkwood' in John McGahern, *The collected stories* (London, 1992), pp 281–94, 331–49.

antique form; one of which lay folded up on the ground, so as to be portable in a travelling trunk. On a ponderous carved table (which seemed a fixed coeval with the building) was placed a silver *escritoire*, of curious and elegant workmanship, and two small but beautiful alabaster vases (filled with flowers) of Etrurian elegance. Two little bookshelves, elegantly designed, but not clumsily executed (probably by some hedge carpenter) were filled with the best French, English, and Italian poets …[89]

However, sight should not be lost of the fact that while works of fiction offer interesting and often revealing sidelights on changing aspects of big house life, historical accuracy too often gives way to the dictates of publishing, the importance of characterisation and the necessity of providing an audience with a lighter form of entertainment.[90] Works of fiction should not be regarded as substitutes for estate records, parliamentary papers, mortgage papers and such tools of statistical evidence – the logical sources of reference for an historian interested, for instance, in the economic life of an estate or house.

MISCELLANEOUS SOURCES

For those who are specifically interested in the effect of the Irish revolution on the Irish big house, the recently opened Bureau of Military History files are very useful. These are transcripts of interviews carried out with IRA veterans of the war of Independence in the 1930s. They point to attitudes of local IRA members towards the landed class and even offer information on the motivations behind the burning of some big houses during the War of Independence. These also feature references to the forcible occupation of some big houses by the IRA flying columns who were in search of shelter and food and to their later occupation during the Truce period, July–December 1921, when they were used as IRA training camps. These records can be supplemented by sources in the Department of Justice, Department of the Taoiseach, Department of Finance and Department of Justice files in the National Archives of Ireland that contain reports on individual estates during the 1919–23 period as well as correspondence between landlords and these various departments. In September 1922, for example, W.T. Cosgrave received extracts from reports submitted to Winston Churchill by Lord Lansdowne's agent which illustrate the type of pillaging that took place during the Civil War: 'On arrival at Derreen the scene that greeted our eyes beggars description, crowds of every description around the house, men, women and children, pulling, hauling, fighting for what they could take. The house is absolutely destroyed, doors all smashed, every particle of furniture taken.'[91]

89 Lady Morgan, *The wild Irish girl* (London, 1986 ed.), p. 153; my thanks to the Knight of Glin for bringing this source to my attention. **90** Dooley, *The decline of the big house*, p. 15. **91** Report enclosed in Lord Lansdowne to W. Churchill, 20 Sept. 1922 [forwarded by

In the National Archives in London, the files of the Irish Grants Committee provide much more detail on the nature of the loss occasioned by big house owners during the revolutionary period. These are applications made for compensation by landlords (and others). They provide very important information on matters such as contents allegedly looted from houses. For example, on 27 April 1922 Lord Ashtown was ordered to leave his residence at Woodlawn in County Galway when 'all his property was declared confiscated by the IRA'. After outlining his loss of income, the claim application states that

> The lands of Drumharsna containing 745 acres were seized and confiscated about May 1922 after previous attempts at boycotting and intimidation; claimant's herd was fired at and driven out of his house on his lands; many of the buildings were destroyed, and claimant was prevented from making use of the lands until ultimately the conspiracy against him compelled him to sell these lands to the Irish Land Commission. This was a forced sale at a great undervalue and claimant lost ... £3,475.[92]

More information on the revolutionary period pertaining to compensation sought by landlords for damage to their estates and big houses can be found in the Damage to Property (Compensation) Act, 1923: Register of Claims. This register is arranged on a provincial/county basis and is also available in the NAI in the Office of Public Works files.[93] It gives the amount claimed in compensation under the 1923 act and indicates the final awards made. The Office of Public Works files also contain such information as reports of inspecting officers regarding the damage done to estates or big houses. For example in August 1925, J.C. Butler, inspecting officer in charge of the Mitchelstown Castle case, reported: 'I am of the opinion that all the silver was looted and not destroyed in the fire ... I feel perfectly sure that there was considerable looting of furniture and effects. During my inspection of the castle I noticed that the basement rooms were practically untouched by the fire, yet the furniture of these rooms was not forthcoming'.[94]

In time government publications such as the Department of the Environment, Heritage and Local government's *Architectural heritage protection: guidelines for planning authorities* (2004) will become indispensable tools in understanding legislative and administrative provisions taken in the late-twentieth and twenty-first centuries to protect what remains of Ireland's built heritage.

Churchill to W.T. Cosgrave, 22 Sept. 1922] (NAI, Dept. of the Taoiseach files, S/1940).   **92** Irish Grants Committee: form relating to claim of Lord Ashtown, n.d. (National Archives of the UK, London (hereinafter TNA), CO 762/15/10).   **93** These are held in the Four Courts, so at least twenty-four hours notice should be given to the staff of the NAI before consulting them. **94** Copy of report of J.C. Butler, inspecting officer, on damage to Mitchelstown castle for the Office of Public Works, 14 Aug. 1925 (NAI, Office of Public Works files, 2D/62/76); see also McDowell, *The fate of southern Unionists* where the author has made extensive use of the criminal injuries – Irish Grants Committee – records, 1922–30 (TNA, CO 762) to illustrate the plight of southern Unionists (many of whom were landowners) in the early 1920s.

Over the last quarter of a century or so, the Irish big house has begun to attract a good deal of attention from makers of documentaries. In 1995, the Irish Georgian Society was instrumental in the production of *The Irish country house*, narrated by Angelica Huston and still available on video from the Society's Dublin offices in Merrion Square. A documentary entitled *The big house* was made by BBC 2 Northern Ireland, produced by Tony McAuley and screened on 3 March 1994. The following are some of the big house or estate-related documentaries which can be accessed in the RTÉ archives (dates of first screening and archive accession numbers are given in brackets).[95] *Amongst women: ladies of the manor* (24 August 1992, BX30/6809); *An cruiscín lán: Bellamont Forest House* (7 July 1982, 95D00983); *The earl of Longford in conversation with MacAonghusa* (23 September 1968), 94D000098); *Home movie nights: Desmond Leslie* (29 April 1996, 96D00463); *Lie of the land, no. 4: kings, lords and commons* (18 February 1982, 95D00653); *Portrait of Ireland, no. 3: Glin Castle* (21 June 1996, 9600831); *Portrait of Ireland, no. 6: Temple House* (9 August 1996, 9600940); *Rich and rare land, series 4, no. 4* [Kilkenny Castle] (5 October 1994, 95D00335); *Rich and rare land, series 4, no. 12* [Malahide Castle] (21 November 1996, 96D01370); *Silence broken: Strokestown Famine Museum* (15 May 1994, 96D01069); *Six generations: who owned the land?* (5 September 1969, 94D00022); *Time to talk, no. 5: gentry* (18 June 1995, 95D00585). '*Land is gold': Kenmare and the Lansdowne estate* (produced by Sean Ó Mordha for RTÉ's *Hidden History* series) screened on 8 November 2005 examined management policy on that estate from the post-famine period through independence.

CONCLUSION

At present there is no history of an Irish big house that treats of the many aspects of its life – architectural, social, economic, political, recreational, cultural – over its entire life span. Such a study would be immensely important and simultaneously taxing. The sources described in this chapter (particularly when read in conjunction with those in chapter two) suggest the wealth of material, much of which remains un-quarried, that can be used to explore different facets of big house life in Ireland. It should also be remembered that this is by no means an exhaustive list, but then part of the joy of researching lies in the anticipation of discovering previously undocumented sources.

---

95 A more comprehensive listing can be found in Otto Rauchbauer, *Diskurse und bilder zum Anglo-Irischen landsitz im zwanzigsten jahrhundert* (Heidelberg, 2002), pp 385–6.

Conclusion

The study of big houses and landed estates in Ireland is a very challenging one; indeed, the first challenge lies in locating the sources that can be used. As far back as 1848 D. Owen-Madden hinted at the difficulties that would face historians in the future when he wrote:

> There has never existed a taste in Ireland for preserving papers. In this respect, our Anglo-Irish nobility differ very much from the peers of England and Scotland. I was once told by a living distinguished peer, the representative of an Elizabethan family, that he remembered a room full of family papers at his grandfather's seat. Among them were the correspondence and letters of a celebrated Irish lawyer of the seventeenth century, one of the ancestors of the family, and very eminent in history. 'But', said Lord —, 'my brother and I made kites of them. I perfectly well remember that when we were schoolboys we tore up the judge's letters.' Similar instances of destruction could be told. This paucity of family papers is a great loss to the historian.[1]

This work has pointed to the fact that there are many reasons for the dearth of family and estate papers in Ireland other than the mischievous deeds of young boys but has also suggested that what scarcity there is can be offset by a rich variety of other primary sources so that paucity should not be used as a pretext for avoiding the study of any big house or estate (or at the very least some aspects of their history). In recent years the appearance of numerous invaluable databases of estate (and other) records, the cataloguing of previously unrecorded collections, the rediscovery of family archives and the exertions of historians to find records in the most unlikely of places have all contributed to the opening up of the whole area of landed estate and big house studies, as is evidenced in the number of secondary works referenced in this work, which, of course, by no means represents a complete listing.

But if much has changed since 1975 when J.S. Donnelly jr. wrote: 'Despite their supreme importance the rural economy and the land question have claimed relatively little scholarly attention',[2] there still remain many gaps to be filled and possibly a good many areas to be reappraised for whatever timescale one may choose. There were, after all, probably in the region of 6,500 big houses in pre-famine Ireland. The vast majority of these have not featured in histories, local or national, published to date. Therefore, endless possibilities exist for future research given that while all big houses shared similar characteristics (at least within each

---

1 D. Owen-Madden, *Revelations of Ireland in the past generation* (Dublin, 1848), pp 80–1; my thanks to Desmond FitzGerald, Knight of Glin, for bringing this reference to my attention.
2 Donnelly, *Land and people of Cork*, p. 3.

classification), they were all as individual as the personalities who shaped and reshaped them according to economic circumstances and changing social trends over many years.

The study of an individual big house is possibly more daunting that the study of an estate for while one can study an estate without necessarily dwelling on the big house, it is not as practicable in reverse since much of the history of the house was tied up with the establishment, growth and decline of the estate. Aspects of the history of a house can, of course, be studied in isolation but even something as specialized as the accumulation and dispersal of a family's art collection should take into account the wider historical contexts explaining why certain paintings were collected at particular times, what financial windfalls facilitated buying or what outside influences forced the sale and break up of collections. It should also be an imperative to consider carefully the architectural transformation of a house with due consideration to the social, political and economic history of the time. And while big house architecture has received a good deal of attention, studies of individual architects are all too rare.[3] Notably, Richard Castle, the most important country house architect of his day has not yet been the subject of a major biography.[4]

Similarly, while the material culture of Irish country houses has attracted a good deal of scholarly attention,[5] little has been published on the planning, layout and use of space. Important research into this whole area is currently being undertaken by Patricia McCarthy who is using annotated architectural plans (executed or not) to examine the intentions of an architect and/or his patron in designing a house and bringing this design to fruition. Such a study will shed much light on how

---

3 See, for example, Paul Atterbury, *A.W.N. Pugin* (New Haven, 1995); Maurice Craig, 'The quest for Sir Edward Lovett Pearce' in *Irish Arts Review Yearbook*, xii (1996), pp 27–34; Desmond FitzGerald, Knight of Glin, 'Francis Bindon (*c.*1690–1765): his life and works' in *Quarterly Bulletin of the Irish Georgian Society*, x, nos 2–3 (1967), pp 1–36; Edward McParland, *Vitruvius Hibernicus: James Gandon* (London, 1985); idem, *The architecture of Richard Morrison (1767–1849) and William Vitruvius Morrison (1794–1838)* (Dublin, 1989); Jeanne Sheehy, *J.J. McCarthy and the Gothic revival in Ireland* (Belfast, 1977); see also Terence Reeves-Smyth, 'An Elizabethan Revival house in Ireland: Edward Blore and the building of Crom, Co. Fermanagh' in T. Reeves-Smyth and Richard Oram (eds), *Avenues to the past: essays presented to Sir Charles Brett in his 75th year* (Belfast, 2003), pp 321–52; G. Wheeler, 'John Nash and the building of Rockingham, Co. Roscommon' in ibid., pp 169–95; for brief biographical sketches of architects who worked in Ireland, see Rolf Loeber, *A biographical dictionary of architects in Ireland* (London, 1981); those active after that date are being catalogued in an ongoing project at the Irish Architectural Archive. **4** Desmond FitzGerald, Knight of Glin, 'Richard Castle, architect, his biography and works' in *Irish Georgian Society Bulletin*, vii, no. 1 (Jan.–Mar. 1964), pp 31–8. **5** The reader's attention is firstly directed to Barnard's *A guide to sources for the history of material culture in Ireland*; see also Anne Crookshank, 'Portraits of Irish houses' in *Irish Georgian Society Bulletin*, v, no. 4 (Oct.–Dec. 1962), pp 41–9; idem, 'The visual arts, 1603–1740' and 'The visual arts, 1740–1850' in Moody & Vaughan (eds), *A new history of Ireland, iv, eighteenth-century Ireland*, pp 471–98, 499–541; Peter Francis, *Irish delftware* (London, 2000); Hill & Lennon (eds), *Luxury and austerity;* Claudia Kinmouth, *Irish country furniture* (New Haven & London, 1993); Michael McCarthy, *Classical and Gothic: studies in the history of art* (Dublin, 2005); Jeanne Sheehy, *The rediscovery of Ireland's past: the Celtic revival,*

public and private spaces evolved, on when and why the function of certain rooms changed, on how architectural planning was used to minimize the intrusion of servants into family and guest life, as well as providing an insight into a variety of other aspects of big house social and cultural life.[6]

What did the construction of a great mansion such as Carton or Castletown mean to the local communities of Maynooth or Celbridge (or for that matter the laying out of villages, landlord investment in the building of roads to improve access to markets and fairs, the building of canals and the building of multi-storied flourmills in the eighteenth century)?[7] How many people were involved in these processes from beginning to end? Dickson quotes from the *Cork Gazette* in 1796 commenting that the construction of Castle Bernard in Cork would provide employment 'for some hundreds of poor for a year or two at least'.[8] Tradition has it that Castle Oliver in Limerick and Dartrey in Monaghan, both constructed during the Great Famine, were built to provide local employment during that great crisis. But were workers favorably rewarded or merely exploited? What were the local spin-off industries which benefited most? To what extent were the raw materials used bought locally? Undoubtedly, foreign timber was used but local or at least Irish quarries possibly provided the stone material.

At the most basic level, much research remains to be done on the actual cost of building an Irish country house but this is an area that will require a great deal of searching in order to identify, locate and accumulate relevant sources, which seem to be particularly scarce. Lots of other related questions remain unanswered: was the funding for the construction of big houses derived solely from landed wealth or were there other sources? (The most obvious case of Thomas Conolly of Castletown comes to mind.) Did, for example, the ownership of West Indian plantations, as in the case of the marquis of Sligo, allow for the building of a much grander mansion at Westport than might otherwise have been the case? (L.M. Cullen makes the interesting point that 'Englishmen and Scotsmen who had made a fortune in the East Indies sometimes bought estates in Ireland, set up as landed families, and set out singlemindedly to forget their origins'.)[9] Marriage arrangements were undoubtedly important and not only revived a family's fortunes but often

---

1830–1930 (London, 1980).   **6** My thanks to Ms. Patricia McCarthy for providing me with this information.   **7** See, for example: B.J. Graham and L.J. Proudfoot, 'Landlords, planning and urban growth in eighteenth- and early nineteenth-century Ireland' in *Journal of Urban History*, xviii, no. 3 (1992), pp 308–29; Lindsay Proudfoot, 'Landlord motivation and urban improvement on the duke of Devonshire's Irish estates, c.1792–1832' in *Irish Economic & Social History*, xviii (1991), pp 5–23; idem, *Urban patronage and social authority: the management of the Duke of Devonshire's towns in Ireland, 1764–1891* (Washington DC, 1995); idem, *Property ownership and urban and village improvement in provincial Ireland c.1700–1845* (Edinburgh, 1997); idem, 'Placing the imaginary: Gosford Castle and the Gosford estate, c.1820–1900' in A.J. Hughes & William Nolan (eds), *Armagh: history and society. indisciplinary essays on the history of an Irish county* (Dublin, 2001), pp 881–916; idem, 'Markets, fairs and towns in Ireland, c.1600–1853' in Peter Borsay & Lindsay Proudfoot (eds), *Provincial towns in early modern England and Ireland: change, convergence and divergence* (Oxford, 2002), pp 69–96; Prunty, 'Estate records'.   **8** Dickson, *Old world economy*, p. 98.   **9** Cullen, *Modern Ireland*, pp 127–8.

contributed to the remodeling of an old house or the building of a new one; the apparent widespread coincidence of the building or embellishment of a big house and the arrival of a new bride and concomitant spending spree requires more systematic research.

There is a glaring lacuna with regard to the role of women in Irish big houses, both upstairs and downstairs. Very few ladies of the house have been the subject of biographies.[10] Their rôle in the running of the household, the management of staff and setting trends in embellishing interiors or purchasing household items has yet to be systematically analyzed. Family and servant life in Irish big houses awaits the type of study carried out for England by Jessica Gerard in her *Country house life: families and servants, 1815–1914* (Oxford, 1994). Servants in Irish houses require much more attention with regard to their duties, their social lives, how they were hired and fired, their working conditions, their interaction with family members, what they faced after retirement and so on.[11] Indeed, it can also be said that the post-independence generations of big house men have been less enthusiastic than their forebearers in publishing autobiographical works or memoirs.[12]

This work has also pointed to areas of landed estate life which are worthy of more systematic examination. W.E. Vaughan has made the point that 'Local studies are the best way to study the Famine; of that there is no doubt …'[13] In this respect, there is ample scope for work on the effects of the Great Famine on individual estates. The fundamental question of how individual landlords reacted to the plight of their tenants has yet to be systematically addressed. While new evidence suggests that there were many landlords who survived the Famine in a strong enough position to consolidate their own holdings through the purchase of property belonging to insolvent landowners, not enough is known about who these landowners were and why they had managed to remain solvent. How, for example, did the likes of the absentee sixth duke of Devonshire manage to increase remittances from his Irish estate to £26,300 in 1846, augment his rent roll by 12 per cent from 1842 to 1859 and then embark on the lavish embellishment of his Irish home at Lismore Castle in 1851?[14] Did those who used assisted emigration as a means of relieving distress do so for paternal reasons or were they motivated by a stronger desire to consolidate their holdings and, thereby, realize greater long-term profits? Undoubtedly landlords and the lower orders viewed the economic and social rationale of assisted emigration very differently but what evidence is there of this? To what extent did the stronger farmers on an estate collaborate in this process knowing that their own future would be better secured? During many of the pre-famine decades, these large farmers had suffered at the hands of local secret agrarian

10 See, for example, FitzGerald, *Emily, duchess of Leinster* and Elisabeth Kehoe, *Fortune's daughters: the extravagant lives of the Jerome sisters* (London, 2004).   11 For an introduction to the same see Dooley, *The decline of the big house*, pp 146–70; also Hearn, *Below stairs*; Pamela Horn, *The rise and fall of the Victorian servant* (Dublin & New York, 1975).   12 Exceptions include Henry Mount Charles, *Public space – private life: a decade at Slane Castle* (London, 1989).   13 Vaughan, 'Reflections on the Great Famine', p. 7.   14 Proudfoot, 'The management of a great estate', pp 40–9.

societies composed largely of the rural poor who had attempted to prevent them exploiting the local market economy. Quite a few landlords, particularly on estates located in the west of Ireland, behaved in a businesslike, non-sympathetic manner when they purchased bankrupt estates after 1849, evicted the existing tenants and consolidated vacant holdings to form more viable profit-making farms.[15] Traditionally many of the new purchasers were seen as greedy men out to make a quick profit at the expense of the less fortunate. In some cases this was undoubtedly true, so how were such landlords perceived over time? Was there an element of resentment that lingered long in the collective memory of the tenant community with repercussions during the land war, the Plan of Campaign or even the revolutionary period?

The first four decades of the nineteenth century should not merely be regarded as a prelude to the Great Famine. In relation to land issues this period was important because of the growth in various agrarian societies. In the 1980s there was an impressive amount of publication in this area that transformed much of our understanding of pre-famine underground agrarian movements.[16] However, as Gary Owens has since pointed out, 'publication on this subject came to a near standstill during the 1990s', leaving a great deal of ground yet to be covered in terms of full-scale analyses of many of the most significant outbreaks such as that of the Rockites in Munster and Leinster from 1822 to 1884, as well as a variety of much less well known ones.[17]

Similarly, until the 1990s historians had largely neglected landlord and tenant relations from the Great Famine to the land war. In 1994 the publication of W.E. Vaughan's *Landlords and tenants in mid-Victorian Ireland* helped correct this imbalance but as yet relatively little has appeared in print regarding individual estates during this time. As with Dr Vaughan's national study, local studies could inform on 'evictions, rents, tenant right, estate management, agrarian outrages, and conflicts between landlords and tenants' and help provide correctives to generalizations found in national surveys.[18]

On the other hand, the period of the extended land war has received a great deal of attention from historians. However, much of this focus has been on the Land League, its composition and aims. The effects of the land war on individual estates have yet to be fully examined. Why did tenants on an estate react to this economic depression when they had not done so in the early 1860s? How did the Land League function on individual estates? What about the estates on which there was no Land League agitation? Their history has yet to be told and would make for a very interesting study. L.P. Curtis jr. has, for example, rightly enquired whether the non-payment of rent was in deference to Land League policy or: 'something to

---

15 See, for instance, Joseph Hone, *The Moores of Moore Hall* (London, 1939), pp 158–60; Lane, 'The general impact of the Encumbered Estates Act of 1849', pp 45–50. **16** See chapter 1. **17** Gary Owens, 'Social history' in Geary & Kellegher (eds), *Nineteenth-century Ireland: a guide to recent research*, pp 38–9. **18** Vaughan, *Landlords and tenants in mid-Victorian Ireland*, p. v.

do with economic exigencies and not just with political imperatives'.[19] There is
evidence to suggest that tenants who supposedly supported rent strikes paid their
rents secretly. During the troubled years of the mid-1880s when the plan of
campaign was initiated on his estate, Lord Granard wrote to his mortgagees, the
trustees of Maynooth College, disingenuously informing them that he was not
receiving any rents from his tenants. However, it transpired in a court hearing in
1888, that he had, in fact, been receiving rental income above his rent roll.[20]

What held the rural alliance of the late 1870s, early 1880s together is as
important an area of study as what the movement attempted to achieve. What type
of relationship existed on individual estates between large farmers, small farmers
and labourers and in some cases between the rural tenants and the urban tenants
who had the same landlord? The story of those evicted during the late 1870s and
1880s has yet to be told but they certainly were not forgotten, at least not in
nationalist lore, where they remained the perceived martyrs of the agrarian question
until post-independent Irish governments decided to reward them or their
representatives with substitute plots of land (the 1903 Land Act had previously
attempted to do likewise).[21] Moreover, we know little of what happened between
the ending of the first phase of the land war in 1882 and the outbreak of the second
phase with the adoption of the plan of campaign in 1885. Did a different leadership
emerge at local level? Were the same estates targeted but for different reasons and
if so what does this tell us about the wider pretexts behind local agitation?

Much work remains to be done on the operation of the plan of campaign on
individual estates. We know that it was put into effect on around 200 estates, but how
did the initiation of the plan on a local estate impact on neighbouring estates?[22] Why
were certain estates chosen over others; in many cases there were presumably other
factors at play than the level of encumbrances of a landlord. Similarly more
information is needed on the working of the United Irish League during 1898 to
1902 and again during the later ranch war (and, indeed, during the UIL's resurgence
in certain areas during World War I). Because of the myth that the land question in
Ireland died out after 1903, little has appeared in print about the history of individual
estates after that year. However, the case of the Clonbrock estate, partly documented
in other parts of this work, shows that its history was more traumatic after 1903 than
at any time before. Equally, a much fuller analysis of the land war of 1917–23 awaits an
eager scholar. Was there, for example, any link between the Plan of Campaign estates
and the estates targeted (or big houses burned) during the revolutionary period? The
whole impact of the various land acts on individual estates from 1870 through to the
last quarter of the twentieth century would make for an interesting study.

In attempting to come to an understanding of any aspect of the history of an
estate or big house, it is imperative that sources be approached in as objective and

19 L.P. Curtis jr., 'On class and class conflict in the Land War' in *Irish Economic & Social
History*, viii (1981), p. 88.   20 'The mortgage papers of St Patrick's College, Maynooth', ed.
Dooley.   21 Dooley, *'The land for the people'*, pp 74–81.   22 For a list of these estates see
Geary, *The plan of campaign*, pp 154–78.

unbiased a manner as possible. In this guide primacy has been given to estate
records, the argument being that where available they are the most illuminating of
all sources. Their reliability means they can be used as correctives to other sources
and, indeed, to ideas once or presently propounded on aspects of estate management, for example. In 1950 K.H. Connell argued that landlords promoted subdivision in order to increase their rental income – a mass of smallholdings was more
profitable than one larger one.[23] However, more recent research by historians using
estate records has shown that landlords were generally unaware of what middlemen
were doing and while certainly their apathy in not rectifying the situation earlier
than they did can be criticized, one must consider whether they had the power to
do so if they wanted.

While this work has highlighted the fundamental importance of estate records,
it has also indicated that they will not tell the whole history of a house or estate –
from an economic, social, cultural and political perspective – so all the while the
researcher should be considering other supporting and corroborating sources of
evidence. To take but one example, again in relation to estate management: the
perusal of a set of estate rentals may suggest to the researcher that all rents were
extortionate, or that some tenants on the estate were being rackrented as their rents
per acre were substantially higher than perhaps Griffith's valuation or those of
fellow tenants on another part of the estate. To assess the real significance of rent
levels, a broader context must be considered and a number of factors taken into
account such as agricultural prices at the time (not always available in the estate
records, except perhaps in farm account books, but readily available in newspapers
and published agricultural statistics since the 1850s), the size of the holding, the
quality of the land, and the general ability of tenants to pay. As W.E. Vaughan
observed regarding earlier studies of rent movements: 'How rents could be discussed
without constant references to prices and production is a mystery, which must stand
as one of the triumphs of faith over reason.'[24] In studying the movement of rents a
lot of factors need to be considered. Lindsay Proudfoot in his examination of the
Devonshire estate concluded that 'the general lack of complaints about individual
rent increase suggests that, for whatever reason, most renewing or incoming tenants
were prepared to tolerate them as reasonable'.[25] The reason should be obvious
enough; as individuals they could not afford to do otherwise, particularly in an
agricultural society where land was also the main access to social respectability. It
was only when tenants discovered the power of collective agitation that they could
question rent increases and hopefully avoid the consequences.

Likewise, it would be dangerous to perceive a landlord as a 'good' landlord or a
'bad' landlord based primarily on the level of rents on his estate. As Barbara Solow
has pointed out:

23 K.H. Connell, *The population of Ireland, 1740–1845* (Oxford, 1950). 24 Vaughan, *Landlords and tenants in mid-Victorian Ireland*, p. 53. 25 Proudfoot, 'The management of a great estate', p. 41.

If we say that land is rented at a price below market price, we do not attribute a necessarily generous nature to the owner of the land; the consequent resource misallocation may be very harmful. Moreover, we should be unwilling to assert that a man who accepts a market price for his land is by definition a 'bad landlord'.[26]

What is necessary is a careful examination of rent increases in relation to their real affordability, the reasons for evictions, landlords' responses to tenants' difficulties, and even the general personality of the landlord himself (or in some cases his agent) to determine whether as a landlord he was 'good' or 'bad'. Estate management policy varied to at least some degree from one generation to the next for personal reasons, if not because of external factors dictating change. A number of witnesses to the Bessborough commission in the early 1880s showed their awareness of this. Robert Reeves, a land agent in Limerick and Queen's County, claimed that 'a landlord today may be a good man, but his son may be a very different one, or he may be in good circumstances now, and may in a few years get into difficulties'.[27] John Gamble, a seed merchant from Derry, contrasted the notorious third earl of Leitrim with his father who, Gamble claimed, was 'considered one of the best landlords in the country' and 'indulgent as a landlord to an extraordinary degree'.[28] One is, therefore, often forced to look outside estate records to unearth sources of tenant grievance and to understand what underpinned collective agitation.

It is only through the study of local landed estates and individual big houses that historians can truly foster an understanding of the system of landlordism and the rôle of the big house in Ireland. As L.P. Curtis jr. has rightly pointed out regarding landed estates in Ireland:

> Irish estates varied greatly in size, resources, credit, and management practices, and generalizations about their operations often founder on exceptions so numerous as to disprove the rule. Ideally, the study of landlordism in Ireland, as elsewhere, requires an aggregate approach. Case histories of great estates – usually so much better documented than small estates – may reveal many important facets of the landlord system; without knowledge of how medium and small-sized estates functioned in the same period, the extent to which the great estate was typical of the whole can never be fully understood.[29]

The same very much applies to big houses. The continued study of more estates and houses can only encourage comparative studies and, therefore, help to expose the anomalies and act as correctives to national histories which, because of their very nature, tend to hide such anomalies in generalizations.

---

26 Solow, *The land question*, p. 43.   **27** *Bessborough commission, minutes of evidence*, vol. i, 77. **28** Ibid., 307.   **29** Curtis, 'Incumbered wealth', p. 333.

Index